M000317995

Awakening Glory

Trilogy

Published **2020** by
Awakening Glory Ministries
Prophetic Publications & Worship
www.awakeningglory.com
awakeningglory@gmail.com

Special Acknowledgement to my wife
Shauna who made this possible
Special Dedication to my mother Susan Wirtz
who passed away days before release of this book

Front Cover © *Brandon Sproles*
used by permission

Awakening GLORY

TRILOGY

VOLUME 1

Awakening Generation
The Day Is Dawning

"Not in darkness"

VOLUME 2

Awakening Genealogies
The Resurrection Code Revealed

"That the day should overtake you"

VOLUME 3

Awakening Glory
The Mysterious Days of the King

"Like a thief" 1 Thessalonians 5:4

Awakening
Generation
The Day Is Dawning
VOLUME ONE
"beloved you are not in darkness ..."
1 Thessalonians 5:4

Awakening
Genealogies
The Resurrection Code Revealed
VOLUME TWO
"That the day should overtake you ..."
1 Thessalonians 5:4

Awakening

VOLUME THREE Glory

The Mysterious Days of the King

"...Like a thief."
1 Thessalonians 5:4

7. **Preparing**: Maturing the Harvest
2 Peter 3:9

8. **Calculating**: Awaiting the Arrival
2 Peter 3:10,12

9. **Expecting**: Overspreading the Heavens
2 Peter 3:11,13-14

AWAKENING GENERATION

The Day is Dawning

1 VOLUME

CJ Michaels

"You are not in darkness that the day should overtake you like a thief." 1 Thessalonians 5:4

1

Awakening:
The Origins of Discovery

THE NOW

*"'Behold **NOW** is the acceptable time', behold **NOW** is the day of salvation."*   ***2 Corinthians 6:2***

*"Seek the Lord **while He may be found**; call upon Him **while He is near.**"*   ***Isaiah 55:6***

*"I must seek Him whom my soul loves ...when I found him whom my soul loves **I held on to him and would not let go.**"*   ***Song of Solomon 3:2-4***

*"**Today if you hear** His voice ..."*   ***Hebrews 3:7,15***

God isn't needing to be awakened, it is us. For He isn't MIA ***"He who keeps you will not slumber ... nor sleep"* Psalms 121:4**, we are for the most part. For us to get this backwards would be a colossal mistake! Instead of stirring ourselves, we would be persuaded He needs to be stirred. In my mind this may very well be the last divide of the wheat and tares in those professing faith. True revival versus one only for show. Elijah versus the prophets of Baal trying to get their gods attention, appearing very devoted to the cause. Those trying to present a kingdom here on earth to Jesus, when Jesus already victorious brings the kingdom from heaven!

For it is the easiest cop out to our responsibility to awaken, to put this whole thing back on God who seems arbitrary in the first place about returning. We easily can find new narratives and replacement theories for why God has *"delayed"* **[cf. Hebrews 10:37]**. Yet neither is He random or waiting on us but as this book will show He is on a perfect schedule for His return to earth! One that was decided before time began!

For from our inductive focused study of **2 Peter,** into all scripture pertinent to the end of this age, comes our baseline principle, ***"This is Now"* 2 Peter 3:1**. Since prophesy is revealed over time and deals with time, Peter is bringing the early church to a NOW moment, demanding a decision to believe the report that Jesus isn't just historical but eternally alive and the culmination of history! Here I am today, **2020**, giving you a NOW report as well. I am glad to be an end times fishermen with key information for the church, His bride just like Peter was. For this is a NOW MOMENT!

THE FUTURE MATTERS

What we believe about our future will affect our present which will affect our destiny!

For if I can prove to you, by our vantage point in history, that we can NOW see that Jesus Himself told us when He is returning; then how would that affect your response? For did you catch that, Jesus Himself left us with the truth, not Peter or Paul or the latest "prophet"? Truths that can be supported by two or three witnesses in God's word as well and various other supporting casts. My point is this book starts and finishes with a decision we all must make.

As Peter will conclude with in His second letter, *"What sort of people ought you to be in holy conduct"* **2 Peter 3:11** because we actually choose to believe the bible is real, reliable and life changing in what it reveals about our future.

For those solid in faith this book will make no difference in the way you live your life. For you make the most of every moment, regardless of the truths of the future. Yet how much more if we know the truth of our times, that in fact we are closing into the final years of this age, would we not walk with embolden purpose? Would that not speak volumes to the prophecy of the *"late rains"* **James 5:7** and the words *"after this I will pour out My Spirit"* **Joel 2:28**? Paul seeming to think that knowing was our destiny, spoke to the church that they were *"not in darkness"* **1 Thessalonians 5:4**. Could it not be that a people who know their God & His purposeful end, would be more effective in sharing their faith when thrusted before Kings & courts for answers others so desperately desire at the very end of this age. **[Cf. Daniel 11:32-33, Luke 21:12]**

TODAY'S CONCLUSIONS ARE NOT TAUGHT IN SCRIPTURE!

- No one can know anything
- Therefore searching for a seasonal time placement is wrong or misguided
- If the Apostles couldn't figure it out neither should we believe we can
- It's because Jesus can come at anytime so He won't unless your ready
- What's the point in knowing,
    - Knowing will corrupt us
- It distracts from now

On the flip side of this is the question, how costly will it be for you who pretend we can't know anything? If we are that generation of promise then what will it be said of us? Or more importantly, how will we stand before God to answer for our neglect of having such a golden opportunity. How much more confidence and with how much more appreciation will we have when we discover the BIBLE was harmonious all along in what it conveyed concerning time! Would it not leaves us with such clarity and assurance? Would it not leaves us with emboldened faith to partner with the Almighty? The choice is ours to sell out, to bring Jesus to the lost, before all is over. Yet small is the suffering to do so compared to what is right around the corner [chapter 9]! This isn't the case if you continue to be lied to about what really occurs at the end of this age.

This book isn't the answer to everything but we are told Christ in us, empowering us is. A people who know their God and know His plan and know the day they live in, become a mighty instrument and fire set upon a hill! As Daniel foretold, they **"shall be strong and carry out great exploits" Daniel 11:32 (NKJV).** The origin of discovery always starts with our choice, not the early churches, prophets of old or Jesus but ours! No NOW moment matters more than the one right before you. My job isn't done until I can offend your comforts with the Word of God. For this is not just information I am giving you but a call to awaken to the reality of the Word of God. The question in our generation soon will not be can we know or when but how will you respond to the chase for the Kingdom coming?

THE PROJECT

*"**About the time of the end,** a body of men will be raised up who will turn their attention to the prophecies, and **insist upon their literal interpretation, in the midst of much clamor** and opposition."*

Sir Isaac Newton

Maybe my God actually still uses people like me all messed up from childhood. Maybe I am one of those, who this famous man spoke of prophetically, if so, there are yet others. I don't pretend to be alone in this or know everything. As His body of believers we are called on together to find answers. For I believe like others, everything has meaning in the bible in one way or the other. God doesn't speak recklessly. Since prophecy unlike the rest of scriptures is a mystery revealed over time, I have chosen to include a historical approach in writing this book, in order to highlight how revelation has grown brighter while being kept concealed by God from the masses.

Starting with one pinpointed key period in the early churches understanding of what was occurring in God's plan in reference to prophesy in the writing of **2 Peter**, we will see how God's Word shaped the landscape from theirs to ours. For in Peter's second letter, which is a defense for things yet future, we have all we need to remove the obstacles to understanding the truth on this subject. We are not even talking about the powerful words contained in this letter, but its placement in church history. For what was written previous to it by Peter in His first letter, show the clearest picture that revelation was increasing and getting brighter.

For our eyes must be opened to appreciate how God is now revealing what was previously concealed. What better place to work from than the time in history where the church overcame its short sightedness. By doing this, I desire for the majesty of the Father to be appreciated, who both chooses simple vessels like Peter to speak complex prophetic ideas and conceal them enough so arrogant men may doubt, run in circles.

This book comes with the conviction that God still speaks! Every generation is given what it needs for its time, with this in mind would not God speak concerning matters that affect us in our day. If indeed we are that generation to see His return, then we qualify to know? Some would say the bible can't speak to us, we are not to know anything. I say, let the blind lead the blind, but you are reading this today because God has been speaking to you. Something has been telling you your preachers have been selling you placebos. To this end let me help point you to the light shining in a dark place **[cf. 2 Peter 1:19]** to lead you to greater awareness of your day!

For the basis for our knowledge isn't found in our own private interpretations or encounters or even the latest recent world events. It is based on two or three witnesses from the Word of God agreeing when understood in context and meaning of the original language. Prophetic revelation has always been meant for the church to dialogue concerning and be in watch for His coming. Even the idea of having knowledge can make us arrogant **[cf. 1 Corinthians 8:1]** thinking we know something someone else doesn't can in itself be a blindness. Kind of like I got here first haha. So do we give up the search, because others make a mess of it? Do we not move forward even though no-one seems to be open to search? For on the other hand God warns, *'My people are destroyed for lack of knowledge"* **Hosea 4:6** and encourages us to *"seek and you shall find"* **Matthew 7:7**

In fact, the prophetic word from scripture is clear that at no other time in history as ours will there be a series of deceptive voices and yet insight as well! Everyone wants to have an answer, but what is crazy is God isn't speaking anything different from what He has already spoken in His word; accept that now we have a clearer vantage point of sight and hopefully can gain greater faith! At a time when most have lost confidence in His word to answer what is going on, Peter declares that, **"the day dawns and the morning star arises" 2 Peter 1:19** For those slow on the uptake this means, our generation should know more than any previous.

For Peter and Paul that day was dawning as seen in **2 Peter**, that one would think if they hadn't died so soon after this letter much more would have been discovered and released in the Canon of scripture. Maybe it was God's plan not to allow that, we can all sit and wonder but here we are. With hindsight, we above any previous generation can see how this act of concealment for reasons found in scriptural context was reserved to be unlocked today! Consider how much weight the disciples of the disciples should have to point us back to the Apostles teaching and advance it. Yet no one pays attention because today it isn't considered *'Canon or scripture'*, as if no one had any voice back then, even though they were the disciples of the very disciples! Yet in this book we will show the testimony of connecting relationships to the truth.

In this second letter written with urgency to leave a legacy, we find a wealth of guiding principles. From the reality of Christ coming kingdom, the non-imminent nature of His timing due to precursors, how revelation works, what are considered our sources that need to be harmonized, the distinction between prophesy and the rest of scriptures, the importance of foreshadows and types and finally God's chosen prophetic time code for the big picture **2 Peter** is a treasure chest for Eschatological teaching. Peter doesn't leave much out and resolves the major stumbling blocks of their day and maybe ours as well if we choose to listen and observe.

This three part series, **Awakening Glory,** is a very systematic approach building from basics to details, from the issue of our limitations of knowing, to the grandeur of God's plan to how all this will end for this age. From times and epochs, to the day and hour, we will examine what the Prophets, Apostles and Our Lord Jesus had to say. If anything is gained from reading this book it is my hope you see the Beauty of my God who both in concealing and in revealing is purposeful in giving what is best at the right time. Just think, if God is perfect in His timing, than He can be trusted in with your life and destiny as well for this short period we have left.

This project is presented as if it were being read in court, for defense of the biblical harmony of things yet future. It is birthed in my heart over many years of study of scriptures both New & Old Testament and inspired by my love for the scriptures itself. Allowing scriptures alone to interpret scriptures, our standard must become exactly what scripture itself tells us it should be, *"on the evidence of two witnesses or three"* **Deuteronomy 17:6**. This standard itself is spoken in scriptures again by Jesus & Paul as if God is making a point of two or three witnesses, *"On the mouth of two or three witnesses every fact may be confirmed"* **Matthew 18:16 [cf. 2 Corinthians 13:1]**.

When nothing can be deemed true unless an agreement can be made within the scriptures themselves, then prophets truly become subject to prophets as the word says. **[Cf. 1 Corinthians 14:32]** It's this simple premise that in fact morphed what I believed about the end times into a more precise picture of what I have come to believe. I have allowed myself to be governed by His words, and I invite you as well to come under His rule. Did you catch that, I was wrong in many ways when I started this project. Even I had to change my mind.

By the final part of this series, **the Mysterious Days of the King**, my hope is to have unveiled scriptural proof of a unique perspective of the timing & nature of His return. Resolving mystery after mystery as to why Pre, Mid and Post Tribulation theories all have significant issues harmonizing; I finally landed softly on the unshakable harmony that only one answer remained one I hadn't discovered before this project. Yet there it was as clear as day! Which makes me ask God why such a mystery concerning His bride & Him, that it would take me so many years to unlock it. A mystery that seems now so obvious to behold, that I hope not to be the only one who advocates for it in our short future.

So to arrive at this mystery revealed I am taking you on the journey with me from the start to the finish. To do this, I have divided the writings into three parts following the three points in Paul's words to the church.

I. **Awakening Generation**: The Morning Star Arises
   "Brethren, you are not in darkness" - The Mystery Past

II. **Awakening Genealogies**: The Resurrection Code Revealed
   "that the day should overtake you" - The Mystery of the Ages

III. **Awakening Glory**: The Mysterious Days of the King
   "like a thief" **1 Thessalonians 5:4** - The Mysterious Future

7

THE AUTHOR

*"Ten years was my argument with God. If no one writes
that Jesus actually indicated to us Himself when He's
returning, then I'll write. 20 years later here we are"*
My Journey

So without any bible degree, I come to you as God's fishermen of this century. Maybe it is very apropos that God's original fishermen, the one we follow along with in this thesis, Peter, was the one to reveal to us the key to understanding God's timing for His return. If this is God's plan, then let my life be a stumbling block for those who believe they alone have all the answers already, who glory in steeples, complexities, biblical degrees, appearances and the like. For I sure don't have all the answers, just some key ones. How do I know I do? Well, the Scriptures themselves agree with themselves so I can put my confidence in them. This has worked well for me, for finally I have a profound peace over my future, and I just want to share that with you.

The question of how all this came to be crosses my mind though. Remembering back to my early days after God courted me and He revealed Himself to me in high school. I felt like I had just awoken from a dream to really live in relationship with God. It was 1980. People were telling me right away Jesus was coming, because of Hal Lindsey's predictions. So I understand the feeling of people telling you, you don't have long to live. Yet back then the message was always scary. I remember saying, *'Hey I just got here, and now you're telling me the world is ending with crazy events?'*

Back then, they would hand "chick tracks" that depicted harsh realities of the end times. I didn't know what to think. Others were caught up in the fear of being left behind (after the rapture of the church). The chasm was great between those that believed differently between Post & Pre Tribulation positions. Even today, I have never found a book committed to harmonizing the bible and exposing disharmony when it comes to our prophetic future, for most just gravitate to a side. I should know I have read so many horrible ones and great informative ones as well. They always left something on the table unharmonized or added or taken away from the picture or scriptures. Often times just a piece was revealed by God, so a book was written but the rest of the information was stuck in traditions and not harmonious.

Not sure where I would be now though if God didn't sovereignly show up in my life. Few years later as a senior graduating, God came to me in a dream in which I saw many wheat fields perishing in the sun without workers to harvest them. I was concerned. Then I saw a city glowing in the distance. As I got closer it got dark bronze until I was led to a park in the heart of the city. The park was a virtual garden of Eden. On a bench others shared fellowship with me, I knew I was amongst believers. Yet suddenly I was drawn up out of the park above the city until I saw all the fields again. This time I saw a storm on the horizon. Lightning flashes and fire burning up the fields. I was terrified. Squinting as if that is possible in a dream, I saw a star, a speck of light above the fields as they burned above this unusual lightning storm.

Baam! In an instant, that light filled my eyelids and a form of a man appeared. I awoke suddenly full of the Spirit of God, sweating profusely and thus began a journey. For the next thing I found myself doing was prophesying on paper what was filling my heart at that moment. I was just a young boy mind you and never imagined speaking in the first person for God. God called me that day to warn His people of the coming storm, the need for laborers in the field and the hope that star brings from above the storm. I believe that storm is already brewing around the world. I pray this book awakens something in your heart for that which He has destined you in this day. For that star that awaits us above the storm is our King Jesus!

Today is really all we have. For *"Today if you hear His voice!"* **Hebrews 3:7** for NOW is the day which God has purposed for your destiny. Therefore get ready for your heart to be enlarged and softened to His call on your life by understanding the day you live in! I don't believe you will be disappointed or waste your time reading what God has revealed to me. Instead I believe, you will grow more confident in the majesty of a purposeful God who took to the effort to leave us bread crumbs to the truth.

THE MISSION

"To those who have received a faith of the same kind as ours, by the righteousness of our God and Savior Jesus Christ... make certain about His calling and choosing you;"

2 Peter 1:1,8-10

Hopefully my mission is the same as Peter's when he penned those words addressing those of *"a faith of the same kind as ours"* **[above]** with the express purpose of later saying His purpose was *"to remind you"* **v12**. For this reason my project got delayed a year to refocus, and learn how to speak to the right audience, you, His betrothed! For Eschatology, the study on what the bible speaks of next or future is very divisive and controversial in our present day Christian circles. That is because it has become the interest of many a "Christian" Pharisee as it did in John the Baptist days, who said, *"who warned you to flee from the wrath to come"* **Matthew 3:7**. The whole search easily becomes about <u>WHEN</u>, not <u>how to be ready</u>!

Yet in their day it was full of importance, like-mindedness and careful search for the one they loved so dearly. So the key element in this was Peter was directing his message to those who shared "*his kind of faith*" **2 Peter 1:1** (paraphrased). Lord knows I am not looking forward to many being upset over their reaction to this book. My heart isn't into arguments although I am making a case for truth so I should expect them. Instead I want to see the Bride awaken, and His people acknowledge how beautiful God is in perfection! What I am seeing is perfection!

That said the word is clear, *"Spirit of truth has come He will guide us into all truth ...and He will tell you <u>things to come</u>"* **John 16:13** From this passage a few things become quickly self-evident. One there shouldn't be such divisiveness if the Spirit is drawing us into unity of thought. Having read and studied and heard much of the banter of hardliners and understanding their scriptural support it surprises me that no one can stand up and say, *"wait a minute, You both can't be right, let's keep at it!"* This is more reflective of our times we live in then anything else. Jesus declaring to us, the enemies plan would be to sow tares amongst the wheat before He returns **[cf. Matthew 13]**, giving voice in the Christian world to unbiblical ideas by those lacking a desire to be held accountable to contradictions they leave in their wake scripturally. Maybe that's why this project took so long. I didn't want to keep correcting myself with further revisions.

So why tackle such a difficult topic where the introduction of a clearer belief system based entirely on harmonizing the scriptures might further divide the chasm that already exist between parties holding partial truths? For instance, we just read it is the Holy Spirit's job to convict us of what is to come. What makes me think I can help the current situation or should *"do the Spirit's job"*? Here we see the underlying difficulty in interpreting the subject in the first place; which lays underneath everything in life, culture, politics, and religion. God chose us to do His work through the Spirit. God is working in time with people in spite of people and He still gets what He wants! He wins! No, I can't do the Spirit's work, neither do I want to. We are all just instruments, messengers; but beware if God has actually called me for some reason to this task. What if He has chosen for me to be the one for you to know more and receive a greater sense of purpose in your day? Will you listen at least to the scriptures?

Looking at the ideologies of how we view God involved in time & our participation or partnership with that is critical in understanding Eschatology. Do we do nothing and keep our own convictions in fear of being controversial upsetting what is popular? The great debate of whether God controls time and in what fashion and to what degree do we play a part cannot be divorced from Eschatology. Does He need or desire assistance? Yes, if not us then who? For He already has appointed another if that is the case! *"If these become silent, the stones will cry out!"* **Luke 19:40** David is David because, David didn't wait for another. Elijah as well didn't wait for another, and so on ... We will see Peter a mere fisherman didn't wait but steps up!

However before we get too far ahead of ourselves let's just return to the Christ idea of **Matthew 13** where there are tares *[mentally ascending believers]* amongst wheat *[truly regenerated born again ones]*. So within every local body of believer's dwells those govern not by the Spirit of truth to whatever percentage or mix depends on the level of shepherding. Jesus being the best shepherd of all still had one, Judas Iscariot. Yet Jesus was the leader not Judas. What really gets deceiving is when our leaders themselves are tares. Nothing like well educated analytical minds acting spiritual without revelation. *[Peter will have much to say about the threat of false teachers in this same letter* **2 Peter 2***]* Even Paul recognizes this threat saying, *"For the time will come when they will not endure sound doctrine; but after their own lust shall heap to themselves teachers having itching ears"* **2 Timothy 4:3**

In the end we cannot discount the enemies strategies to whisper his agenda and carry this out on the winds of the carnally minded. Surrounded by this present day culture for easy answers and fixes to problems it isn't hard to relate to the words above *"itching ears"* **2 Timothy 4:3** and how the paradigm of popularity and success is driven by the need to please our supporters of our 501c ministries.

However the biblical mandate is to be a Berean who *"examined the scriptures every day to see if what Paul said was true"* **Acts 17:11**. That is not to say that those who are Born of God are not genuinely mistaken until a better idea comes along. The Spirit ability to nudge us towards truth is amazing. For what makes a teaching or doctrine *"sound"* **2 Timothy 4:3** in the first place? Is it not proven by careful study of context and supported elsewhere in scripture from another witness and finally and most importantly expressed by Jesus Himself in His life and words.

Next, we should be challenged by Jesus warning to us, *"For this reason you also must be ready; for the Son of Man is coming at an hour when you do not think."* **Matthew 24:44** So it shouldn't shock us if all the popular answers are wrong. Maybe God is more wise and clever in concealing than we have imagined, yet just as amazing in revealing this right before the end.

Even the most anointed men have struggled with this subject, so we need much kindness and grace. Yet when we understand most of our failure has been our poor vantage point in time, we should rekindle our hearts toward the search. God hinting to the truth that only the last generation would start to piece together the *"big picture"* enough to place the details correctly **[cf. Daniel 11:32, 12:3, Matthew 24:34]** as was the case in the first coming of Christ. Certainly one thing we all can agree on, we are closer than any generation before us. BUT! We are the final generation, Jesus showed us how to know! There's really is no excuse for us to not to get excited for His return as if it were in some other lifetime. The boy cried wolf too many times is God's way of making this a challenge for us. He is looking for your faith! It doesn't matter that others have searched and been wrong. This is your hour, this is your time!

With this in mind, we should all sit up as smart folk and not allow the adoption of views verbatim without searching the scriptures first. In fact maybe do what I did, throw out everything and start from scratch! My mission is clear, I must give you my piece to help you finish your puzzle. **[cf. 1 Corinthians 13:9]**

2

Knowing:

The Shifting Sands

THE ELEPHANT

"Knowing that the laying aside of my earthly dwelling is imminent as also our lord Jesus Christ has made clear to me... ."

2 Peter 1:14

We ought to be the most envied people on the planet. As His daughters and sons, we always have something to look forward too. No matter what the affliction of our present state, that we endure, our death should be a triumph. Our last breath will be our first breath with Jesus! Our death would amount to His second coming especially if we all *"have fallen asleep"* **1 Thessalonians 4:15** until He comes. In this way our hope in the future, should always drive and effect our now. For no matter what generation experiences the second coming of Christ, it most likely be experienced for all generations at the moment of their death. I mean this is a legitimate possibility.

Also, there should be no uncertainty or shadow cast on something so great as what God has in store for us beyond this divide. For we are talking about a Great God coming to reward the apple of His eye, His bride. So how did we, His people, come to this place of such confusion and ambiguity over our future? Who is diverting our attention? Who is watering down our expectation of His promise when He returns? Are we not concerned that His bride are only those who are found ready or *"eagerly awaiting Him"* **Hebrews 9:28**? Maybe there has been an Elephant distracting us in the room!

13

The early church miscalculated their estimations in scriptures. This shouldn't argued since we live 2000 years later. Why should we think we can estimate anything better than they did? In fact, we wrestle that anything they said in scriptures could be wrong! This is the elephant! For us to clear this elephant from the room we must travel back in time much like the popular movie sequel of the 80's *Back to The Future*.

For lying around this whole topic of why the Apostles got it "wrong" is this period when **2 Peter**, **Hebrews** and **the Gospel of John** were written during a key transition time for God's people. However, the beast in the theatre of modern thinking is why does the bible say through the apostles that Jesus coming was *"near"* and *"soon"* **[ex. 1Peter4:7, James 5:8, 1 John 2:18, Romans 13:11-12]** when from our perspective roughly 2000 years has transpired? I would not call that accurate prophecy if in fact that was what their intension was to predict?

1

NOT ALL SCRIPTURE IS PROPHETIC
"NO PROPHESY OF SCRIPTURE IS A MATTER OF ONE'S OWN INTERPRETATION"
2 PETER 1:20

Prophesy works differently
then the rest of scripture

2

PROPHESY GETS CLEARER WITH TIME

"So we have the prophetic word made more sure, to which you do well to pay attention as to a lamp shining in a dark place,
UNTIL THE DAY DAWNS" 2 Peter 1:19

However we find out from Peter himself here in this amazing letter in defense of the accuracy of prophecy, that not all scripture is prophecy, saying, *"No prophecy of scripture"* **2 Peter 1:20**. Don't miss this! Peter wants us to know what was previously thought, *"the end is near"* **1 Peter** was based on imperfect data, and an estimations made by obedience to Christ command and not a prophetic statement. Further he distinguishes the nature of prophecy as getting clearer the closer you get to its fulfillment **[cf. 1:19]**.

Last I checked, 2000 years seems a whole lot closer to the fulfillment seeing how no where has every eye beheld Him yet **[cf. Revelation 1:7]**. In our current Christian climate, we find many conclusions in the matter of viewing the Apostles inaccuracies. Unfortunately, inconsistent views of who God is biblically have been the result. Their logic goes, first everything in the bible is true, so the Apostles were correct when they said He was near. He just changed His mind because He can come at anytime.

Of course these assumptions are being made all over the place. Starting with the denial that the men of faith who made estimations out of obedience to Christ command **[Matthew 24:43,45-46]** can never be wrong. Trying to protect the pedestal of these founding fathers, we change the nature of God and bring into scripture something entirely disharmonious with the written testimony. All of these notions have produced a total loss of interest or confusion in a subject that takes up about roughly a quarter to a third of the Bible. At a time when, we all should be going back to the drawing board due to the conflicts in the popular belief systems concerning the End of this age. Instead we are being lulled to sleep not to care at all by a false narrative. I mean if the Apostle couldn't get it right who are we to think we can.

These "brilliant ideas" are so popular you might think me to be the heretic for challenging them, but they are not supported by scripture. Here are just some of the unsupported beliefs. First huge one, God can come at anytime. Next, the world will see Him when He comes at first. Even this one, that there will be seven years of tribulation isn't directly taught in scripture. How about this one, God is waiting on a victorious church to return. Maybe we should rephrase that, that God knows the church will be triumphant but He isn't waiting on anyone.

None more popular than this one, no one can know the year of His return, etc. All these are interpretations of scriptures yes but man's interpretations based on isolating passages with inserted assumptions placed upon them. Much like evolution which has a missing link between the most evolved ape and the most primitive man, there are glaring gaps and scriptural contradictions to these beliefs. At some point we gloss over glaring inconsistencies for our chosen narratives.

In light of Jesus own words themselves, ***"You too, be ready; for the Son of Man is coming at an hour that you do not***

15

expect." **Luke 12:40** might we suspect that our popular belief's of the end times will fail men who trust in them! What is Jesus saying? In **Matthew's** account the statement includes the words, _**"for this reason"**_ **Matthew 24:44**? What reason? He had just told the heads of the church, God's households they wouldn't know at what literal _**"day"**_ **v42** or _**"time of night"**_ **v43** the thief was coming, but if they stayed attentive _**"alert"**_ **v42** they would be ready. In fact, Jesus says in another place, if they are awake at some point they would will know the hour _**"I come to you"**_ **Revelation 3:3**. So the Apostles did their best to warn and keep the church alert by saying they thought His coming was near. They just weren't making the statement you think they were making - a false prophecy.

So the logic doesn't hold up. The same people who say we can't know anything because He can come anytime, use these missed estimations to make their point. Yet these missed estimations prove the point that we are allowed to give our best estimations in every generation, thus my book! So my question is how much do we translate our duty to be watchful to actually watching for when He is returning?

For example, Jesus chides the Pharisees that they couldn't even tell history was happening right in front of them! _**"Do you know how to discern the appearance of the sky but cannot discern the signs of the times?"**_ **Matthew 16:2-3** Remember these are the Rabbi's who held the actual count from the earliest known Masoretic texts of **Daniel** & Creation but they were covering it up with chosen ignorance. So now Jesus rebuke makes sense. It wouldn't if they had no way of knowing the timing, but they did! So the same with our generation as it was with the generation of the first coming, we have enough information for a logical narrowing of the time of His return!

Within this very context above, Jesus is commanding the disciples to steward the readiness of the church for the reason of not letting the enemy in. **[Cf. Matthew 24:45]** Which is the best explanation for why we see so much ESTIMATIONS being made in their correspondence to the church making its way into scripture. One, they really EXPECTED Jesus based on many deceptive points of references given them. Two, they had a stewardship left to them by Jesus command, to ready the church. Three, God wanted us to see their struggle and devotion to know, and, four, encourage us all to live like Christ could come tomorrow.

We can argue later how much we are allowed to know and when by examining the context for phrases like _**"of that day and hour no one knows"**_ **Matthew 24:36** in His discourse on the Mount of Olives but one thing is clear, we need CONTEXT here. Consider how important this is when we are being told later clearly, He is only returning for those who are *"eagerly awaiting Him"* **Hebrews 9:28**. What will be your argument as your left behind because you failed to be fueled by the hope of His return, because in your mind you were taught it would all just pan out? *[Cf. Peter Pan Theology popular after the false predictions of the 1980's]*

Let's repeat those words, *"to those who eagerly awaiting"* **Hebrews 9:28** and that's it. No one else! Can you say you are eager for His return? Awaiting someone, comes with some level of expectation based on *"paying attention"* **2 Peter 1:19.** For starters, to say today that we are confused and out of touch with what really happened in the landscape of biblical times or even worse what the bible teaches on this subject is an understatement. For we have completely neglected it and called it off limits. For most of us, the proposition of the Apostles getting it "wrong" within our sacred canonized scriptures is blasphemy as well. There must be another reason we think.

Consider though their estimations were an act of obedience to Christ to keep the church alerted **[cf. Matthew 24:44-45]**, this should be sufficient reason for their inclusion to the Canon of scripture by the church centuries later. All scripture is for inspiration **[cf. 2 Timothy 3:16]** and reliable doesn't mean they got it right or now nothing can be trusted BECAUSE WE THINK God *"changed His mind"*. If God changed His mind, thus He could have come but didn't why? It wasn't that the church wasn't victorious during these times.

Some site Paul's words that, *"time has been shortened"* **1 Corinthians 7:29,** saying this proves God was thinking of coming then changed His mind. The context though is to implore married men to serve God more mindfully than pleasing their wives because Christians were being persecuted and lives were being cut short. Again the context wasn't the coming of Jesus Christ, yet we try to support our narrative by pulling scripture out its context.

Within all this confusion, I believe we have been led down a very ugly path of construing what really is the narrative and using heretical notions that are unbiblical and dishonoring to who God really is! If God is really Sovereign in time then he isn't *"delaying"*, changing His mind, playing games and making random decision based on *"the bride's readiness"* OR ANYTHING? The scriptures is clear, He already knows and orchestrated this present age to conclude at a *"fixed times"* **Acts 1:7**. Yet many try to circumvent this obvious statement for the end of the age with the belief the rapture occurs before the end separate from the second coming.

Again the notion that Jesus can return *"AT ANY TIME"* comes from the idea that the Apostles were speaking truth's that He is always near because He can come anytime. Or better yet He hadn't made up His mind. Of course God has the ability to come anytime, that is not what we are debating here! The question should be does God come before He says He will? Is God now indecisive? Does He not know the end from the beginning? Has He not spoken in His word when? Yes, He has. So then the preacher should preach how much will He inform us and when will He show us not that he can come anytime or is the next thing to happen.

Yet instead of searching scriptures, we love easy outs to what seems like a lofty concept, His return. Interpreting *"all scripture inspired"* **2 Timothy 3:16** and all things canonized as *"thus saith the Lord"*, we prefer to rationalize or defend the Apostles as though they were prophesying and correct but GOD changed His mind. We lift men up and lower God. Does this not erode God's sovereignty! Peter is clear when speaking on this topic of understanding future events, the necessity to separate prophesy from the rest of scripture, saying, *"no prophecy of scripture"* **2 Peter 1:20**. Why is Peter compelled to do this? Within the context it should be crystal clear. For we find the church shifting its perspective to a much larger picture of God's plan. Peter needing to explain why this was happening and can happen.

Why is this so important to Peter to make a delineation between prophecy and the rest of scripture? Think about it! He is about to defend in this letter his use of the phrase *"in the last days"* **Acts 2:17,** 12,000 days earlier. For we see him refer to it again in **2 Peter 3:3.** Given Peter just wrote in His first letter, *"the end is near"* **1 Peter 4:7** a conflict was occurring amongst the churches for context. When we look at his statement in his first letter, we view an honest evaluation of the times they lived based on their partial knowledge of prophecy.

All this appeared to many at the time as delays given approximately 12,045 *"last days"* had occurred from Pentecost to his first letter. This created a climate for false teachers, to which Peter spends the whole second chapter in his second letter on **[cf. 2 Peter 2]**. They would have said, *'I mean come on Peter, this is 30 years later and 12,000 days or so; so what did you mean by "the last days"* **Acts 2:17?**' However, Peter will be clear to reveal that prophecy was getting clearer and will, but that they were living in *"a dark place"* **2 Peter 1:19** at that time. Hopefully I can show you, just how confusing a period they lived in. My main point though is they made estimations not prophecy.

What we fail to see in our pursuits of truth is that God was comfortable allowing the human condition and struggle to understand His coming to be apart of what He deemed *"inspired"* **2 Timothy 3:16** scripture. It revealed their pursuit to know and stay alert, and it should inspire us. By understanding the amazing way God concealed it from them while they never stopped pursuing knowing more; are we not being taught a truth, a powerful truth? Every generation is not afforded the same vantage points to seeing the big picture but God desires every generation to long and seek His return!

If that isn't enough for you, then consider approximately 267 years later, great learned Christian bishops found no problem with their estimations being canonized as *"inspired"*. Yet by that period of time when the Council of Nicaea in **325AD** Canonized, many in the church held to Amillennialism, a belief they were already in the Millennium reign of Christ. Thus the reason for the Apostles estimation was the end did occur in **70AD** with Jerusalem's destruction, and now God was done with the Jews and replaced by a new order of a conquering church through their Emperor Constantine. This being just an example to us how time changes our perspective.

Today we face the same threat of perspective as a growing number in our generation, are reinterpreting *"Last Days"* as a revelation to the Apostles of the final days of the Law before the Age of Grace would fully be transitioned at 70AD. I don't hold to this view, but in respect they will site, *"in these last days"* **Hebrews 1:2** and *"in these last days"* **James 5:3** as proof since they were spoken before **70AD**. This leads us into very dangerous territory of reinterpreting Jesus coming as already occurring in our age, or the Millennial Kingdom will be brought in by us. This comes with a growing disinterest in the failure of previous generations to give solid reasons for all the Apostles words, *"he is near"* and *"last days"* mentioned in scripture. Remember we are 2000 years later, after many failed attempts to prognosticate his return, the boy just cried wolf too many times!

So many conclude the Millennium reign of Christ must have started through the church, and at some point Jesus will join our party. It's just so much easier to believe in NOW and not something into the future. Yet at no time has Jesus been seen by *"every eye"* **Revelation 1:7** Not at the transfiguration, not at His ascension before His disciples, not in 70 AD, never! So the real question is can the Millennial reign of Christ somehow lose its contexts from the book of **Revelation 20:4**. Can Jesus not be here and His reign start? I deal with those doctrinal issues in chapter 4.

Yet what they fail to see is the full impact of the term *"last days"* with its context which originates from **Joel**. Peter had it right, the Holy Spirit guided Him to declare it had begun on the Day of Pentecost **[cf. Acts 2:17]**. Yet the full extent of this word is taken from **Joel 2:28-32** which includes *the Day of the Lord* and *His return* to Jerusalem in **Joel 3** as the period of time lesser than the whole of human history. Again the sun and moon did not become dark during **70AD**! No superman return was ever recorded, that is because it is still future.

So let's look at this amazing prophecy in **Joel.** God's spirit will begin to be poured out in greater measure until the whole world will experience it in the Millennium future **[cf. Joel 2:28]**. Phew, let's take a breath. What I am getting at here is that *"last days"* aren't literal days, but a part of a prophetic week of each day consisting of thousand years. That would make the final 3 days or 3000 years lesser than the whole, 7 days or 7000 years. The perspective is huge not small.

For example, Paul tells Timothy. *"In the last days difficult times will come"* **2 Timothy 3:1** as if it were still in the distant future, and this is just the tip of the iceberg. Many old testament references point to it linked to stuff still future. **[Cf. Isaiah 2;2, Jeremiah 49:39, Ezekiel 38:16, Hosea 3:5, Micah 4:1]** And finally we have Peter here in his second letter connecting *"the last days"* **2 Peter 3:3** to the coming judgment of fire **[v5,10]**. Well, this hasn't occurred either has it? So why are these linked events not showing up in our history books, if they indeed are past? When did you ever hear that a man showed up above the world like superman and every eye beheld him? No, the last days are not over, they are just a longer period than first thought. So we are back to the hard truth, the Apostles got it wrong. They weren't prophesying.

Some don't just agree with me but they think the Apostles were keeping the early church in line. They will say, *'Fear or uncertainty is needed to keep us alert'*, therefore we are not to know when He returns. I obviously reject this notion, that fear ever accomplished God's righteousness, or that God would keep the generation effected in the dark, its just unbiblical **[cf. *"God does nothing unless"* Amos 3:7, *"Not in darkness"* 1 Thessalonians 5:4]**. For those who say if we know when He's returning we will get lazy, again I reject this notion as well. The fact that we are the last generation changes that formula. For if I love God I would be more excited and motivated to finish the mission if I know His coming is in my lifetime, in fact I would be more motivated. Early church obviously wasn't ashamed to give their estimations, seek for the timing or discuss this topic.

However, consider if what I am defending in this book from the scriptures is true, that only the final generation is afforded knowing the season of His return *[period of a few years]* and we are it. This would have the affect Jesus says it should. It would cause us to *"lift up your heads"* **Luke 21:28** and increase the push to bring in every last soul. In fact if God expects us to sit up and take notice and we choose ignorance, what will we say to Him when He comes? What will the early church have to say!?

Even as I speak the truths I will demonstrate to you in this book, it is not a private interpretation but based on research everyone can access in His word, in historical records, in plain sight confirming a very timely end. In spite of this, the bible tells us an incredible truth. Jesus says even if angels should appear some won't believe, and even the ten virgins are caught asleep when He returns! **[Cf. Matthew 25:5]** So I write with fervent heat of passion saying, "AWAKE!" Stop believing these lies that God has become somewhat disinterested or would allow His own to be in the dark, or in fact we all just missed it as though He returned already!

For what started as only the Heavenly Father knows in the statement, *"But the Father alone"* **Matthew 24:36** has grown to include Jesus now enthroned in heaven with His Omniscience! What started out for the disciples as *"not for you to know"* **Acts 1:7** grew to be *"you yourselves know full well"* **1 Thessalonians 5:2** and you are *"No longer in darkness that the day should overtake you"* **5:4**. What started out as *"the end is near"* **1 Peter 4:7** for Peter ends with *"day is a thousand years"* and *"God is not slow"* **2 Peter 3:8-9** in His follow-up letter. Can you see where I'm going with this? Revelation is never stagnant, and the waters must flow again.

This should not be a surprise since **Daniel** prophesies that, *"Knowledge will increase"* **12:4** because time changes our vantage point in seeing the big picture. Yet here we are today settling for naïveté, because no one is challenging the sacred cows, the elephants in the room that Satan has planted while we slept. So here it goes .... Jesus cannot come at anytime, in fact we can narrow down His return to a period of years from two signs Jesus Himself gave us. What we can't do is know the very day.

Yes, that's correct you heard me correctly Jesus Himself told us! Does that matter to you? Your savior is trying to speak to you prophetically behind the obvious in the shadows of God's chosen codes, for God always leaves behind two or three witnesses agreeing. The issue as I roll out this revelation won't be the evidence but your hearts readiness to receive the word of God.

In rolling out this harmonious comprehensive look at God's timing for events yet future, **2 Peter** more than any other place in the Word of God clarifies the direction we should be headed in understanding the revelation of God's plan, timing and details. For no other place does it give clear rules for interpreting prophecy and insight into the shift the church made at the time of its writing. So I choose to make it our focal point.

THE SHIFT

Before the Shift
*"The end of all things
is near; ..."* **1 Peter 4:7**

After the Shift
*"The Lord is not slow about
His promise ..."* **2 Peter 3:9**

So much like the Doc Brown's pinpointing calculations to send the DeLorean Fusion car back in time to an exact point in time; I want us to focus at the period between the first and second letter of Peter, approximately **60-67AD.** This is right before the destruction of Jerusalem, and Peter's death to Nero. It is actually believed his second letter was written very soon after the first letter to the same churches only because Peter knew he had little time left, declaring his death **[cf. 2 Peter 1:14]**. Peter will die around **66-67AD**. Remember Paul will be martyred as well.

So back in time we go to help answer these questions, we must, as Yoda would say. Let it be said, **2 Peter** was chosen by this author, because it sheds light into what I refer to as *"the shift"*! A period of time when we see the big picture of God's timing coming into view for the Apostles, after their tunnel vision wore off. All dated within this period of **62-65AD** we have the emergence of ...

1. **Hebrews** with its seventh day theology paralleling creation with human history **[4:1-9]** with the literary style of the Epistle of Barnabas (100AD) written later expounding on that theme into 7 ages or prophetic days of thousand years each.
2. **2 Peter** with its thousand years is a day prophetic code and God is not slow **[3:8-9]** and
3. **The Gospel of John** which clarifies false notions the Apostles wouldn't die before His return **[21:23]**. Note the **Book of Revelation** had not yet been revealed either giving the Thousand Year period of God's seventh day rest for earth.

Starting with this second attempt to write to the churches of Asia, we find answers from all kinds of angles concerning God's timing & the insight into the difficulty they faced to understand it! For a dynamic shift from viewing Jesus return as *"near"* **1 Peter 4:17** to being a part of a big picture that could be further out than expected is seen clearly in *"God is not slow"* **2 Peter 3:8-9**. For example, the letter seems to climb to its pinnacle as Peter finally mentions his *"one fact"* that a *"day is as a thousand years"* which is a big picture idea for God's overall plan, or as Peter argues *"from the beginning"* **v4**.

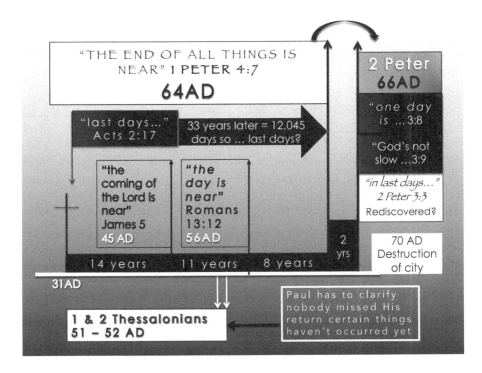

We can't ignore this development when Peter insist in the same letter that prophecy is getting clearer! **[1:19]** We must assume Peter found something new. Peter is now changing his tune saying, God is not slow. Addressing the issue of *"those who count slowness"* **3:9** as a bigger issue than the church not being ready because He is *"near"*. What did Peter discover? We will never know exactly.

However, it does sound like Peter is trying to say in his second letter, *'I know we have been saying we are close to His return and it feels like it's getting old hearing it. For I know I said these are the last days over 12,000 days ago. However, we have received more insight into what God meant by* **"in the last days'** Acts 2:17 [cf. 2

23

Peter 3:3] *for starters I must die,* **[cf. 1 Peter 1:14]** *other things must happen first and Jesus never said this would happen in our lifetime, so you are going to have to pick up the baton of seeking answers."*

When we bring the Gospel of John into this picture written during this same period, we begin to see the church misinterpreted Jesus words **[cf. John 21:23]** What words? Jesus had promised within the Apostles lifetime they would see His Kingdom, *"some of those standing here who will not taste death until they see the Son of Man coming in His kingdom."* **Matthew 16:28**

All of a sudden Peter mentioning of the Transfiguration **[cf. 2 Peter 1:16-18]** as proof they saw His Kingdom majesty **[cf. Matthew 17:1]** makes historical sense. This coupled with Peter mentioning Jesus prophecy of his own death in the same context **[cf. 1 Peter 1:14]** there really can be no mistake. Peter is shifting the church from this idea of a *"soon"* return to a bigger picture.

Notice the focus has changed from the first letter of being prepared to not being discouraged or losing faith in His return just because it seems delayed and now Apostles are about to die. Here's one of the big issues of life and seeing prophecy. Without knowing or being convinced God has this whole thing finished before He started it, what we are facing doesn't make sense with the shifting perspectives. Especially, if we don't have faith in His word to reveal that mystery, we tend to give it another narrative. We tend to view everything as an accident that even God is subject to, or we go the other way to say He's a Sovereign who changes His mind.

Instead of building unbiblical narratives to support flimsy foundations that can be easily refuted in the Word of God, we must challenge ourselves to ask questions and build on His foundation of two or three witnesses believing somethings are not given to change namely the Word of God or more substantially, Jesus own words. For example, in the prophetic community today there has been this *"Jonah principle"* that if someones prophecy or their version of the end doesn't happen it was because God changed His mind or the church made a better or worse choice just as with Nineveh and Jonah's preaching. **[Cf. Jonah 3]**

This is very convenient for false prophets to fall back on and keep giving words that don't align with the Word of God or what was previously accepted by the church as unshakable. In the case of Jonah, Nineveh's choice either way does not or would not effect God's prophecy or timeline in scripture. The same as what the message is here, your decision to chase God doesn't change what is about to happen scripturally, but it does define your place in history and affect a lot within that.

Those who hold strong to alternative endings are losing faith in a God who keeps His schedule, yet they may enjoy my main driving point of the timeline. It was in part created due to Israel rejection of Christ and a choice.

From the Almighty's perspective though all this is done, but that doesn't mean He isn't exercising *"patience"* **2 Peter 3:9** as Peter will tell us. Or that men of God aren't allowed to have mistakes or get things wrong. In God's defense though consider this. He allowed just enough in scripture for others to find the truth, while concealing the knowledge Peter & Paul were onto at that time by the timing of their very death's. Just clicks away in the perspective of time, Peter & Paul will die soon after this letter in **67AD**. God is all business about concealing and revealing at the right time. I am here saying the time is funneling into our NOW!

For example, even Jesus knowing His return would exceed the timeframe most would assume gives a parable stating, *"While the bridegroom was delaying"* **Matthew 25:5** and *"a man planted a vineyard...and went on a journey for a long time."* **Luke 20:9** Remember parables often exaggerate the truth, Jesus truly is not delaying. What He is saying is, this will be the perception at the time of His return. Why am I confident in this? Well, let's turn to another manuscript from this time period which in plain speech says, *"He who is coming will come and will not delay."* **Hebrews 10:37** There you go, the early church did not believe God was random but on a schedule.

So which is it? Is He taking His time, waiting on us or has it always been determined before time existed when God would act? This is the decision you must make to move forward or stay stagnant in the dark. For no matter whether we sleep or stay awake, I contend He is actually on schedule and the schedule is printed in the bible! One careful look at His first coming would tell you, He came *"at the right time"* **Romans 5:6b** Why would His second coming differ?

So again it bears repeating for emphasis, He is on His seventh day lawn chair according to **Hebrews 4** because from *"foundations of the world"* much if not all things were planned, decided, orchestrated or destined! **[cf. Matthew 13:35,John 17:24, Hebrews 4:3, Hebrews 9:26, 1 Peter 1:20, Revelation 13:8, Revelation 17:8]** History has been completed for Him to be done and rested! From our perspective everything tends to feel out of control, still in process because it is. From His perspective He is already resting from His works. **[Cf. Hebrews 4]** Consider there is not *ONE SCRIPTURE* that speaks clearly this message promoted by the church that Jesus can come at anytime, or is the next thing to happen. The opposite, in fact, is spoken and proven by more than one witness in scripture. **"He has fixed a day"** **Acts 17:31** The sooner we get on board with this fundamental truth, the sooner we too will enter His rest. We can trust Him with our lives, He already worked out everything for good **"to those ..."** **Romans 8:28**

The absence of something clearly spoken is critical here, for if the Apostles believed for one moment His coming was at any moment, then what prevented them from just saying so like, *'His coming is at anytime'*. Granted there are a lot of things unsaid that are still true, like *He cannot come anytime*, because other ways of saying the same thing are plainly said such as, **"times and epochs which the Father has fixed!"** **Acts 1:7** or **"unless the apostasy comes first"** **2 Thessalonians 2:3**. You don't have to be a genius to understand if events must come first and the timing is fixed, then Jesus cannot come next but at the appointed time on a schedule with other events!

Many shout out that the **"unless"** passage was about the start of Day of the Lord not Jesus coming, which I agree! Yet this exposes another fallacy that there can even be a Day of the Lord without Jesus being present above earth, therefore His coming, therefore His day! Notice Paul's theology lumps three events in one saying, **"with regards to the coming of our Lord Jesus Christ and our gathering together to Him"** **2 Thessalonians 2:1** then goes forward with the churches concern that, **"The Day"**, had already started. This one contexts gives in fact two precursors, or events that must **"come first"** **2:3** There are five in total, one of which we see starts Peter's argument - His own death **[cf. 2 Peter 1:14]**. Again these are called *PRECURSORS*, events that must come before, making it impossible for Jesus to come at any time. Some scholars find more.

Most of this "Anytime Return" is driven by the crowds of "experts" who hold to an idea that the rapture is separate from His second coming therefore need not be apart of the timeline Jesus spoke of with precursors to His second coming. **[cf. Matthew 24:15-27]** In this reconstruction without rules not found in scripture like I am using of 2 - 3 witnesses, they have created license to chaos with imposing their own ideas. Yet if we focused just on this theory that the rapture is separate from the term *His coming*, we will find ourselves in conflict with none less honored then the Apostle Paul who taught, **"After that those who are Christ's at His coming then the end"** **1 Corinthians 15:23** When are we raptured? At His coming! Not before or after but <u>but AT</u>!

For example, does not Jesus come to earth to take us? Would

that not be a coming especially if He meets us in the lower atmosphere *"aer"* [cf. 1 Thessalonians 4;17] which is a different greek word from the higher atmosphere? Next, **1 Corinthians 15:23** reference to His coming above and our exit being the same is followed immediately by *"then the end"* **v24**. No break in time! They are sequential, linked together in that order! There can be no space in time from the rapture to judgment! **[Cf. Luke 17:29]** The obvious is also staring us in the face. Would this not create a third coming for Pre-Tribulation theorist when the word for coming *"parousia"* is a future definite article in the singular?

Then there is this issue. We are told we never leave His side. **[cf. 1 Thessalonians 4:17]** So if we go off to heaven He must leave as well, thus what follows cannot be the Day of the Lord because He is not present for it and when He returns with us a third coming! What I just showed you is how you create stuff that isn't directly taught in the bible, like a third coming or a rapture separate from His coming. Or isn't logical like separating the day of the Lord from Him being present on earth.

When we return to the *"dark place"* **2 Peter 1:19** the Apostles lived in, I am so glad Jesus told us the truth it wasn't for them to know, saying, *"not for YOU to know"* **Acts 1:7**. How far do we interpret this context as well? Do we take this to mean every generation that followed wouldn't know, when Jesus is very specific saying, *"for YOU"*? If Jesus was speaking to all believers throughout this age would not He have phrased His statement different? What is the context but the mission of evangelizing the whole planet! Under those guidelines, we can expect God to conceal to every generation who knowing might cause them to sit on their butts. That isn't the case with the last one as I have shown logically!

Historically speaking we see a fisherman like Peter given prophetic revelation way above his ability to comprehend it at Pentecost, later having the mentality to see the prophetic literature more clearly. We have been calling this having a better vantage point! Peter is now grappling with the length of days that have past and the insight from his study of scripture. When this all started the Holy Spirit took over speaking through him, *"These are the last days"* **Acts 2:17** applying **Joel 2** context to their day. Only now in **2 Peter 3:8** He understands its in connection with a big picture of God's plan, most likely due to Paul's influence and wisdom.

What we learn is truth is relative to when it is spoken, to whom it is spoken and for how long it was meant for, and the bigger storyline it fits into. For example, Peter preaching in **31AD** concerning these *"last days"* **v17** goes unto mention another event in that period of time, when *"grant wonders in the sky above and signs on the earth below blood fire and vapor of smoke. The sun will be turned into darkness and the moon blood before the great and glorious Day of the Lord shall come."* **Acts 2:19-20** So when Peter mentions Jesus return is *"near"* in his first letter, he is actually revealing they agreed with the Apocalyptic Jews of their day [cf. Essences] that the Messiah was coming to judge soon. So what changed? Peter must have found Moses' **Psalm 90** for his **2 Peter 3:8** revelation, which told him to "*number our days"*! The answer is Peter turned analytical given the popularity of I Enoch's prophecies as well.

Peter's second letter to the same churches revolves around reintroducing the phrase again he spoke at Pentecost saying, *"In the last days"* **3:3** and defines what those days might represent within the context of what was previously spoken of in scripture by Moses in **Psalms 90:4**. Notice how Peter's wants this letter to be known as after the first pointing to, *"This is NOW"* **3:1**. As if he is saying, I know I said in my first letter *"end is near"* **1 Peter 4:7** but... Thus we see in such detail his explanation for the way prophecy is a process that gets clearer. This is contrasted with *"mockers"* **3:3** who settle on losing faith & hope being cynical at the first sign of disappointment.

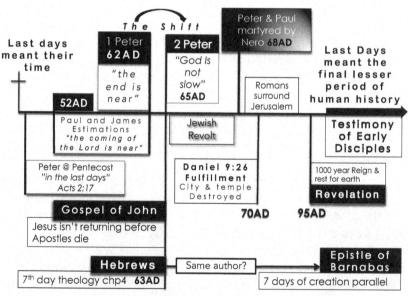

APOSTLE'S TIMELINE OF REVELATION

Again Peter wants for future generations to know this letter came after the first exclaiming, *"This is now beloved the second letter"* **3:1** So no one is ever confused later which letter represented the shift in thought. He could have written this in his greeting portion of his letter but he places it directly before his big revelation in **2 Peter 3:8**! This idea of a simple fisherman gaining a wealth of information is found back in his first letter when he points to others before him who did the same, *"The prophets ...made careful search ...seeking to know what person or time"* **1 Peter 1:10-11**

By the second letter he declares the success of his searches as, *"we have the prophetic word made more sure"* **2 Peter 1:19** and evidence they searched far and wide for answers in the way he incorporates 1 Enoch ideas in both letters. Aware of his impending death, He urges the church to receive the baton of revelation, *"to which we would do well to pay attention as to a lamp shining in a dark place"* **1:19**. This means we are shifting into the daylight or full revelation of what was previously spoken through reliable sources, which he carefully explains what those sources are, not new stuff but old seen more clearly **[cf. 2 Peter 3:2]**.

Peter's objective was to reveal how they got to where they were by first showing how they were *"eyewitnesses"* of a foreshadowing of His second coming **[cf. 2 Peter 1:16-17, Matthew 17, Acts 1:10-11]**, the dress rehearsal if you will. This is important, they were clearly shown the identity of the future Son of Man was indeed their master, Jesus! Because they saw Him lit up on the Mount of Transfiguration fulfilling His words to them that they wouldn't taste death before seeing His kingdom! **[Cf. Matthew 16:38]** God choosing to reveal the nature of His second coming so their confidence and hunger could drive generations to follow.

So Peter leaves the legacy to others instructing them how through, *"words spoken beforehand by the holy prophets and the commandments of the Lord and by your apostles."* **3:2** Our letter writer, even goes as far as to support Paul's superiority in his letters on the subject of God's complex plan **[cf. 2 Peter 3:16]**. It was as if, Peter is establishing for legacy what should be doctrine and Canon (accepted). This attention to being careful how we decide on truth is very important in light of the warning of *"private interpretations"* **2 Peter 1:21** leading us into a whole chapter on false teachers **[cf. 2 Peter 2]**.

All this seems to be laid out to remove obstacles for future generations to search for answers when *"the day dawns"* **2 Peter 1:19** or approaches and everything is clearer. *1 Enoch*, Jewish popular apocryphal writing, [not canonized scripture] themes show up throughout his letters revealing how far they went to examine everything in their day. Hence in this tradition of Apostolic leadership, we too will look for truth based on two or three witnesses from scripture only referring to *1 Enoch & Early Church quotes* to demonstrate further support for biblical truth's based on what influenced the minds both before and after the Apostles era.

As to this shift, we need only consider within this time period what transpired. **John's gospel** was written in **[circa 65AD]**, and with it we see clarification that Jesus wasn't returning before they died **[cf. v21:23]**. Peter also affirming that by his mention of his prophesied death, deals with Christ return as not as imminent as others supposed **[cf. 2 Peter 1:14]**. Next **the book of Hebrews [circa 60-65 AD]** introduces us to the big picture Eschatological view in both correlating Mt. Sinai to His future return **[cf. 12:18]** and a future rest for the people of God called God's seventh day **[cf. 4:1-11]**! Even Peter's argument for the end is based on *"from the beginning"* **2 Peter 3:4** The church had shifted in regards to seeing God as having a plan that wasn't reactionary but carefully plotted before the foundations of the world, and measured out in His Sovereignty.

It is from this point of reference, we see more and more evidence of a belief system in the church that follows taking literally Peter's mention of *"a day is as a thousand years"* **2 Peter 2:8** as later seen in **the Book of Revelation 20:4 [circa 95AD]** and the writings found during that period that followed. The prophetic week of seven ages equaling thousand years each was beginning to be birthed. What amazes me in this timeline is that Jesus authored **Revelation** after **70AD** and confirms where the church was already headed in **20:4** in their understanding of the big picture!

THE LIMITATIONS

*"Of that **day and hour no one knows**, not even the angels of heaven nor the Son **but the Father alone**."*

Matthew 24:36

In this section we will look at the difference of knowing the big picture from the details. Revisiting Peter's connection to the Transfiguration as having the prophetic words of His second coming *"**made more sure**"* **2 Peter 1:19**. Peter might as well be saying, 'Soon I'm going to die, and you're going to have to trust our first hand experiences that yes He is the Messiah who will come, *and it it still future.'* Admitting it had begun to get clearer and eventually would be very clear, he still admits they were in a dark place concerning prophetic fulfillments.

Yet one thing seems glaring to me by the second chapter of his letter, Peter's concern with false teachers coming was that they would replace the hope of the second coming promise with an earthly hope that leads to sinning. For what was Peter's assurance, that until we see what they saw in the transfiguration, we aren't there yet!

For many of us looking at their struggle, the question is should our experience be defined by theirs and how? We say, *'Well if they couldn't get off the ground with it, why should I expect to see anything different'*. That is assuming we are all living in the same vantage point in time that they were, **"a dark place" 1:19**! Ignoring Peter's teaching on revelation getting brighter, we seem to have chosen to sleep in the light of our day!

Yes, we hear it all the time. *'No one knows the day!'* As if that resolves the issue, or rescinds the command to **"look for ... the day" 2 Peter 3:12**. Everyone knows exactly what is meant, no one knows the day relatively, or the period of time. In their defense, many try to lump two bible references as two witnesses against knowing anything about His return. These two ...

THE DETAILS OF KNOWING
"But of that day or hour no one knows, not even the angels of heaven, nor the Son, but the father alone. For the coming of the Son ..." **Matthew 24:36**

THE BIG PICTURE OF KNOWING
"It is not for YOU to know times or epochs which the Father has fixed by His own authority." **Acts 1:7**

However both references are dealing with two entirely different areas of knowing as I show above, so they can't be used as 2 witnesses to the same thing. One limits how detailed you can get, and the other which generation who will know. One deals with the very starting day of His coming and the other the calculation for the years until His return based on measured timetables for ages revealed in scripture. To make this two witnesses saying the same thing, they aren't. The contexts are not the same, and the context are not even saying what people want them to say.

Both give real limits but both give an answer at the same time by giving those limits. For example, we can't know the day opens the door to knowing month year since He would have said so. Again, if Jesus was making this a universal statement for the church to not know the timing of the epochs and see chronology from creation correctly, then it would have been said differently. Jesus wouldn't have singled them out. *"Not for YOU to know"*

The first reference is connected to what was described earlier in the discourse, from a period of *"those days"* **Matthew 24:21** would come the coming of Christ entirely hidden **v27** then evident by **v29 [cf. Revelation 6:16]** later seen physically in **v30**. *"Of that Day ...No one knows"* **v36** is defined in the next verse as connected to the commencement of that period called *"the coming of the Son of Man"* **Matthew 24:37**. The contexts will continue by defining this coming as being mysterious until *"the day that Noah entered the Ark"* **v38**. I always ask, did Noah enter the ark in a period of time or on a single day. Well, the closest thing we get to a period here is the seven days prior to the flood when he loads the animals so I guess he's going in and out during that time; as in *"those days before the flood"* **v38** but then He concludes with the very *"day"* Noah enters and God seals the door and the floods start, a single point in time.

In either case we are discussing a pin pointed time in history or the start of that period. Jesus includes the word *"hour"* to indicate how unusual the surroundings of that day will be which were still unknown at the time of Christ. Whether it is the start of the Coming or the start of the flood/fire judgements or that whole period of days that parallel to Noah's loading period, the focus is placed on how difficult and unknown the discovery of the very start is. Jesus could have easily said, *"no one will know anything ever."* For our emphasis here is on the ungodly attempt to reinterpret this passage as a safe haven from searching His coming. As if knowing is illegal, we ignore the obvious throughout the context. Jesus wants us to know, giving us as much ways and information allowed Him by the Father at that time!

There is no question what we are talking about in knowing is a literal starting time therefore on a single day. For Jesus had just given the disciples an absolutely clear way to know once it starts; *"For just as lightning ..."* **Matthew 24:27**! This being the case we have not excluded knowing beyond that! Say the month, year, season of years! We must wake up to this fact! The world the bible lives in may not match up with what is being popularly preached on Sunday's but it better be soon because the clock is ticking! For the whole context for Matthew 24 is around literal 24 hour days!

So let's just look at this once again. Many believe the term *"day and hour"* is a phrase that is referring to the whole period of time in Jesus discourse from the Beginning of Birth Pangs on. What is certain is the word *"day"* is constantly used in a literal sense throughout the whole discourse. For example, He says, *"Unless those days had been cut short"* **Matthew 24:22** giving us a plural use for a literal day. It is here we find the most logical reason why no one will know a literal day if God is shortening what is expected. For something to be cut short there must be an expected count. **Daniel 12:11-12** is that count, saying from the Abomination of Desolation there will be **1290 days** and then **(45 more)1335 days** *[Note: this count must be literal days in **Daniel** for nothing fits 1290 years from the Abomination of **167BC** or the wrongly perceived one in **70AD** as an ending any wonders].* So there is a count of literal days at the very end.

Now in the context, Jesus reminds us of this expected time code by mentioning **Daniel** the prophet in **Matthew 24:15** specifically and then by the early churches addition of *"know accurately"* within the same verse added. We see then their admission to this fact of a count. So the whole context is with this in mind and spoken in a chronological order e.i. *"then" v23*. Which leads us to *"so will the coming of the Son of Man be" v27* as actually happening in the period being spoken where *"day"* is used in a literal 24 hour sense. Noah used directly as a reference for the *"day and hour"* didn't take days to enter the ark the final time, but did take days entering to load it. All this is in reference to an instance in time, or a very short period when Noah loaded the ark that is deceiving as heck. One which the context speaks loud and clear is after the Abomination of Desolation. Understanding most of this isn't rocket science, we should all just sit up and pay attention.

Consider surrounding this *"day"* much is mentioned in the reliability of witnesses and whether Jesus will come seen at first. The whole context suggest the trouble locating the start of His coming because He is not revealed physically at the onset, and at a time when many use these signs in the heaven to declare themselves the coming of Christ. In the midst of this environment of much deceit and danger, God says the very elect could lose their salvation. **[Cf. Matthew 24:22]**

The importance in this message is focused on not missing the rapture, our departure, our exit right. So my question is, does not knowing the season of years help us stay focused amongst all this confusion coming when it comes down to literal days, count from the prophet Daniel? The churches hope was *"the appearing of the glory"* **Titus 2:13** as seen in **Matthew 24:27**, not in something obvious like His physical presence to the world which is later. **[cf.**

Matthew 24:30]

The reference for what *"the day"* represents is clear. The moment when Jesus return to earth in **Matthew 24:27** missed by many. This is distinctly different then *"the day of His revealing"* **Luke 17:30** in sync with the next verse **Matthew 24:28** which is when *"one is taken one left"* **Luke 17:31-35.** One need only follow the parallel verses to sync these. So from a larger period of *"the days of the Son of Man"* **Luke 17:26** which parallel the time when Noah was loading the ark seven days before the floods arrived and the flood itself came a more specific day referred to as *"the day of His revealing"* **Luke 17:30** which parallels the flood. Do you see how much already I am speaking that you aren't hearing from anyone! The floods started after the signs of its coming began. Which is obvious looking at the difference between the harmless glory flashes in the sky **[cf. Matthew 24:27]** versus the sky split open in the Sixth Seal **[cf. Revelation 6:14-17]**.

In the **Matthew 24** context, we might assume no space in time exist between the **Matthew 24:27** event and the **v28** event. However **Luke 17's** account speaking on this time suggest it. **Matthew** will later support this idea of a longer period for Christ arrival before our departure saying, *"For the coming of the Son of man will be just like the days [plural] of Noah"* **v37**. Of course Noah spent seven days loading, knowing the day of the flood, while the pre-flood world was unaware. This is the very first major revelations you must get in your head, Jesus doesn't just show up physically and all is over! His coming is days plural!

The rapture/fire judgment event **Matthew 24:28** comes after His arrival and clearly separates two distinct tribulation periods. **[Cf. *"after that tribulation"* Mark 13:24]** as it did for Noah as well. So we now know a little better the context of *"no-one knows the day"*, and possibly why? However maybe Jesus is just stating a truth that was time sensitive, I mean nobody did know then. Just a side note, Noah knew the day of the flood seven days prior so there's no telling how detailed we can be in the final years months and days leading up to.

That said, the Jewish tradition of the Wedding and how Jesus uses it in the very next chapter **Matthew 25,** speaks volumes to what is really going on here. I tend to believe strongly in the beauty of the bride not knowing the very day for her reward, for her own readiness and reward. For instance, this parable story of the bridegroom coming **[v1-12]** is followed by the same *"day and hour"* **v13** statement. Yet what most don't catch from the story is it describes what happens after He has already come as seen in, *"Behold the Bridegroom"* **v6** and then the effort of all the virgins to trim their lamps or get right with God.

We will later consider when this period occurs. Whether the faithful have already been gathered, then this awakens others who go last before the fire judgments or just get left behind and are taken at the end. The context for all 10 virgins making final preparations cues us to the fact they all were as the text describes *"sleeping"* and not ready! Scripture is clear, he is coming for only those who are eagerly awaiting Him **[cf. Hebrews 9:28]**. Yet, we know God is gracious, so we can easily see this occurring from His arrival **Matthew 24:27** but before His gathering of His faithful **v28** which is before the Day of Judgments, the Trumpet Period.

As for this book, I just give possibilities, ask questions and defend that which is clear. If God alludes to a dreadful conclusion that some will be left behind then by all means, don't go there! It's your choice to be excited about His return.

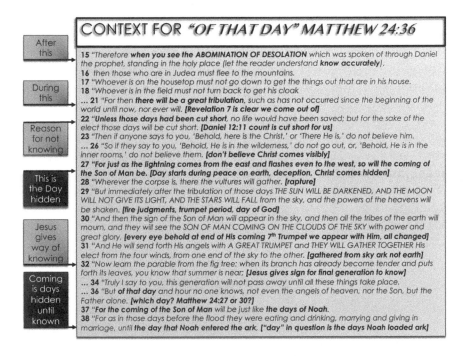

The parable of the Bridegroom serves more as an emphasis to His earlier points on readiness. However it also points to the parallel God created between these events spoken previously and the storyline which interests this author completely, the Groom's coming and the bride's departure. In Jewish tradition, although in the betrothal the feast was a fixed time, the groom would come at His own timing not shared to the bride right before the feast. In this case one could estimate pretty close to the day based on the timing of the feast but again never know the very day. This is exactly what we are heralding in this book. The bride should know the timing of the feast!

Notice the phrase *"day and hour"* is like saying, the very date *"day"* and that which surrounds that day the *"hour"*. Jesus within the context of this sermon mentions *"hour"* like this. I'm *"coming at an hour you think not"* **24:44** and *"whether he comes in the second watch or even the third ... you too be ready; for the Son of man is coming at an hour that you do not expect."* **Luke 12:38-40** The different watches indicate whether He comes during difficult times or easy deceiving peaceful ones; I.e., Night or day.

Jesus intended use for *"hour"* is seen in His reference to a *"watch"* **v38** which the common reference goes to a watchmen at a prison or wall for defense over a city. The second or third watch gets into the details of which part of the night He will return. Just how dark spiritually will things be, just how far asleep the world will be. Don't be fooled by the idea we are talking about a *time* when He says, *"hour"* given its context. For why would there need to be an added description. The phrase *"no one knows the day"* would be enough. Yet Jesus is very careful with His words and means to add another dimension to how treacherous and mysterious His timing actually is.

Since we know the *"apostasy"* occurs before the end, this might give us insight into type of the spiritual darkness being more about apathy, then persecution. If *"Peace & Safety"* **I Thessalonians 5:2** is revealed as the mantra of the time, then it is even more imperative to know the signs and the Word of God revealing His schedule. Again there would be no need to write this book if the hour was plain.

THE COVER UP

"It is not for you to know times and epochs which the Father has fixed by own authority; but... " **Acts 1:7**

In this broader second reference, we can understand on many levels why they couldn't see in the natural what we see today. From the difficulty in understanding God's bullet point list in **Daniel 9:26** as seen in the disciples assumption in their question to Jesus in lumping the Temple's destruction with the end of the age in **Matthew 24:1-3**, a common fear of their day. Yet none of this addresses why God didn't want them to know.

However the simple answer is in the context itself, the mission, the spread of the gospel of the Kingdom a verse later in **Acts 1:8**. Yet notice Jesus is singling them out in **Acts 1:7**. This is very personal and specific. Yet notice Jesus is quick to affirm the Father has a time fixed. Why would God not allow His return to be known to them? For remember Peter admits they were in '**a dark place'** **2 Peter 1:19**. Jesus will tell them why in the context. God's priority is for them to **"be My witnesses" v8.** In other words, *'this doesn't concern you, so don't get distracted from the mission that drives the very timing of the end itself.'*

How would that work if they knew Christ wouldn't be returning for 2000 years, especially since this mission affects the timing of the end? For we read, **"The gospel of the kingdom shall be preached in the whole world as a testimony to all nations and then the end will come." Matthew 24:14** Which we know now from mission boards is fast approaching. This also gives us a further insight. If God's reasoning for concealing the timing is to protect against the stagnation of the spread of the gospel. Then this statement, **"not for You to know"** could be seen as connected to why it has been concealed to every other generation but the last. Walk with me through this logic, if you will. The context is the completion of the mission so ...

Here's my train of thought. Jesus says while on earth, **"I have called you friends for <u>all things</u> I have heard from My Father I have made known to you." John 15:15** So if Jesus knew then the disciples would have known jeopardizing the mission. Hence the reason Jesus wasn't told while on earth. However now He knows why the Father is silent on this and tells them it is just **"not f<u>or You</u> to know the times and epochs which the Father has fixed" Acts 1:7** Which is to say the truth, that not only did God have a perfect time, but also reserved the right to conceal and then reveal it only for the generation for which it would happen **[cf. Daniel 11:32,12:4,9-10].**

Why would we believe it is even for the final generation to know? For one, because it wouldn't affect the mission and most important His word declares He speaks before doing anything. **"Surely the Lord God does nothing unless He reveals His secret counsel to His servants the prophets." Amos 3:7** Consider we are a generation that knowing will not diminish the urgency of this mission but in fact increase its push by knowing! For its one thing to know its not in your lifetime and another to know its within yours and time is running out.

We might even at this point be certain that Jesus now ascended to His former state of Godhead knows when as He is talking to the disciples here. Paul speaks in **Philippians 2:7** that Christ had *"emptied* [to make void, laid aside equality with God or His omniscience] *Himself taking the form of a bond-servant and being made in the likeness of men"*. So here in **Acts 1**, Jesus is really saying, *'I get why you can't know now! It would mess up the mission reaching its goal on time. It would jeopardize souls being reached! Now that I know being back in my Omniscient divinity.'*

Investigating this matter of concealment, we see how God went to great lengths to accomplish this cover up? We need not look any further than the prophecy that drove the storyline of Jesus day in predicting the Messiah's coming, **Daniel 9:24-27**. Simply put, by the time we get to **Daniel 9:26** and **27**, we are experiencing the masterpiece of vagueness that ended up stumbling many.

Understand God is risking telling the Jews when their Messiah was arriving on the scene in the verse before, *"until the Messiah the Prince" v25*. This is like Christmas for the Jews, the hope of a deliverer from the oppression of the nations. But instead of speaking in clarity concerning the remaining *"week"* or seven years, out comes a vague bullet list itemizing a sequence of events that are very troubling. The first of which would come *"after" v26* the start of the final 70th week, the crucifixion of the Messiah.

The obvious advantage for us is seeing the second event in that list, the destruction of city & temple in **70 AD**, fall way outside the 490 years that make up the 70 weeks. Yet for us, the Messiah arrived right on schedule with the beginning of His ministry following **v25** and death at the mid-point of the 70th week following my interpretation in **v27**. In hindsight we can see a lot from this. Since **70AD** Roman massacre did not occur within even the time frame of a continuous **70 weeks** from the decree in **v25,** God has left bread crumbs to suggest the 70 weeks either was dissolved or paused.

2 Peter, was written before that destruction occurred, they were in still in dark times, thinking the Apocalyptic Events might be coming with Christ second coming as well as a possibility. Since again they thought the temple in the bullet list of **v26** was at the end of the age from their question back in **Matthew 24:2**. So again here's where we see better 2000 years later, how **Hosea**'s prophecy is working hand in hand with **Daniel**'s as we approach Hosea's time fulfillment. We can ask the question really did God give Israel a choice that either way fulfilled the prophecy? I believe He did! Yet for the Apostles they were caught in this shift, yet Paul does an amazing job recognizing it in his presentation of how God threaded this current age (Olive tree) without rejecting Israel's purpose and promise **Romans 9-11**.

So let's slow down and look at this carefully. **V26** the key word is *"after"* the sixty-ninth week starts the Messiah would be *"cut off"* or *"having nothing"* not necessarily on the start of the final week but as we know three and half years later or *"after"* what was previously mentioned as the marker for the completion of the **69 weeks**. This vague way of concealing the truth is one of many in the prophecy. In the statement *"Until the Messiah"* v25 marks the beginning of His ministry not His death. So although many disagree with me that Jesus died in the middle of the last week no other version of interpreting **Daniel 9** fits the narrative I will show in this book of Israel's choice! I contend that God intended for a seven year ministry to be continuous, instead it got cut off as revealed in **v26**. God allowing choice yet still sovereign wrote the perfect ending to the story!

In all this confusion Peter called *"a dark place"* **2 Peter 1:19**, we see the disciples wrestling with their own assumptions, that the temple destroyed would bring in the end of the age **[cf. Matthew 24:3, Daniel 9:26]**. For God's purposes the whole prophecy was setup so Israel could accept or reject her King. For if Israel received her King then immediately the Romans would have been threatened and thus crucified Christ. Jewish nation would have had an uprising, then temple would have been destroyed with Jesus resurrected coming with vengeance to deliver Israel 2 days later. The rest would have been Israel spreading the message to the nations.

Understand God is challenging Israel's corrupt priesthood and idolatry as well, in **verse 26**. As seen in *"Herod the king heard he was troubled and all Jerusalem with him. Gathering together all the chief priests ..."* **Matthew 2:3-4** when word of a Messiah baby came around. Don't tell me this didn't drive everything in their day. The priest were working with the rulers to suppress any Messiah, and why would they do that? Because they knew the prophecy included the destruction to their power base, the temple, with all of its corrupt system of robbing God's people and suppressing them.

Notice how the disciples only knew to think what everyone was thinking, the **Daniel 9:26** destruction of the temple prophecy would usher in the Messiah! So they link the end of the age with the coming Messiah to the fallacy of the temples destruction **[Matthew 24:3]**. This is important to see, because **Daniel 9:26** preoccupied the fears of Jerusalem. Yet no one had the revelation what God was really after wasn't Jerusalem liberation but their hearts to their King. God put a stumbling block in the prophecy! Why? The temple was an issue!

Again there are those that argue for **70 AD** destruction of the temple was the end of the age of the Law, but **70 AD** was not even an Abomination that caused Desolation by definition of **Daniel 11:31**, or **Daniel 8:14** and Jesus did not return. However a future temple itself will be an Abomination to God! Why? Did not Christ death and resurrection make an end of the Law and the need for a sacrificial system? Was not the Law crucified with Christ as seen in the destruction of the Pharisaical courts occurring at the same time? And isn't any attempt to rebuild that system going to be met with severe judgment for the offense it would be to God in the Day of the Lord?

So also we see during this period the Essenes, an ultra pure rabbinical order heading to the hills, with the conviction the end of the age was upon them. This again is our vantage point with the discovery of the Dead Sea Scrolls. Peter in the middle of this vague period points to Paul **[cf. 2 Peter 3:15-16]** who had the best grasp on how God had slipped into scriptures hints to this mysterious age of God's grace due to Israel's rejection.

Next and very telling is **Jeremiah** proclaiming three times, **"Do not trust in deceptive words, 'This is the temple of the Lord, temple of the Lord, temple of the Lord"** 7:4 signified that the temple would be built three times, thus once more. Showing how God left us breadcrumbs concealed in scripture as well to this. For **Daniel 9:26** says, **"desolations"** plural giving room in text for a third one built and then eventually destroyed. More on this later, but this is a very telling sign of the very end of this age, a reconstruction of a sacrificial system made obsolete by Christ sacrifice being the ultimate Abomination to God. Any attempt to bring back the sacrificial system by Israel will end in judgment, you can count on that!

Again as we go through each part of this prophecy, it is important to understand how we see things versus the perception of the early church. So here we have the disciples now understanding Jesus as the Messiah only after His resurrection as being the one **"cut off"** in **verse 26**. So they were expecting the rapid fulfillment of the rest of the list and spoke their estimation of His nearness, not aware God had instituted a pause button. Yet today we see something very different, Israel again is a nation having returned to Canaan making it possible for further **"wars; desolations"** v26 Do you catch on now, how seeing God conceal and reveal is important for us! We are approaching the end! What was a mystery is no longer.

So no one expected God to put the pause button on the **70 weeks** of **Daniel 9** how could they. Again just one of many reasons they thought the end was near, was the strict rabbinical count on time had **the fourth millennium** occurring at some point along with the common Jewish thought of an age lasting **2000 years**. Since all this is going on during this tumultuous period between **30-70AD**, there is no wonder we find evidence the Apostles search was broad and included Apocryphal writings accepted by the Essenes. Deeper I delve into the Apostles day, the more I stand amazed they didn't go off course by the radical Jews around them.

The truth is God is amazing in concealment. God left the prophecy so open with a bullet list undefined in its timing as to leave God with a choice based on their acceptance or denial of Jesus Christ! Israel still had to choose to receive her King. God didn't prophesy *'and you will reject Me'*. Instead Jesus weeps, *"If you had known ...the things which make for peace ...they have been hidden from your eyes ...you did not recognize your time of visitation."* **Luke 19:42-44** and again, *"O Jerusalem ...I wanted to gather your children together ...and you would not have it."* **Luke 13:34** all this displaying choice!

The reality is they rejected their opportunity so Jesus cuts His ministry in half, and all of a sudden it takes a great mind like Paul's to unravel what just happened prophetically from scripture **[cf. Romans 9-11]**. Notice **Isaiah 61:2** is only read halfway under the Spirit's leading by Jesus on purpose! **[Cf. Luke 4:19]** His ministry would have been to declare to the Jewish nation who upon receiving their King not only the next 2000 years of bringing grace to the nations *"the favorable year of the Lord"* but how to prepare for their deliverance in the *"day of vengeance"* **61:2** to immediately follow for 3.5 years. God's plan A sometimes looks like a plan B occurred, but the bottomline is it is in God's nature to give a choice, even when He knows what the future holds. God gave a choice and kept the timelines in order and the prophecy as well.

Yet God pulled a fast one on everyone. This mystery of His own bride, the church birthed from Israel's disobedience in God's foreknowledge a message hidden in the prophets. Consider, **Hosea** was chosen to give us the timeline for the bride for he exemplified this mystery. Imagine the lengths God went to have a prophet marry a harlot (Israel) and have children called *"not My people"* **Hosea 2:23** It's here we find the other time table given to an Old Testament prophet. The time that God would reject Israel (putting a pause button on their fulfillment of 70 weeks), by saying He would *"go away"* **Hosea 5:14** and finally return to her later after two prophetic days.

How long does God give for this but 2 days! **[Cf. Hosea 6:1-3]** Well, if that was a literal 2 days then why didn't Jesus return to Israel at His resurrection? Even the early church struggled to know what God was doing, but Peter here starts to figure it out. God is speaking in code, one that He created all over the place. Frankly, we now should see this dawning on us!

THE COMPARISON

*"To which you **do well to pay attention** ... Until the day dawns ..."*   **2 Peter 1:19**

So my ax to grind is this; the early church searched and accepted this stewardship to give their best estimation to keep the church alert as Jesus commanded them, while we who it applies to sleep because we misinterpret their statements as doctrine not estimations. In doing so we sit upon the greatest gifts to knowing His return than ever. Both the Dead Sea Scrolls & the Rise of Israel as a Nation are like two witnesses testifying the same period of years for His return; both the big picture chronology from the Masoretic manuscripts pointing to God's perfection in time, and the last generation being established by the six day war bringing Israel into maturity as a nation **[cf. Matthew 24:32]**!

SOMETHING IS AT STAKE HERE!

"Christ ...will appear a second time for salvation without reference to sin
to those who eagerly await Him"
Hebrews 9:28

"Because you have kept the word of My perseverance,
I also will keep you from the hour of testing,
that hour which is about to come upon the whole world,
to test those who dwell on the earth.
Revelation 3:10

However today, we have created the strongholds allowing no point to search! Is this not the enemies plan! Jesus can return at any moment we say, because what else would explain for the Apostles being wrong, or the misguided idea of the Jewish wedding practices where the Bride has no idea when the groom is returning at all. These unbiblical conclusions that no one can know anything, that He can return at anytime, couldn't be farther from the truth of scripture.

It is based off the assumptions that everything the Apostles wrote in the Bible was doctrine and that the Ancient Wedding Practice of betrothal agreements had no commitment of a timeframe for its finish in the feast, which would have given the Bride a clear season to watch for the day of her honeymoon. Such randomness placed on God and even the Jewish practices is a work of religion trying to use fear not faith to inspire or control. The work of the enemy is at foot, and it doesn't even stop there. We believe in our Christian circles that with all the confusion over the topic of His return that it is religiously correct to avoid the subject entirely. We call it a non-essential.

Well, that non-essential was the final topic of a man about to die who was heralded as the pillar of the church - Peter, not to mention Paul's efforts to write back the church in Thessaloniki. Will not the early church actions judge us, in the day of reckoning? For we see the early churches did not neglect searching the scriptures concerning their future! Enough to cause both Paul and Peter to write back to their respective churches because others where spreading lies. In one case that He had returned already and in the other He wasn't returning at all. It amazes me that now more than ever as God removes the veil over this by the revelation of the Dead Sea scrolls and the advent of the Jewish nation we are sold on giving up the search as if it is an unholy thing, or replacing our hope with temporal kingdoms on earth, or better yet getting carried away with every wind of crazy sign on earth or "prophet".

Come on, if the Apostles couldn't figure this thing out what makes you think you can, they will say? Or they got it right because its really past & done and we are now in the kingdom age, just look at our awesome conferences? Everything in our mind to avoid a subject so entrenched in the Word of God, to make it impossible for God not to wonder where our hearts really are.

The Apostles, they mostly were just fisherman when they started. Even having the learned Paul, they were living the muddy waters of overlapping ages. What a difficult vantage point to seeing God's big picture. Jesus knowing this even tells them, *"It is not for*

43

YOU _to know"_ Acts 1:7 singling them out. Have you ever considered God didn't want them to know, the same way He didn't want Jesus to know while on earth? Hello, if Jesus told His disciples, they would be writing the very word of God and everyone would have known. Everything they knew would be in print for generations. We all would have lost our motivation to go into all the world.

It is this simple, the only generation the end applies to needs to know. The only generation that it wouldn't hurt the mission is the very same one that needs to survive its the birth pangs, going before courts for answers everyone wants. Knowing now is the currency of heaven, for souls! The only generation that the bible declares will know and do great exploits is the very same one Jesus gave a sign to so they would know! This isn't complicated stuff. Someone was going to be the last one and it happens to be YOU!

3

Searching:

The Journey of Kings

THE ATTENTION

"To remind you of those things even though you know ...
To which you would do well to pay attention ... "
2 Peter 1:13,19

Peter tells us to *"pay attention"* **2 Peter 1:19** Why? Because we haven't talked about this subject? No! He had just told them what he was saying was *"to remind you of these things even though you know"* **v13** So they knew the information. The early church was well taught in Eschatology! Instead Peter is focusing on a truth about prophecy. The information that gets clearer the closer you are to its fulfillment is prophecy unlike the nature of all other scripture where everything is the same at any time.

For Peter discloses that the closer you are to its fulfillment and the longer you keep looking at it, it produces a dawning effect. Which means reviewing the information from time to time as we get closer is of necessity. Here we find the idea of searching working hand in hand with waiting, watching and meditating on or as it reads, *"Looking for and hastening the day of God"* **2 Peter 3;12.** For our supernatural new nature should lead us in this pathway.

So we find Peter in an *"Aha moment"* needing to update the

latest development in their perspective. Thus he makes abundantly clear that this is *"NOW the second letter ..."* **2 Peter 3:1** Within the words he uses here in this letter, we find him describing how visual the conception of revelation really is when it is caught, saying it is like *"the day dawning"* **2 Peter 1:19**. Just imagine yourself on that Hawaiian beach watching the sun come up, or even better on Haleakala crater 10,000 feet up seeing the horizon light up! So it is when different pieces of this grand puzzle start fitting together.

Nothing can be mistaken here, this should come together clearly to support God's storyline perfectly. For His workmanship is being revealed in His perfect timing, and you are a piece in that masterpiece. Again imagine you are that jeweler with a magnifying glass looking intently at the diamond for quality. God is asking us to look deeper than the surface of all these individual contexts to His hidden mystery, threaded through the pages of scriptures revealing a time code masked in plain view. Where else would God being God put it but right under our curious noses.

The apostles sought to know these truths, to catch the winds of the Spirit concerning the age they saw being birthed. Knowing *"Where there is no vision the people go unrestrained"* **Proverbs 29:18**, Peter attempts to give them that restraint! For that verse finishes with *"happy are they who keep the Law (principles that govern things)"* **Proverbs 29:18** So Peter will lay out the principles that govern seeing revelation correctly in **2 Peter 1:19-20 & 3:2**. Absent from these governing laws for our search are: instructions to go to the next great conference, or hear a "prophet," because they knew the scriptures alone were the foundation to seeing clearer. Harmony rules prophecy.

Peter who truly was a prophet gives this humble proclamation that they were in *"a dark place"* **2 Peter 1:19,** but soon things would change. It's like Peter is saying, *'The lamp of God's revelation is beginning to shine bright enough for us all to figure some key stuff out. First we must acknowledge more is coming so remember to not give up the search'* Thus we see him championing the cause of Christ return for future generations instead of building up His own resume! So different from most in our times who have boasted their superior knowledge that shouldn't be questioned. Instead I am inviting my brothers and sisters to join with me on this search for truth.

Maybe this is a clear sign many today are false prophets, they love to be right but not to bear with the body to get it right.

Having spent years dismantling what I believed, I became my own worst critic until I abandoned what I previously believed for the only answer that actually answered all hard questions and made everything scriptural to me harmonize. I sacrificed my need to be right. I find my days now filled with a satisfaction and relief knowing the bible for once makes perfect sense. Imagine if I never endeavored this process I would still be wrestling and questioning God's word. Now I don't need to, and I want that for you.

All this underscores the fact that a mystery remains to be solved. This shouldn't be an abstract idea as well. For the New Testament is the fulfillment of many words the prophets of old spoke of a New Covenant coming. This new way was such a mystery to ages past that Paul constantly refers to faith, godliness, lawlessness, the church & Christ relationship as mysteries revealed in God's government at the right time. Some have said these are mysteries for a reason, because they were never meant to be solved. I refuse to believe such garbage. For Jesus tells me, *"the Spirit of truth comes He will guide you into all truth ... disclose to you what is to come."* **John 16:13** They are mysteries so those who seek may find!

For in Christ words and Paul's writings they constantly harp on this theme of the mystery of this present age and its fulfillment becoming clearer. Jesus constantly speaking of the Kingdom hidden to be revealed at the ripe time of the harvest in **Matthew 13, Mark 4:11. [Cf. Romans 11:25, Romans 16:25]** Other mysteries mentioned are the resurrection & its order *"I tell you a mystery we will not all sleep but we will all be changed"* **1 Corinthians 15:51, Ephesians 3:9**, of the very select group considered to Him as His bride *"the mystery is great ...I am speaking of Christ and the church"* **Ephesians 5:32**, *"mystery manifested to the saints"* **Colossians 1:26** *"this mystery which is Christ in you"* **Colossians 1:27**, of the final days of darkness *"mystery of lawlessness is already at work; only he who restrains until he is taken out of the way"* **2 Thessalonians 2:7 [cf. Revelation 1:20, 10:7, 17:5-7]**

Of these mysteries the prophets painted many pictures for us to show the fulfillment of God's plan during and at the end of this age. Peter explaining it elegantly in his first letter saying, *"The prophets who prophesied made careful search and inquiries seeking to know what person or time the Spirit of Christ within them was indicating ...was revealed to them that they were not serving themselves but you ..."* **1 Peter 1:11-12** Wait did you catch that? They sought to know the TIME!

Wait I thought we weren't supposed to know the time of His return. Who are they trying to get this 'time' for? YOU!

As to the **"time" 1 Peter 1:11** of which Peter says they searched, most of the prophets had no reference point for the timing for their picture dreams and visions. Referring instead to them in vague terms such as **'in those days', 'at that time', 'in the last days', 'on that day'** or **'on the Day of the Lord'** while keeping the sequence of events in the correct order as they appeared to them. They had no idea of the timing or duration of these events. However, as mysterious as these word pictures appear at first, they lay the ground work for piecing together the proper order of events foretold by Christ in the Gospels & Revelation, to be placed later within the timeframe revealed by other prophets, giving us two or three witnesses.

For example, the prophets will run a sequence of events and then start again from a new place and run another sequence of events under a new *"oracle"* or theme in descriptive ways. Sometimes these descriptions go back and overlap with a different theme. Like seeing a big picture and then being shown details with a magnifying glass of part of it. Many get confused by this, which is why God does it in the first place, to conceal it from the casual eye.

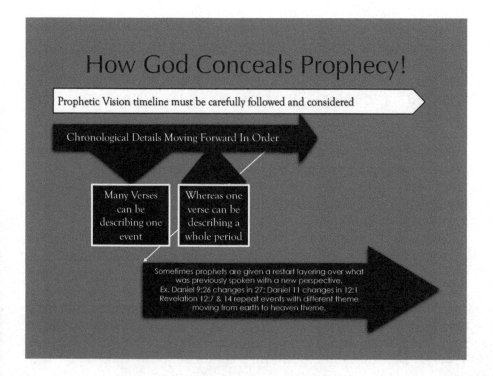

Yet if we pay attention, we start to see correlations from key markers such as **"before the Day of the Lord"** and **"on the Day of the Lord ..."**: tied to celestial markers like the moon being blood versus moon dark. Another technique is by seeing links between the events taking place alongside the heavenly sky pictures. It's always amazing as the last chapter will show how many prophets in the Old Testament described the same event from slightly different angles with different words yet they are really seeing the same thing. However, I always went with what was a firm truth that could not be broken and made sure nothing contradicted itself.

Another form of revealing is through types and shadows. **"Now these things happened to them as an example and they are written for our instruction upon whom the ends of the ends of the age have come."** 1 Corinthians 10:11 God instituting feasts, Sabbaths and dealing throughout Israel's history in a way that later could be seen as a sign to us of His plan for a designed timetable for human history. Along with this, Jesus Himself was led constantly in many ways that laid examples after examples for us, by simple choices the Father led Him to make while He lived.

Jesus weeps yet waits four days to raise Lazarus why? Jesus didn't have to wait three days to be raised why? Again there is purpose in everything God does or did. God's literally begging for someone to ask the right questions, to **"pay attention"**! In order to match the symbolic nature of actions with their counterpart prophetically one must believe God works this way. For example, Joel speaks of what will happen before what many of the prophets commonly referred to as the Day of God, Day of Vengeance, Day of the Lord comes as happening during the **"last days"** Joel 2:27.

This term becomes confusing to the early church after so many literal days passed to question its literal 24 hour application. Here we are at **2 Peter**, and here we are today 2000 years later. Yet could the meaning of **"days"** used here be couched in a greater storyline of the whole of human history? How else can we rectify this problem? No one has recorded in history the Day of God occurring! By this simple acknowledgement would we not be still in the last days even now?

Which turns this use of **"last days"** into the latter part of all of human history [the lesser part thus the last]. Here we have a classic example of how both the analytics and the storyline come together from a different vantage point. For God is

49

speaking of the period of time in which He would step into it history in a very defining way. The spread of His Spirit across the globe to all peoples and stations of life until it paves the way for the King to come. This would culminate or occur at the very end of this age with one still to follow according to the **Book of Revelation chapter 20**! So connecting the dots and knowing the storyline is vital in getting this right as well as some mathematics.

Joel knowing nothing about when this timeframe would occur simply uses the terms, *"after this"* leading up to another marker, *"the Day of the Lord"*. As markers go, **Joel** simply distinguishes *"before"* and *"on"* that day. This mere fisherman Peter overcome by the Holy Spirit uses this context to declare those *"last days"* had just begun on the day of Pentecost that would lead up to the Day of God. He knows little of what he is saying accept the assumption can be made the church meditated on this passage by the Spirit's leading in the upper room together. That journey leads us here where Peter is beginning to understand the gravity of those words as part of something greater than 24 hour periods called "day".

Addressing a church growing under the influence of greek mythology, mysticism, and gnostic influence, Peter gives His last right and testimony leaving a legacy here along with a prophetic warning of coming false teachers. So important was this thesis to the church, **Jude's** epistle will echo or act as a carbon copy of **2 Peter** as though two witnesses needed to support each other for the church to settle doctrine at this time. The church is at a crossroads, new believers are coming into the faith without ever seeing or being with Jesus! The ones that have seen Him are about to die.

So Peter seems to point us in a new direction for *"last days"* **3:3** at the same time clarifying *"the Day of the Lord"* **3:10** as prophetic speech representing anything but a literal day on both accounts. Much the same way Jesus used a reference for *"day"* symbolically standing for something else. In **Luke 13:31-35, John 6:39,40,44** This process of piecing together what God meant in each place brings us to a careful weighing of the context in which they are couched, the form of speech used and its harmony with other revelations. Notice Peter is asking us to take our turn in this process **chapter 1,** then leaves us with His most significant finding, *"__Do not let this one fact__ escape your notice"* **Peter 3:8** in the third chapter. This statement carried so much weight that we see the effect it had on the next generations of disciples of the disciples *[a focus of the next* *chapter]*.

For littered over the landscape of the next two centuries will be clear evidence of this formula of a literal thousand years being a prophetic day in God's economy of time from **2 Peter 2:8**. From Polycarp, John direct disciple **[circa 100 AD]**, Irenaeus **[circa 180 AD]**, Tertullian **[circa 180AD]** Epistle of Barnabas **[circa 100AD]**, Cyprian **[circa 220AD]** and more, we see the convictions of the earliest non-biblical era carrying forward this legacy laid down by Peter & John's vision **[cf. Book of Revelation 20:4]**. Understand that **2 Peter** leads to **the Book of Revelation** which further reveals God's *"seventh day rest"* as a thousand years. **[Cf. Revelation 20:4]** Which is what a person must decide, is God just throwing out numbers literally or symbolically? And if so, which is it in the context written?

What many don't know about Christianity is that many great men fought for the interpretation of these prophetic codes for *"days"* as a **literal 1000 years** referring to, *"they came to life and reigned with Him for a thousand years"* **Revelation 20:4** for two centuries after Christ's departure. It is here I must say, every mention of time numerically has significance in the bible, we just have to understand God's thinking when deciphering them. EVERY LAST ONE! God's word is to be taken very seriously, words and numbers have meaning.

Just as every note and key has a purpose in the sound of a song it creates. Nothing is useless, for one can say that, *"All scripture is inspired"* **2 Timothy 3:16** we just must ask for what purpose, to reveal what to us. All the actions and words of Jesus while He walked on earth were orchestrated by the Father have meaning! None were wasted or without some form of meaning. Jesus lived to be seen! For example even John's vision, Jesus purposefully revealed the book of **Revelation** after **70AD** so there would be no confusion. His return is future! Even Jesus Himself clarifies the thought misunderstanding that the **167 BC** Abomination was what Daniel spoke of, by saying, *"the Abomination of Desolation which was spoken of through Daniel the prophet"* **Matthew 24:15** in **31AD!** When something was spoken must be considered.

So also this present age isn't the last age, for one awaits us at His coming so the end isn't really the end! A time period mentioned of being a thousand years matching **Peter 3:8 to Revelation 20:4** You have a decision to continue to deride these *"biblical coincidences"* or *"time specific revelations"* or allow them to put you an awe and wonder.

For example, this one fact should wake us up. Jesus the

manifestation of the fourth day passover lamb dies on the Fourth millennium of history! Hmmm. Since Lazarus was raised on the fourth day, nothing makes sense but an example was made and it be this one. Jesus died at the right time as part of a complete package God is rolling out on schedule. We should all be like the Berean's **[cf. Acts 17:11]** who checked everything spoken against the scriptures and ask the right questions. Why would Jesus wait to raise His friend?

1239 prophesies OT
578 prophesies New

1817 total
Contained in 8,352 verses

Of the 31,124 verses that's

26.8 %
¼ of the
bible

Remember for the Bereans it was Paul they were questioning. No matter how honorable the preachers who speak we must honor God's word and delight in its power to reveal truth over anything else! What are we going to say to the Berean's, *'How dare you question the Apostle Paul?'* NO! Paul gladly would rejoice His words were tested and found harmonious with what came before. Yet many of us have endured the *"don't challenge the MAN OF GOD"* era; so this might surprise you to learn the early church didn't function in that totalitarian way.

Be mindful it is Jesus who said, **_"every word"_** and **_"every careless word"_ Matthew 12:36-37** will carry meaning on the day of judgment! How then would anything God does or say not have meaning! In the end, we are just hurting ourselves by not examining scripture versus what is being said today, are we not? There is a reason I'm leading you in this direction so strongly, for Jesus will speak something amazing that everyone I know has discarded as having no meaning. **[Cf. Luke 13:31-32]** Walls must come down, our minds must be freed to look outside the boxes religion has created for us to confine ourselves too.

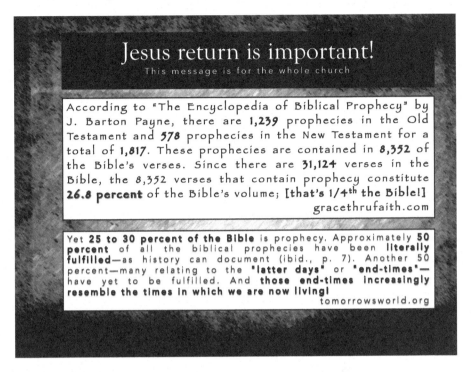

Jesus return is important!
This message is for the whole church

According to "The Encyclopedia of Biblical Prophecy" by J. Barton Payne, there are **1,239** prophecies in the Old Testament and **578** prophecies in the New Testament for a total of **1,817**. These prophecies are contained in **8,352** of the Bible's verses. Since there are **31,124** verses in the Bible, the **8,352** verses that contain prophecy constitute **26.8 percent** of the Bible's volume; [that's 1/4th the Bible!]

gracethrufaith.com

Yet **25 to 30 percent of the Bible** is prophecy. Approximately **50 percent** of all the biblical prophecies have been **literally fulfilled**—as history can document (ibid., p. 7). Another 50 percent—many relating to the **"latter days"** or **"end-times"**— have yet to be fulfilled. And **those end-times increasingly resemble the times in which we are now living!**

tomorrowsworld.org

THE KINGS

"It is the glory of God to conceal a thing: but the glory of kings is to search out a matter"

Proverbs 25:2

For now please stop and just consider that the timing of these events future was important to those who searched for them before us. The prophets and especially **Daniel** sought to know the timing of God's plan, as well as **Peter** here. They did not for a second believe God could come at anytime or that their searching and pursuit of a *"time"* **1 Peter 1:11** was foolishness. Why seek for an appointed time if the appointment can be changed? Does that not make sense to you? God will not change His mind concerning the timetable he creates!

In spite of what Jesus says to His disciples revealing the truth that knowing would not be for them, they still searched for answers as to when because knowing would benefit a future generation! Of course we fail to see that in Jesus telling them a fact, *"not for You to know"* **Acts1:7**; was actually Him suggesting someone else will be allowed to know by singling them out. So Peter is aware of this and thus fights for that future generation which will know! Thinking as He approaches death, it might just be the next one, says, *"pay attention"* **2 Peter 1:19**.

Further Jesus never tells them not to search, thus we see Peter & Paul doing so from their writings. He is merely putting the emphasis of their purpose on the spread of the gospel **[cf. Acts 1:8]**, and a reminder they are not to prioritize knowing over making disciples in all nations. Yet we come back to this passage, *"Surely the Lord God does nothing unless He reveals His secret counsel to His servants the prophets."* **Amos 3:7** Well has Jesus returned yet? Not to my knowledge, so he didn't need to reveal to generations past because God has done nothing so far.

If He was to do something, the word of God is telling us He would reveal to His prophets or servants before such a time! Remember, **1 Peter 1:11** this doesn't just include the search for detail of signs and events but the timing of His return. Of course some will argue that applied to only His first coming not His second. However much of the old testament prophecies are pertaining to the future and Peter here writes in search of the second coming linking what the previous prophets did to His search as a legacy builder.

We see this in Daniel's pursuit which benefited not only those who would lived close enough to the first coming of the Messiah but even to us today by his prayers being granted the revelation of the **70 weeks in Daniel 9:24-27**. Understand Daniel figures out the time of their captivity is almost over, the TIME! Next, God gives Him an answer in a timing vision. A vision whose answered fulfillment is measured in a prophetic code of weeks to years. 490 years equaling 70 weeks.

God isn't answering, *"I'm coming soon"*! God is being specific, analytical here in code, and even follows it up with the answer for our curious minds today as to why the 70 weeks weren't completed in *chapter 11-12* timing for the final 3.5 years of it future after the future abomination. Jesus fills in these blanks by notifying us the Abomination is yet future. Here we are piecing together this beautiful tapestry by searching the depths of God.

Yet consider those words to Amos, God doesn't have to reveal until right before He does something. For when He says He *"does nothing unless"* **Amos 3:7** this doesn't mean He shares with everyone at every point along the timeline, or speaks plainly for all to understand. So when do we see anyone figuring out the first coming but right before it occurred in the three wise men. Why? Because God intentionally made prophecy, so those who find the answer need to dedicate themselves to the search. God wants seekers!

In the case of Daniel, God shares a lot! By the time we are at the last chapter of his book, He has brought Daniel into visions in **chapter 7,8,9**, and **11-12**. It is at this point He declares He is done. *"Go your way Daniel for these words are concealed and sealed up until the end time... those with insight will understand"* **Daniel 12:9** King James version is clearer when it reverses the order of the words to say, *"the time of the end"* **12:9** Okay stop! God is about to go silent for 500 years before Christ's first coming, because in His mind He just gave them indication when He'd be resurfacing in **Daniel 9:24-27**! Yet reveals during the final period much would be revealed. Is this not the pattern I have been advocating here?

Did you catch that! Soon it will be crystal clear for those paying attention during the stretch run to His first coming just as it is now before the stretch run of His second! The truth given is the end of each age brings revelation to God's servants. This is consistent within the context, *"Those who have insight ...give understanding"* **Daniel 11:33** and *"those who have insight will understand"* **Daniel 12:10** Revealing both a necessary search and a needful revealing on God's part who opens the minds of humans. Notice though both references are from **chapter 11-12**, which focus on the second coming not the first! This promise of eyes opened before the very end is NOW!

Is this not a clear message to us living on the brink of the end! The words are clear we will *"have insight and understand"* **Daniel 12:10**, Jesus agreeing says, *"when you see these things begin"* **Luke 21:28** *"when you see these things happen"* **v31** know you are the last generation! *"This generation will not pass away until all things take place"* **Matthew 24:34**. Even going as far as indicating at the Abomination of Desolation we should *"know accurately"* **Matthew 24:15**.

Again this is consistent with the context of **Daniel 12:11** where there is defined number of days mentioned, **1290/1335**. So God expects us to know exactly when inside of the

Abomination. Except that He will **"cut short" "those days"** **Matthew 24:22** for the faithful, this will shock the experts ready to endure the full amount focused not on purity but earthly signs. Again another proof text is here for the rapture not at the end of those days, not at the seventh Trumpet (Post Tribulation Theory).

If your waiting for the Abomination this might be too late, for the measure of deception will be heavy. Imagine Israel waiting too long to understand her time of visitation as well, instead she found herself chanting "Crucify Him!". So where are the kings today, who should be figuring out this stuff before then? Consider Daniel's prayers opened this door of understanding to us! It took individuals on their knees, involved in God's storyline!

However having listened too long to "experts" in the church who have decided they are so smart by adding rules that diminish Jesus words, we cannot even take weight to what Jesus Himself said. Categorizing what He spoke only for the Jews under the law and not the church because they were spoken in a different "dispensation". The assumptions kill us. We never question their clever ideas. When you can decide on what words Jesus spoke that I can take for myself, please get back to me. All this sounds stupid because it is. God is the same yesterday today and forever.

What is the objective in all this but to find a way to separate the rapture from Jesus discourse in **Matthew 24** which includes His coming in **v27**. Thus we are told the rapture is not the Second Coming by Pre Tribulation experts from many seminaries. Yet I come back with, if the assumption is we are gone before any of the events mentioned in which he will personally warn and speak to His disciples in **Matthew 24**, the future church as then where does it say otherwise? Where else in scripture do we have a reference or indication even hinting that we go before these events? We don't! Instead we have to live with mess this dispensational gymnastics creates with scriptures. Now someone must tell me what words Jesus spoke apply to me.

The facts are you won't find a shred of evidence for the rapture being separate from His coming! **Matthew 25** should shout out that **Matthew 24** has to do with the exit of the Bride and its connection to His coming previously mentioned in **Matthew 24:27**. Why? Because Jesus connects the two into one context of being ready as His bride and not sleeping as virgins with a common phrase **"no one knows the day or hour"**

Matthew 24:36 & 25:13 How can the Pre Tribulation use this verse when it refutes their theory being apart of this context. For example, not only does Jesus indicate we are leaving after the start of the dialogue in **Matthew 24** with His words *"when you see these things"* but the day no one knows is within the context of the chapter. So we might as well then say, we can't know the day of His coming but rapture is fair game, in following their failed logic.

My point is every word in the bible is true and for you, don't let Dispensationalist shred apart your right to it. Jesus who warned that, *"Every careless word we would give an accounting for it"* **Matthew 12:36** expects us to not get into the mindset that all this is relative without meaning or open to *"spiritualization"* or *"the experts"* recreations. Peter is direct, *"No prophesy of Scripture is a matter of one's own interpretation"* **2 Peter 1:20** NO private interpretations are allowed! So we are back to how then do we know we aren't superimposing our own will on scripture. Harmony! We allow scripture to explain scripture. So how does this work. Let's take the issue at hand. Can the rapture be separate from His second coming? No, because other scriptures forbid it. **[1 Corinthians 15:23]**

Every prophetic word in God's Word harmonizes at some point with itself, or other passages if we subject ourselves to God's rules **[cf. 2 Peter 1:20 & 3:2]** and not subject God to our rules. Instead of pushing something not spoken in scripture as truth upon scripture, we must yield to scripture for truths. The example I am using is a huge one for this. Dispensationalist will divide periods or ages into differing rules and teach that God is improving His program with each age. As in the law governed and now grace. However, this only leads them to down rabbit holes as in the Law is reinstitute in the tribulation period. The mistake is God never instituted the Law or sacrifices for salvation, but to lead Israel to grace through faith through the sacrifice of Himself. There has never been two ways to Heaven, only one.

All this profoundly affecting our theology of the God we believe in, when *"Jesus is the same yesterday today and forever."* **Hebrews 13:8** Which is the conclusion from the Epistle that declared God's big picture had been spoken *"in many ways"* **Hebrews 1:1** from the beginning pointing to Jesus and then pointing back to Him who is the fulfillment of one grand plan! Not two plans, not many ways to God, but always present throughout all of History was this plan of covenant made by sacrifice. The book of **Hebrews** declaring that the *"better sacrifice"* **Hebrews 10:8,14**, was made for all of history. Consider from the start Abel's sacrifice **[cf. Hebrews 11:4]**.

God has always desired the same thing, chose the same standard of the heart. As early as the times of Moses we hear God's plan, *"I will make them jealous with those who were not a people"* **Deuteronomy 32:21** Verses later we are told the why, because Israel *"would not discern their future"* **v29** Later the prophets would echo these themes, along with the Apostles acknowledgement of what they meant. **[Cf. Hosea 1:10, 2:23, Zechariah 13:9, Isaiah 63:16-19, Romans 9:25, 1 Peter 2:10]** My question to you is will you discern your future? Because the difference now is huge, the sacrifice has been paid, God has interceded to get what He always wanted from the start.

God has never changed! What God desired never changed! What God views as righteous never changed. Who He choose never changed from his perspective seeing the end from the beginning, just the pathway to the end needed a sacrifice made *"at the right time"* **Romans 5:6**! Seeing congruity and harmony in scripture is vital to seeing God correctly and His plan.

The whole point in others creating distinctions in ages was to support a theory that Jesus comes before He actually says He comes in **Matthew 24:27** which is during the great tribulation. For Pre Tribulation Theorist this is very important to accomplish these distinctions. Yet what we sacrifice on that altar is the portrayal of a God given to change, double minded and illogical and the Word of God as confusing. The very thing we attempt to defend, a God who wouldn't allow us to go through Wrath thus in our minds a "good" God, we allow Him to be seen as cruel, indifferent, random etc by our manipulation of scriptures. On the other hand, the scriptures speak plainly, it is our destiny to partake in tribulations. *"Through much tribulations we must enter the kingdom of God."* **Acts 14:22**

Yet Pre-Tribulation Theorist will engage in a semantic war of terms, in which we never seem to question how they got to their conclusions scripturally in the first place. Namely, the rapture and the second coming are different events. How can Christ take us without coming to earth? For when we refer to their main passage for this, we read that we will *"meet Him in the air (aer = lower atmosphere)"* **1 Thessalonians 4:17**. My point here early on is the enemy of discovery is not questioning the experts, not holding fast to the rules God gives harmony & context.

It is here we are given the warning which I will repeat again.

"No prophecy of Scripture is a matter of one's own interpretation" **2 Peter 1:20** and Paul's words harmonize here, *"the spirit of a prophets are subject to prophets"* **1 Corinthians 14:32** Notice this has always been a community effort to understand since God created the church to be just that, a body needing each part. All the key pronouns are in the plural, Peter making very clear by his third chapter the list of sources must be pulled together. There must be agreement, two or three witnesses to confirm, all interpreted in context of course! The greatest enemy of revelation is special knowledge. For example, *'Only I know what they really meant'* and *'God spoke to me personally and He is saying this is what they meant.'*

The assurance the Word of God gives brings peace of mind, knowing ahead.

Today we are bombarded by many proclaiming to be prophets who are teaching on the subjects covered in the scripture but not the scriptures themselves. They seem to be truth tellers who are operating in ways that only cloud us from the truth of God's word. If they manage to use scripture it is to pull it out of all its surrounding limitations and other witnesses to be some easy answer that tickles ears. In the end, they just make a mockery of the bible as if we all can't see the contradictions it leaves us.

For instance, we have believed so strongly the lie that no one can know the timing of the Lord's return that we have created this vacuum in the prophetic. The result is all kinds of mischief and misleading ideas of men who gladly want to fill that vacuum and gain an audience with a Christianized spiritualism. Concluding the bible isn't the authority on our future, we entertain ourselves with witchcraft. By turning to mere men who speak whatever opinions that suit them based on the latest news, suspicions, they prey on your fears and curiosity!

In so many ways Peter is shouting a message in his second letter contrary to our current Christian climate, *"SEARCH, but not to find or create something extra biblical!"* Some create where there isn't a collaborating witness, whereas others just divide up the Word like peas and carrots diluting its intended impact upon our hearts. Either way we are told not to add or take away from His word. **[Cf. Revelation 22:18-19]**

THE PRECURSORS

"For it will not come unless ...." **2 Thessalonians 2:3**
"Until the day dawns and the morning star arises"
2 Peter 1:19

An event that must precede something else is called a precursor. If indeed there be just one precursor than Jesus cannot return at anytime. If that precursor is still unfulfilled, then Jesus cannot have returned already and that cannot be the next thing to happen, since the precursor must precede it. For all the talk of Christ *"Imminent Return"* the word is found only once in all of scripture here in **2 Peter 1:14**.

Peter's first argument for the timely return of Christ is his own death, **'knowing the laying aside of my dwelling is imminent as also our Lord Jesus Christ has made clear to me."** **2 Peter 1:14** So did the Apostles believe in the imminent return of Christ? No! In fact, this statement by Peter concerning his imminent death would have been a shock to most who <u>misinterpreted</u> Jesus words revealed in **Matthew 16:28**. For Jesus boldly declared that, **"some of those who are standing here will not taste death until they see the Son of Man coming in His kingdom."**

Peter knowing the Transfiguration experience mentioned a

chapter later in Matthew 17 was what Jesus meant. For Peter goes onto explain the transfiguration as a comparison to His coming future saying, *"we did not follow cleverly devised tales when we made known to you the power and coming of our Lord Jesus but <u>we were eyewitnesses of His majesty</u>"* 2 **Peter 1:16-18**. The other disciple John, remembered Jesus words like this, *"a little while and you will no longer see Me; and again a little while and you will see Me"* **John 16:16**. Some forgot to interpret this as when Jesus visited them during the period between His resurrection and ascension, for a common believe had to be corrected.

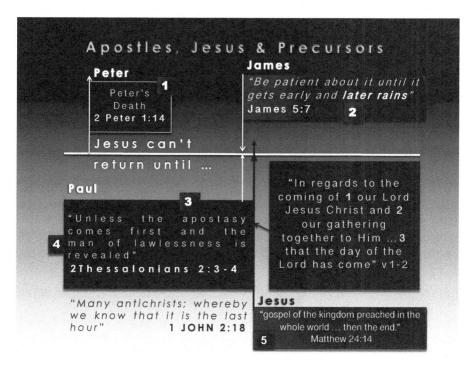

We see this belief to be prevalent as John inserts at the end of his testimony these words; ***"Therefore this saying went out among the brethren that the disciple would not die; yet <u>Jesus did not say to him that he would not die</u> but only if I want him to remain until I come what is that to you?"*** **John 21:23** This misapplication of Jesus words might have been fueled by a longing they had to see Him yet once more! It was sure to be the biggest driving forces in the believing in the nearness of His return before Peter's second letter.

Some may say Peter knowing he would die soon caused the quick second letter to be written. Most people act differently knowing they are going to be leaving their loved ones. This gives us an excellent view into what was most important on the minds of the Apostles. Is not Peter by spending most of the letter on Eschatology, speaking how important what we believe about the future will be to the framing of our NOW! The devil wants to steal your hope in order to steal your NOW!

Consider Paul as well had to write a second letter as well concerning the threat of false views of Christ's return and to clarify what was previously said to the church at Thessaloniki. In that case, it was the false notion that Jesus had already returned and the day of the Lord had started. **[Cf. 2 Thessalonians 2:1-2]**. In both letters precursors are used to defend the timely return of Christ. For Peter it was his death hadn't happened as Jesus had told him it would, in Paul's case, the Apostasy and the revelation of the lawless One needed to occur first **[cf. 2 Thessalonians 2:4]**. This alone would defy the notion that God can come at anytime.

Peter's defense, years removed from Paul's, appears centered more on what was said by him at Pentecost, *"in the last days"* **Acts 2:17** then in Paul's case a disturbing letter. In both situations the Apostles reveal that much had been already discussed on the topic of Jesus return to earth. Paul states, *"As to the times and epochs, brethren you have <u>no need of anything to be written to you</u>. For you yourselves <u>know full well</u> ... <u>you are not in darkness</u> that the day would overtake you like a thief."* **1 Thessalonians 5:1-2,4** Peter states, *"to remind you ... even though you already know them"* **2 Peter 1:12** Why? Because they knew the Precursors and signs surrounding that day, and taught them throughout the church. What they didn't have was the correct chronology to count for the big picture, because they leaned on the one written in Greek the Septuagint with its erroneous Chronology. {More on this later}

In Peter's letter then we see he is merely compiling what they had discussed in one place for legacy, to refute all false claims and pseudo writings that might come up later. Notice there's another element here. In the **third chapter**, Peter now must remind them that this is the second letter **[cf. 2 Peter 3:1]** because what he is about to speak is the most updated version of understanding Peter has received, a shift!

Even in the **first chapter,** Peter alludes to this, *"We have the prophetic word made more sure ...as to a lamb shining in a dark place ..."* **2 Peter 1:19**. Peter is literally by the end of this verse suggesting Jesus is the *"morning star"* returning at a time when revelation is the brightest *"until the day dawns"*! Are we not there right NOW! Are we not on top of this open door!

In Paul's case he may have been alluding to the fact that Jesus had singled them out concerning *"times and epochs"* **Acts 1** that they wouldn't know the timing of the big picture *[like three wise men]* but that they knew enough to discern the signs *[like Anna or Simeon].* So Paul lends a reminder to them that they would see it clearer the closer they were to it. My point the church lived in expectation, they searched and they weren't even the generation of promise! No, that didn't stop them, they weren't going to let *"the day overtake them"* **1 Thessalonians 5:4**!

Jesus had instructed them how to look for the signs, *"when these things begin to take place, straighten up and lift up your heads because your redemption is drawing near."* **Luke 21:28** However in our present world believers have been made to be unconcerned because they have been promised to be taken before anything Jesus even spoke of.

Further what has gone unnoticed by many is upon explaining the *"abomination of desolation"* in **Matthew 24:15**, the church added these words, *"accurately know"* **v15**, because it is within the framework of that count **[cf. Daniel 12:11-12]** that we can deduct a month is all that lies between the Abomination and the King finally going crazy **[cf. Daniel 11:36]** starting the final 1260 days of the Beast Authority as mentioned in **Revelation 13.** During this short period, the restrainer will be lifted by the event of the last precursor *"until ... the man of lawlessness (being) revealed... who exalts himself"* **2 Thessalonians 2;3** A month is not a day or hour is it?

So in writing back to the Thessalonians, Paul is crystal clear how they knew the Day hadn't started by including mention of this precursor event, the Abomination of Desolation or the King going crazy. Here we ask the question does he not get revealed when the setup of the Abomination interrupts daily sacrifice? Could we not be smart enough to tie together his armies actions with his identity before he goes crazy? So really the bible is in perfect agreement with itself, and the kindness of God to prepare us. Daniel revealing how many will rise up with understanding at that time, point to how clear this sign should be to the believer. Jesus speaking how at that point, we should know accurately our departure is in that very same month!

Some might have found more, but my count is 6 such precursors exist in the BIBLE to His second coming. 2 have been completed *[cf. Israel a nation mature, Peter's death]* and four are still out there *[cf. Every nation hearing Kingdom message, Apostasy, Man of Lawlessness revealed, Later Rains of Revival]*, they all must take place before Jesus returns.

THE AWARENESS

"Those who have insight among the people will give understanding to the many; ..." **Daniel 11:33**

"Seal up until the end time ...Those who have insight will understand" **Daniel 12:10**

The question now changes hopefully in your mind from not whether there is a fixed time but to whom does He reveal this timing? How much does He plan on sharing and when? If Jesus is going to give us a sign only the last generation is going to know how to decipher in **Matthew 24:32** then maybe, we should see this as an indication of God's willingness for us to know information in a broader scope than the obvious limitation of a very *"day"* **Matthew 24:36**! Certainly, this is the indication God gives **Daniel** in his final words in **chapter 11-12 [seen above]**.

So consider this: because we live when we do and only because we do we now know this! Israel is a nation **1948** now tender & mature with possession of Jerusalem in **1967**. The meaning of the parable of the fig tree can be deciphered by paying careful attention to its wording. Two words are key, *"tender"* **Matthew 24:32** for the fig tree and *"pass away"* **v34** for the generation. The parable acts as a revelation and a promise to only one generation, the last. Counting from the time Israel became mature or independent as a nation **1967** and not just simply a nation in **1948**, and the length of one generation's lifetime biblically defined as *"seventy years"* **Psalms 90:10** we come to **2037**. Is Jesus not promising when He will have all the transition of the ages wrapped up by? This being a mere **17 years** away from the writing of this book.

Backup the period of time for the Day of the Lord being **3.5 years** and Jesus would be indicating for us that the rapture must occur before **2033** mid year, which is only **15 years** away. One could stretch the meaning of a lifetime to *"due to strength eighty years"* **Psalms 90:10** and therefore **2047**. This is highly unlikely, given not all have strength and the promise is to the whole generation those strong and not strong. Notice soon either Jesus returns or we cannot be taking the prophecies to have precise meaning. The window of opportunity for God to prove Himself exact in prophetic code measurements is upon us.

The next act of God shown to us is in revealing! Only one generation was afforded the insight of the discovery of the Dead Sea scrolls in **1946** archived circa **1956-67**, and during the exact same period the revelation by Israel's independence as a sovereign nation as the mature fig tree represents **[cf. Matthew 24:32]**. For within these caves are almost mirrored transcripts to the ones translated from the same origins in **900CE** called the Masoretic Texts from which we get most the major translations. What does this reveal? Does it not reveal a high level of attention and respect to accurately transcribing the Hebrew

For the Rabbinical Order who archived them, thought to be the Essenes, believed the return of the Messiah was upon them because of the arrival of the fourth Millennium. So chronology would have been important to them for this reason alone. This points us to which thread of translations was truly reliable source for counting time from creation. That God would keep this debate unresolved over proper Chronological dating between the Septuagint manuscripts not found in the Dead Sea scrolls and the Masoretic ones until now is very telling. God wanted only the last generation to know.

Having these Dead Sea scroll manuscripts dating back to the first to third century BCE preserved in Quorum matching the ones from other sources later translated has raised such questions. We must ask why the varied chronological dating of the Patriarchs lifetimes and events in the Septuagint vary so much from the Masoretic texts. For example, the Septuagint was translated in Egypt during a time when boasting heritages would have influenced results, and corruption in the Rabbinical Order was rampant. One would only need to see the contradictions within the text dating and the timing of the flood to see this. Some ask why does this matter? It does!

For one we can see how God concealed chronology from the early church, but most important is what the early church was prevented in seeing. Jesus died at the perfect time. Understand this creates a domino effect of faith in His second coming being perfect as well. When we observe chronology dating varying so much from different text sources, God is most likely behind the concealment. In this case, we are being asked to use common sense, to search out this matter deeper.

One can give up the search and just say, *'See no one knows, they were all making this up so none of them should be trusted'.*

I find this often times the obstacle of many from getting saved, loss of faith in all humanity and therefore truth. Or we have the option of questioning why the difference. In which case, one would tend to believe the manuscripts that comes from the groups that are ultra conservative concerning translation accuracy and Hebrew purity.

The Essenes were such a group who archived the dead Sea Scrolls although misguided by prophetic fulfillment of the Messiah. What advantage this gives us today is we can now see how Jesus may have actually been crucified on the year 4000 itself by the statistical average of those who painstakingly estimated these manuscripts for chronology *[next chapter]*. My point for now is we, the final generation, would be the only ones to discover this as significant and lead us to this marvelous view of God's perfect plan.

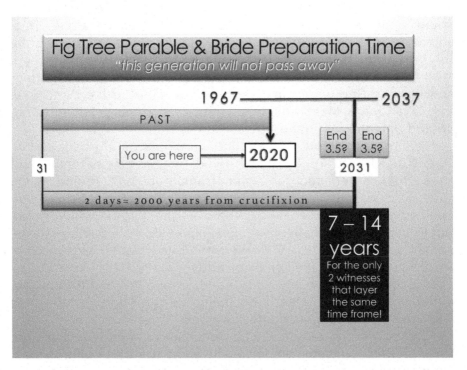

Then comes the clincher, Jesus own words giving us **2 days** when He will return added to **the four days** equaling **4000 years** previous to His death; for the start of the perfect seventh day Millennial Rest on a prophetic week for human history! Just think, why did God create the week being seven days? Why create the world in seven? For just add the mysterious 2 days of *"today and tomorrow"* **Luke 13:32** as **2000 years** by Peter's definition, and you have **2031** or **2033** depending on your method of interpreting the data for dating Jesus death & resurrection. Does this now get your attention, why one thing leads us to another until finally it all makes perfect sense! For roll out **3.5 years** forward and you will see how both signs meet together.

Throw in that we are the only generation that knows the fulfillment of the gospel reaching all tribes is upon us. Estimated around **the late 2020's**, this number is close enough to **2031** to be awe inspiring. The list goes on and so shall this treatise on His second coming and what amazing events are in store for us who believe!

As we search for answers we should not fear getting answers that come close to narrowing the time in which He will return. Just ask yourself is this not my heritage to narrow down the expectation for my groom's return! As a believer walking in this powerful revelation will I not win people to Christ! People want solid answers to what is going on.

THE APATHY

*"Who will secretly introduce **destructive heresies** even denying the Master ... many will follow their sensuality and **because of them the way of the truth will be maligned**"*   **2 Peter 2:1-2**

When it comes to the question knowing or not knowing and how that affects the faith of His own people consider this. Uncertainty or certainty motivates people differently. Jesus gives a parable in **Luke 12:45**, for when they didn't know when He was returning reasoned He would be *"a long time coming"* and *"began to beat the slaves"*. Maybe this is why God choose to conceal the timing of His return for those it would be a long time coming. Yet for us He has no problem revealing. The early church proved through their testimony that being in a *"dark place"* (uncertain) didn't hinder them from finding out as much as God would allow. Here we are doing the same.

The rational in many Christian circles in settling for Eschatological uncertainty is that, that has been the norm for every generation prior to some degree. We say why should things change? We joke about the man on the corner with the sign that says, *"The End is Near,"* saying, *"you don't want to be that guy do you?"* Saying again, *"What's the point in trying to figure out something generations couldn't?"*

Ultimately they will say of this book without consideration, *"How can you say Jesus told us?"* This battle to care about the subject and turn hearts to look again is real folks! This is the great commission **"to make disciples" Matthew 28:19** or what I am doing - giving you the discipline to be watching and looking for Him! Peter saying, **"in the last days mockers will come... "where is the promise of His coming?" 2 Peter 3:3** and I am saying, it's here it's here!

Here I am with a book that shows statistical averages point to a timely first coming thus a timely second, as part of a prophetic week of thousand year days. A book revealing the phenomena of having three symbolic references with the same ratio showing the highly unlikely *"accident"* for the very end, the Day of the Lord. However I am not shocked that God left us ways of discovering the truth? So glad I took those math classes in college because I got some fun things to reveal later. Here I am with a book that melds all the pieces together into a beautiful picture for our future - The coming mysterious days of the King.

Yet, I am kind of disturbed that Satan is lying to God's people so well, that many if you show them amazing proofs still won't listen to anything but what they have been fed on for years! As Esther was told what was at stake for her people as a Queen to intercede, we all must make a decision **"for such a time as this" Esther 4;14** because **"at such a time [when] the prudent person keeps silent ... is an evil time." Amos 5:13** So we must endeavor to take up this search and share our findings.

So back to the words of Christ, let's see how clear some of this really is. For when He says, **"When these things begin to take place, straighten up and lift up your heads because your redemption is drawing near" Luke 21:28** So this can't be at the beginning or the end of the context from which it is couched. The chronology Jesus is speaking of in the context starts with the birth pangs and ends with His appearing to the world.

So it can't be as the Post Tribulation Theory argue at the very end or seventh Trumpet which is seen at the end of Jesus chronology **[cf. Matthew 24:30-31]** and it can't be before everything as the Pre Tribulation Theorist argue. The only ones left who have progressed out of Pre-Tribulation position with their unique take on Post Tribulation/Pre-Wrath position are very close to my belief as to the timing of the rapture but have failed to leave some of the other fallacies of the Pre position from which they departed from.

Those would include the seven year Tribulation period **[cf. Daniel 9** wrong interpretation of the pronoun and purpose of the prophecy**]** and separating the Great Tribulation from the Day of the Lord **[cf.Revelation 7:14** if were come out of the Great Tribulation then it continues after we are gone into the Day of the Lord **as Mark 13:23** reveals another Tribulation continues**]** So the end result is Post tribulation theorist argue that we are sealed through the wrath of God which is found in the Trumpet period calling the Seventh trumpet the end of the Tribulation period, whereas the Post Tribulation- Pre wrath crowd defines the beginning of the Trumpet period the end of the Tribulation period. Everyone agreeing though that the Trumpet period begins God's wrath but not in full and some disagreeing over to the duration and start of the day of the Lord.

Returning to Jesus words used here are *"redemption"*. So what we must ask is what is being redeemed? Are not all God's redemptions based on the blood of Jesus and therefore believer's? Would this not be referring to the rapture? So how can we apply this for Post rapture Jews under the law, or those left behind as Pre Tribulation Theorist will want us to believe? Under Hyper Dispensationalism, we are back under the tyranny of the Catholic church where we need a priest to tell guys how to interpret the Word. How can we tell others what passages belong to us and don't, someone please give me a roadmap. LOL

So going with this failed logic of making **Matthew 24** only for those left behind, would we not be throwing out as well then that favorite passage of Pre-Tribulation Theorist, *"no-one knows the day and hour"* **Matthew 24:36**? Since that day is now within the context for which the Pre-Tribulation Theorist have made off limits to us? And of course, we see that statement of *"day and hour"* included in the parable of the 10 virgins? No, *"these things"* contextually are connected to not missing the Bride's departure and YOUR *"redemption"*!! Yes, we enter the tribulation period but not for long! There cannot be disharmony in scripture which we create by our pet doctrines! Remember, *"these things"* have to begin first! **[Cf. Luke 21:28]** a real problem for The Pre people.

Even the Partial Preterit view, the theory that all the bad stuff is behind us now and that the Millennium has begun in part, linking the **70 AD** destruction of Jerusalem to the Abomination in **Matthew 25:15**, would suffer issues with Jesus statement here. Since **1930 years** have transpired from **70AD**. Remember the period after the Abomination is the *"great tribulation"* and we leave quite quickly after that! Just think, God wanted us to be *"lifting our heads"* for **1930 years**?

Imminent Return as well looks foolish in light of *"these things"* **Luke 21:28** since these things becomes a clear precursor to His return, meaning He cannot return at anytime but AFTER *"these things"*. We just quickly eliminated and destroyed most of the theories out there with just one statement from Jesus lips. Consider the New Testament writers constantly refer to the church as *"who will bring a charge against God's elect"* **Romans 8:33** Even Jesus says, *"God will bring about justice for His elect who cry out to Him ...However when the Son of Man comes will He find faith on the earth?"* **Luke 18:9** We are talking about faith here not the law! Paul applying Jesus words to the church in **2 Thessalonians 1:7** revealing we will undergo tribulation as an actual sign of His return. My point obviously is we are the elect after the Abomination that God takes at His coming in **Matthew 24:27**. Once again my point for you is this isn't really complicated once we remove the obstacles put in our way. We are the elect of **Matthew 24:22** not those left behind or Jewish people.

Many argue that the passage, *"this generation will not pass away until all these things take place"* **Matthew 24:34** was the one He was speaking in front of. [cf. Partial Preterits theory who want you to think they saw Jesus come in **70AD**] Remember *"all these things"* includes Christ appearance to the world at the very end in **Matthew 24:29-31** not just the Abomination which people try to reinterpret as **70AD** past. To name a few more of *"these things"* we have: red moon, no sunlight, Jesus seen by the whole world, etc. Does this sound like things already past? So we find another interpretation needed for *"this generation"* and it is right there in the previous **verse 32**. The final generation is the one that sees Israel as an independent nation which is the definition of a mature fig tree. We are then to start counting 70 years!

Consider Israel was not a nation when Jesus spoke, they were a Roman territory not independent! Israel was never a nation since then until **1948**! What things can Jesus be speaking of really, but those in the context above it. The big context of the Mount of Olive chronology is very limited to the time right before the end **[v5-14]** which include the Abomination of Desolation and the period immediately afterwards **[v15-26, cf. Daniel 11:35]** followed by the fire judgments **[v27-31]** so which ones of these is in His mind when He says, *"when these things* *begin"*, and *"this generation ... "*?

In general, the whole discourse from the birth pangs to our departure in **v27** seem to occur in rapid fashion as I will demonstrate later. This is emphasized by our Lord in the warning of **verse 38**. *"For as in those days before the flood they were eating and drinking marrying and giving in marriage until the day ..."* **Matthew 24:38** Thus the need for this book to define the scope of years prophesied by the harmony and code of scripture to allow our senses to be heightened when all others are put to sleep. Because the final run up is quick and deceptive and not a long drawn out seven year tribulation period. Again another very important reason to search answers in scripture.

Above we see Peter's second letter defense for God's perfect timing hinged upon addressing false teachers, *"those who count slowness"* **2 Peter 3:9.** Warning of coming *"destructive HERESIES"* **2 Peter 2:1,** thus connecting a self serving earth bound hope gospel with mocking His second coming. Do you think he is speaking only of the salvation message when he refers to these heresies? For Peter uses an example, *"God... preserved Noah a preacher of righteousness"* **2 Peter 2:5**. Going on about the seven that made it through the flood with him, Peter shows the importance of hearing the right message of the future which apparently Noah preached!

If the example God laid down for all of us is Noah then that includes the message of the ARK! God's answer! The only safe passage through the flood is what I am preaching to you in this book! God's canopy around the globe is coming, heaven is coming to earth. Noah's message was very eschatological for their day! Do you not think that those who laughed at Noah's preaching is not the example being set by Peter in the next chapter of mockers?

Notice all these elements of a rapture are present in Peter's words, *"preserved Noah ...rescued righteous Lot"* **2 Peter 2:5,7** And further the evidence of tribulation, **"Lot oppressed by the sensual conduct ...felt His righteous soul tormented day after day" 2 Peter 2:7-8** and finally the exclusion of the wrath of God in, *"did not spare the ancient world but preserved Noah ...for the Lord knows how to rescue the godly ... "* **2 Peter 2:5,9** Is not Peter standing against those who would preach that we will be left not taken, or not got through tribulation, or be alongside the wicked during the wrath of God, or not need to be rescued but triumphant, or any of these popular opinions that are just not Biblical?

Paul uses the concept of sleeping for spiritual darkness says, **"Knowing the time that it is <u>already the hour</u> [climate for change] for you to awaken from sleep; ... the night is almost gone"** **Romans 13:12** Paul was equating seeing clearer to being awakened, tells another church they shouldn't be **"in darkness, that the day should overtake you like a thief; for you are all sons of light... we are not of night nor of darkness; so then let us not sleep"** **1 Thessalonians 5:4** The firm belief of both Peter & Paul was we are not to play stupid. It's time to change the spiritual atmosphere we are in, to one of great expectation and solid bible teaching.

THE COMMAND

*"Should remember the **words spoken beforehand** by the **holy prophets** and the commandments of **the Lord** and savior spoken **by your apostles**."*

2 Peter 3:2

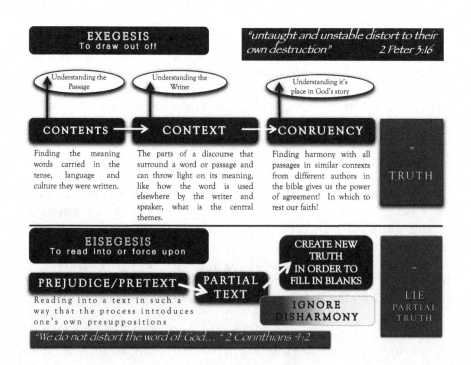

EXEGESIS
To draw out off

"untaught and unstable distort to their own destruction" 2 Peter 3:16

Understanding the Passage

Understanding the Writer

Understanding it's place in God's story

CONTENTS → **CONTEXT** → **CONRUENCY**

| Finding the meaning words carried in the tense, language and culture they were written. | The parts of a discourse that surround a word or passage and can throw light on its meaning, like how the word is used elsewhere by the writer and speaker, what is the central themes. | Finding harmony with all passages in similar contexts from different authors in the bible gives us the power of agreement! In which to rest our faith! | = TRUTH |

EISEGESIS
To read into or force upon

PREJUDICE/PRETEXT → **PARTIAL TEXT** →

CREATE NEW TRUTH IN ORDER TO FILL IN BLANKS

Reading into a text in such a way that the process introduces one's own presuppositions

IGNORE DISHARMONY

= LIE PARTIAL TRUTH

"We do not distort the word of God..." 2 Corinthians 4:2

THE SOURCES

I. Old Testament Prophecies give us ...
   1. Descriptions of events in picture dreams and visions they had, helping us attach future prophesy to Jesus words
   2. Sequences for those events helping place the order in harmony with future prophecy
   3. Time codes given in few instances **[I.e. Daniel 9, Hosea 6]**
   4. Linkage of God's promise to Abraham etc to the future fulfillment

II. Old Testament examples gives us ...
   1. Types and shadows such as divinely instituted feasts and sabbaths and laws as confirming witness to the timing of God's plan
   2. We attach them to what they symbolize

III. New Testament gives us ...
   1. Jesus authoritative revelation
      A. three Gospel accounts of Mount of Discourse **Matthew 24; Luke 17,21; Mark 13**
      B. Jesus explanation of the Big Picture **Luke 13**
      C. Parable pictures of the time of harvest **Matthew 13**
   2. Apostles piecing together Jesus words alongside the prophets

---

THE METHODS

1. *Harmony of Reliable Sources* (2-3 witnesses) **"words spoken beforehand by the holy prophets ... our Lord ...by your apostles" 2 Peter 3:2 "by the mouth of two or three witnesses every fact may be confirmed" Matthew 18:16 [2 Corinthians 13:1]** Also we must give weight but not authority to credible testimony that falls outside the bounds of Canonized scripture.
2. *Historical Precedence* (notice the order given is chronological in **2 Peter 3:2**) We must consider when a theme is introduced how it is developed over time,

73

give importance to when it is first mentioned as well.

3. *Hierarchy* notice everything centers on Jesus since he says the Apostles only are pushing forward His words. *"The testimony of Jesus is the spirit of prophesy"* **Revelation 19:10** So everything points forward and backwards to Jesus words and the demonstration of His life as a revelation of truth above all else.

4. *Hermeneutics* which goes without being said over everything in life. You must follow basic principles of interpreting anything I.e. Context, and finally this all should hold up under trial of peers. *"prophets being subject to prophets"* **1 Corinthians 14:32**

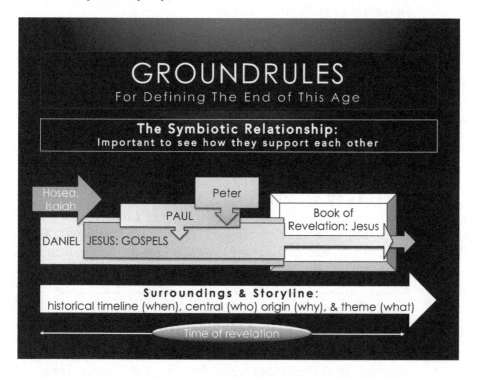

AWAKENING GENEALOGIES

The Resurrection Code Revealed

Volume 2

CJ Michaels

"You are not in darkness that the day should overtake you like a thief." 1 Thessalonians 5:4

4

Mocking:

The Chosen Ignorance

THE FIRST SIGN

*"Know **this first of all**, that in the last days mockers will come with mocking, following their own lusts saying, **'Where is the promise [evidence] of His coming?'"***

2 Peter 3:3-4

Before establishing the Apostles Doctrine on the timely Return of Christ, Peter starts with, **"know this first of all"** 3:3. This shouldn't be a shock that Peter uses the word **"first"**. He had just made it abundantly clear that they were merely forwarding the gospel of Jesus. **"the commandment of the Lord spoken by your apostles"** 3:2 Understanding this connection, we see Jesus starting His discourse on signs of the end of this age by stating a first as well, **"many will come in My name ... and will mislead many."** **Matthew 24:5**

Peter drawing from Jesus words says, mockers will come who know about the promise but mock it. Are we not seeing and saying the same thing? Does this not give further detail to how people will be misled at the end of this age? Are we not clearly identifying a form of Christianity that believes His kingdom is already been established on earth without Him physically present. Remember the church thought this when

Emperor Constantine paganize Christianity.

The connection is clear as day. The sign of the last days won't just be the unbelievers mocking, for why should they care. They don't believe anything we say. However, this will be a big deal as *"Christians"* mock other believers over the second coming. Why? Because of a strong delusion is coming **[cf. 2 Thessalonians 2:11]** to be convinced they are the kingdom being established. **Jude** himself even repeats Peter's words in his letter showing the importance this sign of the end had amongst the early church fathers saying, *"remember the words that were spoken beforehand __by the apostles__ of our Lord Jesus Christ, ...in the last times there will be mockers ..."* **Jude 17-18**

"Christians" who Jesus speaks of as tares (weed look a-likes) guiding others away from their hope, confidence and expectation of His return will be a huge monumental reality the Word of God foretells. Paul likewise tells us without question Jesus cannot return until *"the apostasy* [falling away from the faith] __comes first__" **2 Thessalonians 2:4**. Notice the word "First" is used again! Paul now pronounces his interpretation of it as so severe as to label it an event in history called, *"the Apostasy"*! Paul gives it the definite article *"the"*. This isn't a general falling away over the whole age but very narrowed in time event *"the"*!

So Peter Paul and Jesus are all indicating the same importance to this particular sign. Each giving it a unique detail to it. The sign? There will come a day when those who oppose the truth end up being those who know the promise of His return **[cf. 2 Peter 3:4 above]** and must likely espouse the name of Jesus as *"Christ (ians)"* **Matthew 24:5**. Of these Paul declares this will be so wide scale as to be labeled in history *"THE"* falling away from the faith. Another amazing revelation is Jesus later describes the response of these people as saying, *"Lord, Lord, did we not prophesy in Your name and in Your name cast out demons, and in Your name perform many miracles?'* **Matthew 7:22** and His response *"I never knew you depart from Me you who practice lawlessness."* **v23** paraphrased ...

"You never came under my kingdom authority or control to allow any transforming change in your heart [born again experience] *by my blood forgiving you through sanctifying work of the Spirit. No, instead you adopted a practice of religious entitlement or works wherein your defense here is what you did, not what I did! You never trusted, relied on ME,*

didn't you think to take My word seriously when it required reliance on Me. So I don't know you." **Matthew 7:23**

The question then becomes what does losing faith look like here? For at the time of His return He says, *"I tell you that He will bring about justice for them quickly. However when the Son of Man comes, will He find faith on the earth?"* **Luke 18:8** Jesus is responding to an injustice done to the true believer's who he calls *"His elect"* in **verse 7.** Could this not be the drama played out by those who make the mistake that Jesus is already on the earth through us **[cf. Matthew 24:23, Luke 17:23]** through supernatural manifestations **[cf. Matthew 24:24]** or an anti-Christ figure claiming to be Christ. **[Cf. Didache 16]**

So powerful is this delusion of the true Kingdom Message which must include Jesus physical return for there to be His reign, that Jesus declares, *"Unless those days had been cut short, no life would be saved"* **Matthew 24:22** Jesus isn't talking about physical life being saved but souls of the righteous abandoning their faith in the coming kingdom for one in the Now. In fact when we examine Paul's letters, we again see the importance they took in forwarding Jesus teaching on just what we are holding our faith in. Who made it abundantly clear that many *"false Christs and false prophets will arise"* **Matthew 24:24** to tell us Jesus has already come either in physical form or through a movement. We are expressly told not to believe them by who else JESUS! **[Cf. Matthew 24:26]**

Jesus will make this easy to understand, you won't see me before you see this! *"Just as lightning comes from the East and flashes to the West so will the coming of the Son of Man be."* **Matthew 24:27** Thus Paul keeping on the same theme says, *"looking for the blessed hope and appearing of the glory of our great God and Savior, Christ Jesus"* **Titus 2:13** What are we looking for? Jesus? No, look carefully, we are looking for the GLORY! Notice the world does not even notice Jesus has come until later at the sixth seal. For all the world recognizes is His presence which is His glory, *"fall on us and hide us from the presence of Him who sits on the throne and from the wrath of the Lamb"* **Revelation 6:16**

Of course this leads us to review the argument that Jesus spoke this warning of not believing an earthly report because of the truth that, *"every eye will see Him"* **Revelation 1:7** Which makes perfect sense until you factor in what I just mentioned. Jesus tells us we see *"lightning ... flashes"*

Matthew 24:27 and clearly not His physical form at first. As you will begin to see as we venture deeper into this book, the key to this mystery will be another truth Jesus spoke. His coming will be *"days"* **Luke 17:26** PLURAL, which opens the door for Him to finally appear from the *"clouds"* for *"every eye"* Revelation 1:7 at the end of His coming but arrive with *"lightning ... flashes"* **Matthew 24:27**

So Jesus warning is not about sight but earth hope versus heavenly hope! For why would Hebrews 12:28 tell us to listen for His voice!

Notice that by the popularity of the Pre-Tribulation Theory many will surmise Jesus should have arrived already by the sign of the Abomination, and be looking for Him on earth. Either the Anti-Christ will deceive them or the reactionary prophets will be saying, *"no really He's over here!"*. Consider how many will die because of traps set to herd the gullible. Try to understand that before this point in time there is only mention of wars & pestilence much like there has always been. **[cf. Matthew 24:38]** People will be carrying out their normal life.

What Jesus is showing us is the most important sign to understand in the final stretch to His return because the end is not otherwise clear. It's the highest deception possible, *"Christianized"* rejection of a future return. Followed by substitute narratives and supernatural men claiming to be Him. All this with signs forming in the sky making it seem like we missed something. This great falling away from the hope of a bodily resurrected Jesus returning and removing us is very clear in Jesus warnings, *"then if anyone says to you, 'Behold, here is the Christ,' ...do not believe him."* **Matthew 24:23**!

Remember when Jesus left the earth before his disciples it was said by angels, *"This Jesus who was taken up from you into heaven will come just the same ways you watched Him go into heaven."* **Acts 1:11** This was the solid teaching of the church, that Jesus would return in the same way He left to catch us up to the lower air with Him. **[Cf. 1 Thessalonians 4:17]** Consider, how closely related our faith in His resurrection is to believing in His physical bodily return not from earth but from the sky above!

How important is our faith is in His resurrection, just read this *"if you ...believe in your heart that God raised Him from the dead you will be saved"* **Romans 10:9**. Won't it be obvious some will argue? Yes, at the very end, *"Every eye will see Him..."* **Revelation 1:7** This written in **95AD** after Jerusalem's destruction cast away any doubt it occurred in **70 AD**. Again this isn't rocket science, emphasizing how all this is still future.

Yet check out how John describes this. First he says, *"Behold He is coming with (among) the clouds"* then specifying, *"every eye"*. When we return to how Jesus describes His coming, there is no mention of Him being seen when He comes **[cf. Matthew 24:27]**. Only later after a period of time **[cf. V29]** does He give us that event when *"they will see the Son of Man"* **v30** paralleling *"every eye will see Him"* **Revelation 1:7** Remember Paul's description of us being caught up to the lower air, never mentions Jesus being seen at that time. **[Cf. 1 Thessalonians 4:17]** Be careful to not read into scriptures our assumptions or what man has taught us to think.

Since Jesus comes hidden but physically we have one of the greatest test of faith ever seen. So Jesus says, *"will I find faith?"* **Luke 18:8** One just has to read the parable of the 10 virgins to realize the stealth nature of the Groom's arrival as sudden **[cf. Matthew 25:6]** and the slim opportunity for an open door later **[cf. Matthew 25:11]** only supplied for *"those who were ready"* **Matthew 25:10** So returning to this sign of the end, the departure from faith, Paul after calling for the necessity of **"the apostasy" 2 Thessalonians 2:4** clarifies it as a world movement led by Satan to deceive those who *"did not receive the love for the truth"* **2:10**. How is this accomplished?

Paul will tell us. *"God will send a deluding influence"* **2 Thessalonians 2:11** Many can relate to the age old trick of deluding the wine toward the end of the wedding when everyone is drunk. No one knows the difference. Maybe the greatest deception is a call to celebrate the wedding before the groom has even arrived? Faith in this regard is lacking patience and devotion. It is lacking respect to wait for the Groom to actually arrive. Two more things are apparent in this context, One is that it is a supernatural movement saying, *"coming ...with all power and signs and false wonders"* **2 Thessalonians 2:9** and two it is fueled by a love for sin *[the self life] "who took pleasure in wickedness"* **2:12**.

Don't be fooled by the mention of Satan in these verse as though you will see a man with horns. For his Anti-Christ & His false prophet will be thought of as a kind loving men much like Jesus Himself but teaching contrary to Christ teachings. Here we see the need for both Peter & Jude to give lengthy descriptions of these coming preachers/teachers who *"who promise freedom while they themselves are slaves of corruption"* **2 Peter 2:19** Simply understood in context with Jesus words, they were never truly saved and prove it by their living under no governing influence. **[Cf. Matthew 7:21, 25:11]**

So in painting this solid biblical New Testament sign that ushers us into the end, more and more I am impressed with how much of it is tied to losing faith in His return is just losing faith. Notice, John who in his letters was so forthright about testing the *"spirits"* of the false prophets by whether they confessed *"Jesus Christ has come in the flesh"* **1 John 4:2** or not. Paul declaring in **1 Corinthians 15:17** our faith *"worthless"* without the physical resurrected truth of Jesus being raised; and with that truth verses later the belief that, *"Christ the first fruit ...those who are Christ's at His coming"* **v23**

Understand the whole letter to the Corinth church comes down to the teaching on the Resurrection in **chapter 15** which morphs into Eschatology. The chapter starts on His resurrection but finishes on the truth of that resurrection being our future hope that we will as well.

THE LAST DAYS

"... In the last days."   **2 Peter 3:3**
*"... In **the last time** there will be mockers"*   **Jude 18**

In starting his defense for a timely return in **chapter 3**, Peter is quick to bring back the term he had used at Pentecost 30 years earlier in saying, *"in the last days"* **Acts 2:17**. This term must have been widely repeated by the church for **Jude 17-18** will echo Peter's words but adds mention to *"apostles"* **v17** in the plural. However, what is curious is **Jude** uses the term *"last times"* **v18** or *"chronos"* substituting it for Peter's term, *"last days"* **2 Peter 3:3**. This is another bread crumb that gives us cause to see the church looking at this term *"last days"* differently than normal days. Sorry Partial Preterit Theorist, these *"last days"* can't be exclusively shoved into their time period as the end of the age of Law.

Consider, that Jesus sacrifice put an end to the Law and the new age had been declared at Pentecost **31AD** when Peter declared *"the last days"* **Acts 2:17** had begun. The period of 30-70AD would be a very short *"age"* indeed. Although this period did seem to serve as a transitional time between ages just as the final the day of the Lord for 3.5 years will at the end of this one.

Remember again, **2 Peter** is a letter from the leader of Christianity knowing he's going to die, trying to leave a legacy. So Peter figures out the mystery of this prophetic speech, by pointing our attention to it being the most important information for seeing the big picture using the strongest language possible, *"do not let this one fact escape your notice"* **2 Peter 3:8a**, saying *"one day is [hos = equal to, or like] as a thousand years"* **3:8b.** The greek word *"hos"* has only two options; so similar that it is just as, or exactly as. Peter by his speech is exclaiming, *"one fact"*, does not give us much room to interpret his statement as anything but as a *"fact"*. He is not speaking loosely here, but analytically.

In the natural mind, we assume that the prophetic will be spoken in a clear everyday language and not in some code. I understand this can be difficult to someone new to the bible. Remember as we covered this previously, God conceals in order to reveal to only His servants who seek to know in the timing He desires. This is why we must pay attention to the context of each discourse and the harmony it has with the rest of scripture. God is looking for faith in His words. He's not here for you, to make this plain as day. Instead, He is waiting for those *"whose heart is completely His"* **2 Chronicles 16:9** to *"strongly support"* which includes our inheritance of seeing what others can't. In seeing God's heart expressed throughout scriptures, we begin to see this big picture from His side. *"A day* being *a thousand years"* **3:8** as an answer for *"last days"* **3:3**

For example of differing uses of *"day"*, Jesus used the term literally throughout His context in **Matthew 24** so we can't expand the idea of not knowing *"the day or hour"* beyond the literal use. Especially when *"the day"* is being defined in the context as a single point in time for its definition. That is not the case in other places in the bible. For example Jesus uses the word *"day"* **John 6** in reference to a final day in the gospel of John when the saints are resurrected and the world is judged. *"I will raise him up on the last day"* **John 6:44** and **54**; *"will judge him at the last day"* **John 12:48.** Yet we know at this point in time another day follows with the Millennial reign of Christ if indeed Christ was talking about the final 24 hour period of this current age as *"last day"*.

Understand in a pre-millennial world, He cannot be referring to this *"final day"* as a 24 hour period. For the Book of Revelation declares another one exist beyond this age!In fact the whole point of this book could come down to that. The end for us is just the beginning of another 1000 years of peace. **[Cf. Revelation 20:4]** Logic is speaking against a normal use for "day". This same logic was hitting Peter concerning the context of *"the last days"*. Logic was speaking louder and louder as more days transpired and their death loomed! As for Peter, we know he is always forwarding what Jesus spoke by saying, *"Salvation which is ready to be revealed on the last day for all to see."* **1 Peter 1:15.** So here, Peter chooses to forward Jesus term.

I have no problem with this statement of Peter in first letter. The rapture will occur at the start of the new age and the end of this one and then revealed to the world during the final age or *"day"* after the first 3.5 years. All this harmonizes with Paul's statement, *"When Christ who is our life is revealed then you will be revealed with Him in glory."* **Colossians 3:4** So Peter's use of *"the last day"* cannot occur on the last 24 hours of history, but occurs as this book will show at the start of the last 1000 year period or *"day"*. Thus, this is a term for the last prophetic day. So our firm foundation is we are yet awaiting this final day for Christ has not been physically revealed to all! **[Cf. Revelation 1:7]**

Understand, God has brilliantly used these unlearned men growing in awareness, to forward the foundations God laid in the Old Testament, by linking Jesus term *"last day"* & Joel's term *"last days"* to this code in **2 Peter 3:8**. It might surprise you that **John 6** isn't the only prophetic reference Jesus uses for *"day"*. Declaring boldly to Herod that He will finish His ministry after 2 days and reach His goal on the third. **[Cf. Luke 13:32]** These three days [3000 years} are less than the four days [4000 years] that preceded His death. They are truly the last days of human history. If there was going to be any question of Jesus use of *"day"* here, He immediately distinguishes real time saying, *"nevertheless I must journey on today and tomorrow and the next ..."* **v33** in the next verse.

It is with this rich tradition of coded time the apostles enter the scene connecting these statements to the prophets who spoke in terms of a day being vague period of time they were seeing in visions, *"I will pour out my Spirit in those days [later]"* **Joel 2:29** connecting it to *"before the great and awesome Day of the Lord"* **Joel 2:31** and even on that day [cf. **Joel 3**]. Peter even including, *"the Day of the Lord"* **2 Peter 3:10** as part of his "last days" discussion which **Joel** does as well. So later we will discuss whether *"the Day of the Lord"* is synonymous with the *"last day"* or a separate entity describing the transitional period of judgment at the beginning of the last day.

This term *"Day of the Lord"* mentioned 18 times in the Old Testament, will be our focus in the last two chapters of this book, however Peter seems to use it as a separate item but apart of the *"last days"*. Much has been debated in the church over what it truly represents for it is a mystery. The prophets refer to it as a period of judgment passing into His kingdom reign. In God's big picture timetable of a prophetic day being a thousand, there seems to be no connection but it being apart of.

Post Tribulation Theorist lean toward a single day on the seventh trumpet when the final judgment occurs, whereas Pre-Tribulation Theorist find it to be synonymous with the Great Tribulation. I will contend that it is the coming of Christ mysteriously revealed over a period of time called *"the Days of the Son of Man"* **Luke 17:26** when the whole world will be tested, judged with fire until He is physically manifested. One could stretch that period of the *"Day of the Lord"* to Daniel's full count of *"1335 days"* **Daniel 12:12.** The main idea you will hear me say though is Christ has to be present for it to be HIS DAY!

So the shift was happening in the church right here in this second letter, Peter saying, *"God is not slow"* as some were *"counting slowness"* **2 Peter 3:9** because we are beginning to understand the big picture. The early church was beginning to see the need to look beyond *"the now"* into the continuum of God's larger viewpoint for prophetic truth. They had been convinced He was returning in their lifetime. Yet even while they were caught up in their day, they carefully weighed their estimation from the study of prophecy. Peter & Paul showing how there had to be events preceding, and that God was on a schedule. Here we see a shift though where all their study in the word of God now pays off!

In four places, **[cf. Colossians 1:6,23, Romans 1:8, 10:18]**

Paul proudly declares their faith being proclaimed in all the known world, which was to them a reality but not a truth. Why? Because again from our vantage point we now know the globe like they didn't! Many use these passages as prove text that we are already in the Millennium *[cf. A-Millennials/Partial Preterit]* since Jesus had said, **"the end" Matthew 24:14b** would come when **"the gospel of the Kingdom is preached in the whole world" v14a** Only problem with that is this. God is the one giving the prophecy. To Him the whole *"inhabited earth"* or tribes and people included those unknown to them at the time. God is the one declaring and sees all! I am going with God on this.

We now know of every tribe on the earth and some Mission boards say we will reach this goal soon by 2030 or soon after. Does this make what Paul said a lie, God forbid no! It is just another case of something not being accurate to our perspective now but to them it was real. Just like their estimations of Christ return soon 2000 years ago seemed real based on unclear prophesy in **Daniel 9,** their disadvantaged viewpoint and Jesus confusing statements.

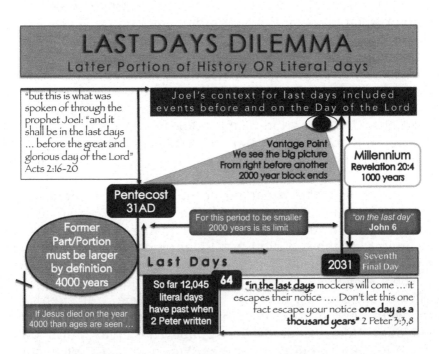

LAST DAYS DILEMMA
Latter Portion of History OR Literal days

"but this is what was spoken of through the prophet Joel: "and it shall be in the last days ... before the great and glorious day of the Lord" Acts 2:16-20

Joel's context for last days included events before and on the Day of the Lord

Vantage Point We see the big picture From right before another 2000 year block ends

Millennium Revelation 20:4 1000 years

Pentecost 31AD

For this period to be smaller 2000 years is its limit

"on the last day" John 6

Former Part/Portion must be larger by definition 4000 years

Last Days

2031 Seventh Final Day

If Jesus died on the year 4000 than ages are seen ...

So far 12,045 literal days have past when 2 Peter written

64 "in the last days mockers will come ... it escapes their notice .... Don't let this one fact escape your notice **one day as a thousand years"** 2 Peter 3:3,8

Most can understand how this works. For if I told you, *"your earthly life has a later end"* and rewarded on the *"last day".* You would take my context or qualifying remark being *"your earthly life"* (as a whole). You wouldn't make it about something smaller like the last days of your job, or bigger like including the after life. The same is here.

Peter's context is going to be human history in total. For example, *"from the beginning of creation" 2 Peter 3:4* and describing the flood paralleled to the conclusion in the fire judgments yet future. **[cf. 2 Peter 3:5-7]** There is no question the context of the *"last days"* is the count of human history. .

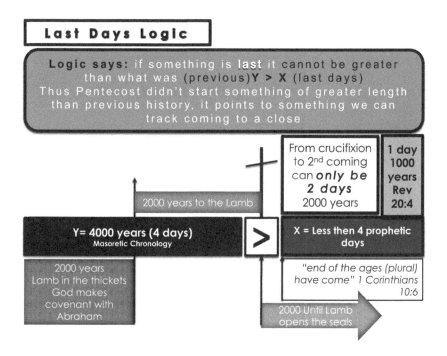

THE CONTINUUM

"all continues just as it was from the beginning of creation"   **2 Peter 3:4**

So here's the problem we all have with the Grand scheme or plan of God. It's too massive to comprehend or personalize our place in it. So we speak what Peter says is the carnal logic, *"all continues"*. Tragic events, yes, but apocalyptic end to this age by an Alien King no! Are you telling me God will step into history?

The straw man argument presented here is found from this statement above. You can hear them say, *'Nothing changed, we have always seen stuff from time to time.'* And *'It's foolish to think that everything will just end. Sure we have natural disasters and wars but this has been going on since the beginning. Those stories of the flood & creation are just fables to teach us lessons'*

This is all a kin to boiling a frog, who doesn't have the sense to jump out of the pot because the temperature is increased little by little causing the critter to get accustomed to it. Just consider the end comes as **"birth pangs"** **Matthew 24:8**, **Mark 13:8** which means it deceptively approaches in cycles of sorrows never seen before, then a return to peace and safety over and over until it defines the new normal, and nobody is the worse for wear.

Notice though when Peter makes his argument based on their unbelief, he introduces the big picture. **"From the beginning of creation"** **2 Peter 3:4** You see the continuum of time has put everyone to sleep. All hasn't been without God's intervention but to them it has! This is the phenomena that exist in our nation with our younger generation. They have never experienced a war or a great depression. Sure there's good and bad, sure nations rise and fall, sure there have been wars, earthquakes and diseases; in all we have gotten use to the ebb and flow of life.

So goes the commonly used phrase, *'Out of sight out of mind.'* If we've never seen an end occur, if we can't find it in our history books then it's not believable. It never happened. It can't happen. Solomon in his wisdom said this is a problem with how God created humans to enjoy eternity before time existed.

> *"He has made **everything appropriate in its time**. He has also **set eternity in their heart**, Yet so that man **will not find out** the work God has done **from the beginning even to the end.**"* **Ecclesiastes 3:11**

Think about it, we were created to enjoy the now. Time did not exist before the fall. Since we focus on our own surroundings, each day as it comes, which causes us to be distracted or unconcerned from the big picture. The mysteries that God has set in motion since the beginning seem a bit above our pay grade. The word for **"eternity"** here in **Ecclesiastes 3:11** in the Hebrew language is **"owlam"** which

88

means *"time out of mind or vanishing point"*.

This continuum gives us an impression of an unending future because we can no longer imagine a beginning to all this. That is why God calls salvation always a **"now" 2 Corinthians 6:2** experience because salvation is *"eternal life"*! The quality of life that's eternal is always found in the present unending. This ability to live fully in the now was a gift from God that now hinders us if we are being asked to *"consider our ways"* **Haggai 1:5,7** and *"number our days"* **Psalms 90:11**. History is loaded with examples, so Jesus uses them: Noah & the Ark, Lot & Sodom, Moses & Pharaoh, and so on. History depends on time, time only exist because of the fall.

For example, if we are bringing God into our *"now"* praying always, walking with Him we are blessed. Our now then serves as a light to keep us awake to the signs of His coming and to be received when He comes. We are walking in the reality of eternity after the seventh day. Yet notice God has to put Himself in us to always keep our "now" fervently ready and connected to heaven not earth, to the Spirit not the flesh. This is a reminder that something greater is coming! Notice the hope isn't that *"Christ is in us"* **Colossians 1:27** but by being *"in us"* we can conceive of the hope coming, *"Christ in you the hope of Glory"* **Colossians 1:27**.

This might be the colossal mistake of these end times, Christians content with the down payment only. Lukewarm and ready to be spewed out according to **Revelation 3:16,** are we living too dangerously to crossing over into an unbelieving heart? Many under the spell of today's hyper grace gospel might as well retranslate that verse as *"the Christ in us the hope of our own glory"*. By removing the aim and goal being one and the same as Christ's aim when He said, *"on the third day I reach my goal"* **Luke 13:32,** are we not departing from Christ's kingdom goals.

His goal isn't our empowerment that is just a tool toward an end. Our goal should be consummating our potential marriage to Christ. The groom wants a bride who is awaiting the Glory because that is when she will see her groom! Here lies the message Jesus was preaching surrounding His future return. There must exist a tension from *the Kingdom Now* that create a longing for *the Kingdom coming*. Both must work together as proof we are actually saved! We are seated with Him above even now, thus we long for that reality to be complete. We must not settle for a version of NOW that exclude our future hope!

Jesus was clear that the arrival of the kingdom was already creating problems for those seeking it on earth. Especially in the final days leading to its ultimate fulfillment, saying, *"Now having been questioned by the Pharisees **as to when the kingdom of God was coming**, He answered them and said, 'The Kingdom of God is not coming with signs to be observed; nor will they say, 'Look here it is ! Or 'There it is! **For behold the kingdom of God is in your midst.'"** **Luke 17:21**

The point our Lord is making is profound, the kingdom never left earth, for Jesus left His Spirit in us. Yet the fullness of it is coming much like the way it is hidden in us will arrive shrouded, *"The kingdom of heaven is <u>like a treasure hidden in the field, which a man found and <u>hid again</u> ..."* **Matthew 13:44** Jesus will arrive mysteriously while people are saying already He's on earth. He will supernaturally grab His bride and hide her in her honeymoon chamber, and all the world will see is dead bodies. Notice Jesus says, *"**Kingdom not coming with**"* admitting at His first coming it had not arrived in full; yet then He turns around and states *"**behold the kingdom of God is in your midst**"* **Luke 21:21** revealing it had already arrived tin part to operate in its superior authority through us.

Jesus first coming was D-Day! Rightly do we preach, that we are God's beachhead arrival, nations are about to fall! We are holding the fort for Jesus! When He arrives above the earth, the Kingdom will not be revealed all at once either by Christ physical appearance notice the parable says, *"**and hid again**"* and Jesus words to the Pharisees says, *"**Kingdom not coming with signs to be observed**"* or clearly defined! Some say Jesus is coming to take us to a place prepared in heaven far away while others say He will come at the very end seen by all. However let's look again. *"**goes and sells all that he has (crucifixion) and buys that field (earth).**"* **Matthew 13:44** Redemption includes the earth, Jesus is buying out the kingdom of darkness!

In the context of Jesus conversation with the Pharisees about the coming hidden Kingdom, He will turn to His disciples and say, *"**You will see ... lightning**"* [the glory of God] *"**so will the Son of Man be in His day**"* **Luke 17:24** Thus *"**the hope of Glory**"* not a physical Jesus manifestation. For Jesus effectively is saying no one will see me a verse earlier! Don't believe them! Instead this inner longing created by the kingdom deposit in us will guide His church to heaven entering our upper atmosphere. It is here that Jesus will encamp around the enemy, and enjoy His bride.

Notice the next verse he turns to his disciples to explain. **"You will long to see one of the days of the Son of Man" v22** Here's the tension, and it must exist. Peter agreeing saying we should long for that day, because it is our honeymoon! **[Cf. 2 Peter 3:12]** Why else would we long for it if it is only judgment! Notice Jesus identifies how it should be when the Holy Spirit is deposited within us. For it is the Holy Spirit [Groomsmen] who will beckon us. The Holy Spirit within us at the time of the rapture will open our ears to the voice calling us to heaven.

Otherwise we will shrink away, for **"who can stand" Malachi 3:2** but the word declares that He will **"make you stand in His presence of His glory" Jude 24**. Jude's context is about the rapture from **verses 14-15** mentioning Jesus coming, to **verse 21** using **1 Enoch**'s term "mercy" for the rapture. The true nature of the rapture involves a decision of faith, more on this later. **[Cf. Hebrews 12:25, 1 John 2:28]** For this reason, we see why Jesus & the apostles spent so much effort commanding us to be **"sober and alert" 1 Peter 4:7**, using terms like **"watchful"** and **"awake"**. To look upward not earth bound. Why? You can miss the rapture. You can be unready.

THE TODAY

*"For the **time will come** when they will **not endure sound doctrine**; but wanting to have their ears tickled, they will **accumulate** for themselves **teachers** in **accordance to their own desires**."*

2 Timothy 4:3

In **2010** Pew Research Institute surveyed U.S.A Christians and what they believe concerning the Second Coming of Jesus Christ. **38 percent** did not display faith in a future Second Coming. This is simply amazing, and we are only getting started. **14 more percent** declared they just didn't know. If we add this up we are <u>over half those who declare they are "Christians" who do not hold to a future return of Jesus Christ</u>. *[Jesus Christ Return to Earth, pewresearch.org, July 14, 2010]*

Of the remaining **48 percent**, **only 27 percent believed** it could happen in their lifetime! Leaving **21 percent** who just don't want Him coming in their lifetime but have been taught to believe it. What was even more startling, was the discovery that so many **[40 percent]** don't believe the bible is the answer to something so major as our future given a third of the bible is prophecy! Historically this may have something to do with the pendulum effect caused by the boy who cried wolf too many times. I mean if the Apostles & Hal Lindsey and so on got it wrong!

Interest in *"end times signs"* arose to an apex with Israel becoming a nation in **1948,** many seeing this as connected to Jesus words. **[cf. Matthew 24:32]** Then came many false predictions starting with Hal Lindsey **[circa 1981]**. Since the Pre-Millennial debate only consisted between two partial truth's *[Pre versus Post Tribulation raptures]* many became disillusioned and gravitated to Pan-Theology *[no one knows so it will just happen]*. As you can see much of this is a reaction to others not forming ideas that are sound enough to harmonize all scriptures concerning the end of this age.

The logic was if the Apostles were wrong and our contemporary experts aren't making any sense then who am I to think I can understand this stuff. Thus the popularity of an Anytime return, because it just took the responsibility away from us to care about something we believed too confusing. Just a word here, most God-loving believers just felt we needed to make a difference in this present world and let God take care of the rest. This push away from an escapism mentality was much needed. Although we must now mention how the pendulum swung to the opposite extreme today.

For NOW here we are in **2020**, we come to a time in history much the same as Peter did, where the illusion is God is delaying His return. What seems obvious to us, are in fact very unbiblical notions. The unbiblical ideas that are circulating are either, He is waiting on us or He in fact already returned we just missed it. Just so easy to believe these lies that get us off the hook for searching the bible ourselves for the answer. However we are losing out on discovering the God of perfection who has destined a time and place for us.

What is very concerning in our day is two of the biggest Christian worship movements hold to these varying views. IHOP, the 24 hour prayer movement leader, Mike Bickle states, *'Jesus is waiting for the church to grow up to loose the Tribulation [thus rapture].'* [https://thekeyofdavid.wordpress.com/

2011/04/07/mike-bickle-on-the-book-of-revelation/] and Bethel
Church prophetic leader Kris Vallotton states, *"I will not
accept an eschatology that takes away my children's future ...I
am opposed to ... the promises of God [Millennial reign] into a
time zone [not this age] ... I don't believe that the last days
are a time of judgement." [https://krisvallotton.com/my-8-
eschatological-core-values/]*

As recent as this last year, Bethel's bookstores have seen
the sudden interest in books declaring that Jesus cannot
return until the church is victorious, or state He has returned
already in part *[cf. Partial Preterit Theory]*. Instituting a new
definition for the Millennial Reign of Christ in the form of a
very contrary narrative of our present and future. Are we
replacing the hope of the church from Christ physically
manifested to "Christian" movements? Notice the shift of
narrative for the future hope moves away from Jesus to the
church organized. The effect on many is tragically a release
from the tension that this world is not our home to a putting
our hope on a movement on earth. When the heart of those
espousing these belief systems say they are only trying to get
the church to live fully now for Christ. I say, *'Awesome but
dangerous!'*

Honestly though this must sound great, God is good so all
the judgment is behind us. Just a victorious church and then
Jesus return. Dang if I was unsaved I would sign up for this.
The popularity of these easily disproven theories, both Pre
Tribulation and Partial Preterit, is they affirm we won't see
judgment/tribulation, no bad stuff. So Bethel, IHOP and
Hillsong push the theology of conquering the seven mountains
of society, focusing on the Kingdom NOW. The focus becoming
conquering the world through love, which is great until you
look deeper under the covers. The hidden leaven of old
Pentecostal Movements *[Kingdom Now Theology, Dominion
Theology, Manifest Sons Doctrine & A-millennial Partial
Preterit]* going far back in the roots of the Pacific Pentecostal
Movements which seem to be being revived. The leaven is
subtle.

The books being sold by Bethel movement are *Raptureless,*
by Jonathon Welton, and *Victorious Eschatology* by Harold R
Eberle to show my point isn't without merit. Included in this
parade is the most dangerous of all, the Passion Translation
which alters theology posing as a legitimate translation. More
and more we will see a conflict here, with every birth-pang
coming. The division between those whose hope is in the

Glory coming and those who are trying to create environments of "Glory" on earth with hope that in their worship, leaders and movements a new age will emerge. The question is do you really want Jesus to return? Not whether there is still tribulation for us or judgment coming. For I am espousing only what the bible speaks and it is a positive future for those still awaiting Him!

However Peter deals with those in his time with unbiblical notions by saying, **"God is not slow" 2 Peter 3:9**. Many in Bethel, to be kind just are hungry for the Kingdom to start now, to see the power and works of Christ happen on the earth. I should know I went to school at Bethel. These have the right idea, as long as there remains a longing for Him to come! Peter combated those **"who counted slowness" 2 Peter 3:9** indicating God has a perfect schedule **3:8**, however in **3:3** a greater danger lies in losing faith in the **"promise"** altogether. My point easily could be made that still believing in a future return could be mocked by those who feel the only hope is on this earth now in the "church". They would easily say, **"where is the promise" 2 Peter 3:3** it's here on earth, don't be foolish, and of no earthly good. You can see by these statements the Christianized way people cover their unbelief!

Peter is very serious about the harm these ideas can do to the body of Christ by calling them, **"destructive heresies" 2:1** taught by those **"who follow the way of Balaam" 2:15**. Which is to teach/prophesy/story-tell for financial gain, what others want to hear. Notice Paul acknowledges this in **2 Timothy 4:3** saying, **"time will come"** when people will pay for others to say what they want. So has this not been going on for years? You get to decide! However the newest trend for the last decade is to charge big amounts for conferences that promote *"Prophets"* that just about tell you what they think God is doing but not what the Word says He is! Is this not Balaam prophesying for a dime?

What I am saying here is it is easy to cave to the itching ears of congregations and movements to sell books that cave to popular opinion in order to keep the movement moving! It is in this vacuum void of clarity that the enemy sows his best seeds. None more clever than manipulating the sudden interest in the presence of God and worship music but slowly deluding the word of God by voiding out the cost to lay at the altar of sacrifice and being **"crucified with Christ" Galatians 2:20**.

By simply changing slowly what our actual hope is in. By

discarding the holy tension that should exist between the Kingdom Now and the Kingdom Coming, we are being deluded into a concept of spiritualism through "worship music" without His Lordship. However, a kingdom without a king is a DOM idea!l Get it King - dom. The Jewish people had the same issues of the need for power and immediate gratification who *"supposed that the kingdom of God was going to appear immediately"* **Luke 19:11** so Jesus tells them a parable concerning His departure and there need for stewardship.

Interestingly enough Jesus uses a different greek word for *"occupy"* [do business trade/bank showing stewardship cf. Mt 25:14] here in **Luke 19:13** than the one he uses in **Luke 14:8** [showing possession] concerning the boardroom of the kingdom when the ages change.

If we believe we are already in the boardroom of power we might be shocked when the ages do change, and we are told to *'occupy'* the last seat because we didn't interpret our mission as stewardship from later possessing. This sudden interest in taking possession of the seven mountains of society is backed by the mindset theologies of taking dominion and not washing feet. No matter what the current movements push, the word is clear Jesus is returning for those whose hearts have been waiting for Him, not some earthly church kingdom to take dominion. As to our stewardship, His great commission was to *"make disciples"* not converts to a movement. Signs only *"accompany"* us they are never our stewardship. The mission of this age isn't Ecclesiastical rule over the earth but evangelism through the organic network of God ordained men and women.

Next, there is a truth found in the early church when they spoke the word *"Marana - tha"* in Aramaic **[cf. 1 Corinthians 16:22, in Did-ache]** to each other. This word identified themselves as Christians to each other in a language not understood by their Roman persecutors. This Aramaic word transliterated in the bible represented two words left in an obscure tense which declared both *"the Lord comes"* and *"The Lord has come"*. I believe this mantra reveals the tension of every believer, to both experience & express His kingdom NOW and long for its fulfillment in Christ bodily yet future.

However driven by the need to be unconcerned with a future that might interrupt our movements agendas, we must question whether we are now *"of this world"* not just *"in"* this world reconciling others. Peter called it *"Following their own lusts"* **2 Peter 3:3** or earthly desires. 'What is all this hoo ha *they say?' 'Where is the promise of His coming?'* **v4** They say, *"You don't understand He is already here with us.'* When we say he is already here in us, as if that solves the riddle of His coming, are we now not becoming friends with this present world which God has already judged? **[cf. John 3:17]** Are we not suggesting we self sufficient since we don't need Him to physically return? Just a question, so please search your hearts?

The apostle John did not mince words states, *"Do not love this world nor the things in this world. If anyone loves the world the love of the Father is NOT IN HIM"* **v15**. Many "Christian" systems and new age movements honestly should have no problem with each other because they hold too much to the same thing. The Christ in us as long as there are no moral laws attached. An anointing making our humanity more enjoyable, a self serving God, we believe much the same mantra of many unbelievers. The globalism speech or Babylonian spirit that will be declared will be built on such freedom from any moral principle. Interchanging Christ with spiritual speech of our Guide to assist our dreams is the spirit of a better humanity.

The word of God is clear, Jesus Himself saying, *"I have chosen you out of this world."* **John 15:19** and the apostles being more specific that we are *"to not love the world"* **I John 2:15** and *"not be conformed to the pattern of this world."* **Romans 12:2** Instead our hope is in the physical appearance of Christ to His awaiting bride when *"we will be like Him, because we shall see Him just as He is."* **I John 3:2** So what are we looking for or at? Jesus or this world?

Paul goes into very clear strong language on first having our minds *"set on things above, not on the things that are on earth."* **Colossians 3:2** Why? Because our hope is in what Paul mentions next, *"When Christ who is our life is revealed then you also will be revealed with Him in glory."* **v4** Notice our life is in Him not this world or any form of peace, any movement tries to offer. Don't miss this either Christ is excluding everyone else from this picture of the Bride being presented at the end of His Day above the earth with us. What about those who made Christ a fire insurance making a room for Him amongst their other stuff? It says, *"Christ who is our life"*!? The bride is those who Christ is their life!

With this plea of Paul, the Apostle, to keep one's hope in the physical return of Jesus Christ with us as His bride comes the instruction to deny sin instead of making room for it in the next verse. **[Cf. Colossians 3:5]** Paul then concludes his thought with, **"Because of these things** [sin mentioned a verse earlier] **the wrath of God will come ..."** **v6** So consider God's wrath is on sin not people. He must remove it from the earth in order to reign with His bride.

However, people want a theology to tell them there will be no judgment on their sin so they can *"sin or live selfishly"* without conviction of the Holy Spirit? Instead they should cling to Jesus for forgiveness where there is no judgment and sin is taken away. Here we are again at the leaven of the Pharisees, pride. We'll do anything to keep our way of life, our autonomy. Even create doctrines and movements to tell us how awesome we are in our rebellion to God.

THE FIRST COMING

*"For **at the right time** Christ died for the ungodly."*
Romans 5:6

Most people overlook the significance of Christ first coming in discovering the big pictures reliability. During the build up to Christ birth, there was a growing hope & expectation as the year 4000 was fully expected by the Rabbinical order.

"Prior to the first century (CE) the Messianic interest was not excessive ...The first century however especially the generation before the destruction of the second temple witnessed a remarkable outburst of Messianic emotionalism. This is to be attributed as we shall see not to an intensification of Roman persecution, but to the prevalent belief induced by popular chronology of that day that the age was on the threshold of the Millennium." [History of Messianic Speculation In Israel, Rabbi Abba Hillel Silver, 1927, Macmillan Co., pg 5-7, ISBN 0-8446-2937-5]

This perfect storm included as well the possible fulfillment of the prophecy of **Daniel 9:24-27** coming true, a Messiah to appear after the decree to rebuild. Again God working to confirm by more than one witness the timing of His Messiah's coming as the Word says, **"For at the right time Christ died** *for the ungodly."* **Romans 5:6**. Notice, the focus is on His death not His birth. For Jesus symbolically represented the Passover Lamb killed on the fourth day of Passover. This is so key! Since if we can show a high probability He died on that very year, 4000, then it brings a new light to much of scripture!

No longer would we mock *"a day is a thousand years"* **2 Peter 3:8**, as a general idea, for Passion week would then become a symbolic representation of where we are in God's plan in the whole of human history. Lazarus coming out of the grave on the fourth day symbolic as well. Just think, could God put all this right in front of our noses without us *"paying attention"*?

For probability sake, I ran the numbers, using Wikipedia research on those who calculated chronology using the Masoretic Text **from the eleventh to the 18th century**. In total there were **22** notable enough to be listed in Wikipedia, who using one method or another came to conclusions who were using serious scientific or analytical methods. As I was taught in Statistics, I threw out the extreme high and lows. 6 were thrown out, 3 to the high extreme where 30 years gap existed from the center bunch and 3 to the low extreme were 78 years removed from the center as well. [See chart next page]

Statistical Average of Calculations

The Average of All Calculations made from 11th to 18th century from the Masoretic Texts throwing out extreme bottom and top, arrives at the year Jesus was crucified [dating creation wikipedia]

1. 3927 Broudard
2. 3928 Mercator
3. 3947 Helvig
4. 3949 Scaliger
5. 3951 Lapide
6. 3952 Bede
7. 3960 Lightfoot
8. 3961 Martin Luther
9. 3964 Malanchthon
10. 3966 Longomontanus
11. 3977 Kepler
12. 3980 Bibliander
13. 3984 Petavius
14. 4002 Calmet
15. 4004 Usser
16. 4005 Cappel

3969.2avg for Creation
= .8 from Jesus death
High Probability for Jesus being the 4th Day Passover And Passion week representing God's plan

Average of highest to lowest
4192BC - 3754BC = 3973BC
or just three years from Jesus crucifixion 31AD

The center group of **16 calculations** had creation on the year **3927** to **4005** BC; a spread of only **78 years**. The average median of all was **3969.2 BC**. This means the year **4000** would have the highest probability falling on **30-31 AD**. In the next chapter we will show Christ had to have been crucified in either **31 or 33AD**. By NASA's study & Daniel's vision we have narrowed that to **31AD**. This is frankly amazing stuff! Jesus not only died on the fourth day of Passover in my mind but the fourth day of History! Yes, there is faith involved but based on seeing all the variables it is an easy prognosis to make knowing God is perfect in time. This gives new meaning to the words, *"at the right time"* **Romans 5:6** And walks us right up to Jesus words concerning His return.

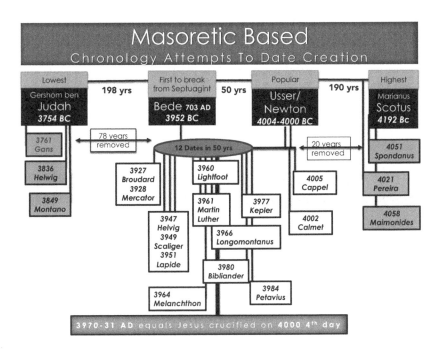

200 years before even Christ came Rabbi Elias wrote of the Jewish expectations:

"The world endures 6000 years: two thousand before the law, two thousand with the law and two thousand with the Messiah."

[Babylonian Talmud, Sanhedrin 96b-99a]

In Mark Eastman's masterwork on this subject He writes,

"According to Rabbi Abba Hillel Silver the beginning of the fifth millennium after creation occurred during the early portion of the first century CE, during the very life and ministry of Jesus of Nazareth!! [A History of Messianic Speculation in Israel, Rabbi Abba Hillel Silver, 1927, Macmillan Co., pg 5-7, ISBN 0-8446-2937-5] [as quoted in, The Search for Messiah, Mark Eastman, MD, p115]

Later in His book Mark Eastman states,

"The rabbis expressed their disappointment that the Messiah had not come during the expected time... 'In the first 2000 years was desolation; 2000 years the Torah flourished and the next 2000 years is the Messianic era but through our many iniquities all these years have been lost ." [Babylonian Talmud, Sanhedrin 96-99)][The Search For The Messiah, Mark Eastman, MD, p116-117]

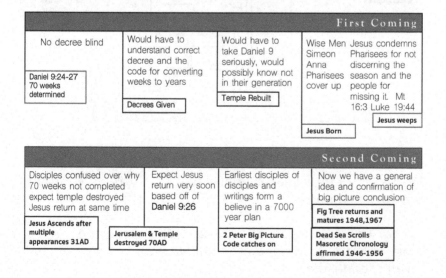

Did you catch that? The heads of ancient rabbinical academies recognized that the time appointed had past for the coming of the Messiah and further by the destruction of Jerusalem and the dispersion all hope was lost! How they could know this yet miss something so amazing as their King - Jesus?! Why didn't they see this? By holding to their conviction of the big picture ages being precise, we have evidence all over for the following years 30-70 AD of an expectation for an Apocalyptic Return of a reigning Messiah based on Chronology of manuscripts now found hidden in caves.

Understand Jesus dying on the year 4000 would put everything in harmony although some level of faith would still be required since Chronology is not a perfect science. God is fine with this, for this pattern of requiring faith is true to His desire to bless you and I. Remember doubting Thomas and Christ words to those who though not seeing they believe. Can you rejoice that on one end, God is giving us enough to see His purposeful design, and on the other end *"we get to"* still apply our faith on the chair we sit in!

Faith is always required! However what we are seeing here points strongly in that direction and would explain all the rest of pieces to the big picture. What a relief to my sense of understanding the Word of God as coming together as a beautiful tapestry of perfection!

So let's review this, the Jewish expectations itself reveal a corrupt Chronology existed in the Septuagint! Second it reveals why the correct Chronology was archived for safety in the dead Sea Scrolls! Third all this points to God's instituted fourth day passover lamb as a prophetic act. Peter's equation of a day is a thousand years now puts all this together on a perfect schedule! We can already see God is on a perfect time for everything with Jesus crucifixion! No, it couldn't be that easy to figure out can it? Are you telling me God displayed His plan for human history through the Passion week? And our future in His resurrection?

THE FIRST DISCIPLES

"Do not let this one fact escape your notice"
2 Peter 3:8

So pulling what we have learned about the Jewish expectation both in rabbinical writings that followed the era and the discovery of the dead Sea Scrolls, we might view **2 Peter** a little different. Peter is dealing with a growing tension and expectation of a coming ruling Messiah based on the Jewish belief of a *"world week"* to deliver them from Roman tyranny. Peter is in no way going to discard this notion of the Jewish big picture but affirms it as found in scripture in **[cf. 2 Peter 3:8 with Psalms 90:4]**. Peter directs his Messianic hope as realized in Christ already, saying they had been eyewitnesses to His glory and kingdom already as proof **[cf.1:17]**. For in a little while all Jewish hope would be shattered, God's judgment delayed **40 years** would come as prophesied by **Daniel 9:26** in **70 AD**'s destruction of Jerusalem.

The city and the sanctuary destroyed by the Romans invasion will implode the hope of the Jewish Apocrypha crowd. Understand, the Messiah had to come before the destruction of the second temple **[cf. Daniel 9:26]**, before the scepter had departed from Judah **[Genesis 49:10]** and according to Jewish tradition before the fifth millennium. All this was accomplished by the crucifixion in **31 AD**! However, with the temples demise in **70 AD** this just meant they had missed it, or as we see the Rabbi's conclude *'iniquities these years were lost'*. You can see the Jewish reaction to delayed expectation the same as the Christian disillusionment, *'God changed His mind'*.

Here Peter sits at the crossroads of history, no longer a simple fisherman, surrounded by speculation and much estimations like his own previous one. Yet now we have shown why expectation was God was being slow. ***"as some count slowness"*** 2 Peter 3:9 Why slow? Because those counting at the time, the Essenes with the Dead Sea scrolls, the year **4000** was now behind them. Speaking boldly and clearly He states his purpose in writing to steer the church in the right direction from all this confusion of Jewish expectation. **[Cf. 2 Peter 1:13,3:2]** Well, we have to ask then the question did he and in what direction did they go? If in fact, prophecy is different from the rest of scripture in that it becomes clearer with time. **[Cf. 2 Peter 1:19]** Did it? What doctrine did they, the church, carry forward?

To say that Peter succeeded in getting the church to carry the torch forward, He sure did! The evidence is in history itself. They firmly believed Peter was not giving a loose example of how time is to God versus us. We read it in the strongest language possible as they did as well, *"do not be selectively stupid on this matter! I'm giving an actual fact!"* **2 Peter 3:8** [author paraphrased version of lead verse above] For when we look at the first succession of the Apostles it was written by Irenaeus in the second century of John's disciples,

"Taking occasion from Papias of Hierapolis the illustrious a disciple of the apostle who leaned on the bosom of Christ, and Clemens and Pantaenus the priest of the Alexandrians, and the wise Ammonius the ancient and first expositor who agreed with each other who understood the work of the SIX DAYS as referring to Christ & His church" [Fragments chapter IX] *and Polycarp another of John's disciples writes "the future world ...shall reign with Him"* [letters to the Phillipi]. *These men inspiring another generation of Bishops, namely Irenaeus, who writes, "borne witness to in writing by papers ...Polycarp ..."* [Against heresies 5:XXIIII:4] *saying, "then the Lord will come from heaven in the clouds ...bringing in the righteous the times (age) of the kingdom THAT IS the rest the hallowed SEVENTH DAY"* [Against Heresies 5:XXX:4]

"As the first seven days in the divine arrangement containing seven thousand years ..."
[Irenaeus, Exhortations of Martyrdom To Fortunatus 4.11]

Even a fragment was found attributed to Papias, John's direct understudy is spoken here. Should it be any surprise to us that the man who wrote God's vision The **Book of Revelation**, John, would have his entire discipleship lineage take the thousand year reign as the time for an age as found in **Revelation 20:4** a step further as part of God's big picture plan. To name a few these are the ones I speak of: Tertullian (200AD), Victorinus (304AD) Papias (100AD) Justin Martyr (130AD) Irenaeus (180AD).

This is not inclusive of John's lineage either. For from one of the earliest writings of the church, thought to have been written by Barnabas who also was thought to have some school for Prophets comes a non-canonical letter, yet respected as Canon for centuries, **The Epistle of Barnabas** writes,

"Pay Attention children, to what it means that, "he finished in six days." This means that in six thousand years the Lord will complete all things. For with him a day represents a thousand years [2 Peter 3:8]... so children all things will be completed in six days — that is to say in six thousand years... this means that when his Son comes he will put an end to the age of the lawless one ...alter sun moon and stars then he will rest on the seventh day." **[Barnabas 15:4-5]**

The First apologist Justin Martyr writes (circa 140AD),

"I and others who are right-minded Christians on all points ... there will be a resurrection of the dead and 1000 years in Jerusalem ..." [Justin Martyr, Dialogue With Trypho 80] *(continues in all of page 81 to support the day being a thousand years)*

In fact, it would appear that all the early church fathers held to the future Millennial Reign of Christ for **a literal 1000 years** as a hope to share in with their Lord. Many taking it a step further seeing a big picture to determine the whole plan of God for human history. Ignatius **(circa 90AD)**, the direct understudy to Peter, himself appeared to be under the conviction as was Peter that they were living in the last days and that the Kingdom hadn't arrived in full. [See Letters to Ephesus 11,16] much like Clement of Rome **(circa 96AD)** who proclaims,

"Shall be made manifest at the revelation of the kingdom of Christ [still future]. For it is written, "Enter into Thy secret chambers [rapture to sky, wilderness] for a little time until My wrath..." [Clement of Rome, The First Epistle of Clement to the Corinthians, chapter 50]

Even in Polycarp's, *Letter to Phillipi*, he makes mention of, *"The future world ... shall reign together with Him."* Add to this list of Pre-Millennialists, Theophilus, Commodianus, Methodius, and Matin Luther when we get out of all the A-millennial dark ages and back to reformation. The following century to the disciples saw no less interests in this idea affirmed by Peter of a prophetic day being symbolic of a thousand years. For the list goes on, Tertullian **(circa**

145-200AD), Lactanctius **(circa a 270 AD)** and Hippolytus **(circa 200 AD)**; all venerated Bishops of the church.

> *"when the thousand years of the Kingdom that is seven thousand of the world ..."* [Lactanctius, Divine Institutes, Book 7 chapter 26]

> *"A day with the Lord is as a thousand years since in six days God made all things it follows that **6000 years must be fulfilled**."* [Hippolytus, Fragments Book Commentary of Daniel 4]

Cyprian, highly respected Bishop of Carthage writes, *"wait for the sudden coming of the Lord ... reign with Christ in His Kingdom"* [Cyprian, Unity of The Church, chapter 27] and even further he goes, *"It is an ancient adversary and an enemy with whom we wage our battle: **six thousand years are now nearly completed** [according to the Septuagint LLX this would have been correct]."* [Cyprian, Ad Fort., Preface 1-2)] Note, they were working off a messed up chronology in the Septuagint, so they thought they were almost there. Don't be distracted by estimations being off, instead notice what the churches was using for a measuring stick scripturally was **2 Peter 3:8**, **Hebrews 4** and **Revelation 20:4**.

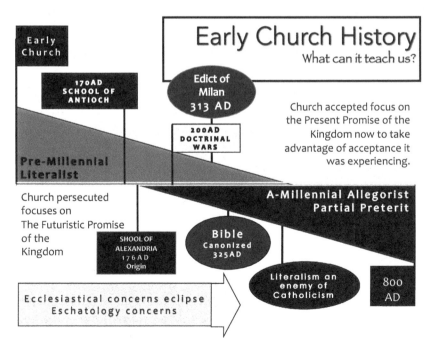

Over time the church replaced its literal interpretation of a future Millennium around **300-500 AD** in direct correlation with the churches acceptance by the Roman world through Constantine. The focus became Ecclesiastical instead of Eschatological in nature. [see chart previous page]

Remember the Septuagint chronology would have passed the **6000** year mark at **500AD**. The sixth Millennium of the Septuagint was approaching as the church rose in power giving the sense they were experiencing a new age already. They couldn't see the bigger picture by following the correct Chronological record. Why? They didn't have access to the Masoretic text. It was left behind in the Dead Sea Scrolls and not retranslated until **900AD**. Besides that the church has always struggled with balancing Eschatology with Ecclesiastical concerns.

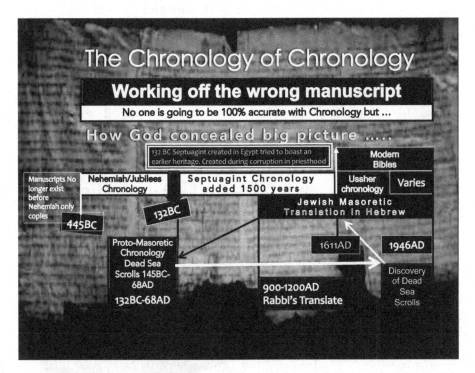

Further problem existed in the fact that great Greek philosophical minds were converted to Christianity bringing with them deep thoughts and analysis of doctrines. This slippery slope of *"higher learning"* led to questions on the literal hope of a coming Kingdom. Origen was the first to challenge the belief publicly **(circa 225)** followed by Dionysius around the same time. Church Historian & Bishop of Caesarea,

Eusebius greatly influenced this departure of faith in Eschatology since he was an authority in reconstructing church history and a huge fan of the Emperor Constantine. Ecclesiastical power had no room for threat of Jesus return and another kingdom. You kidding they thought the millennium was occurring right then and there.

Over the years though Pre-Millennialism & Chiliasm resurfaced as great men of God have stood for the traditions of the early church. Notably Martin Luther & Sir Isaac Newton using their faith in an exact chronology for human history to predict Christ return but now based off of the Masoretic Text being resurrected in **900 AD**.

It wasn't until the nineteenth and twentieth centuries that Pre-Millennial interpretation regained popularity as the go-to for prophecy. Again it is during this time the Spirit of God was returning in fuller measure to God's people.

THE FIRST PREDICTIONS

"Where is the promise of His coming ... as some count slowness"

2 Peter 3:3,9

The very first person to try to predict a date for the return of Christ may have been the person who wrote the disturbing letter to the church of Thessaloniki as early as **52AD**. *"That you not be quickly shaken from your composure or be disturbed either by a spirit or message or a letter as if from us ..."* **2 Thessalonians 2:2** For one thing is certain, many have been fascinated with being the first to rightly predict His return.

However, notice this letter tries to look like scripture, *"as if from us"* instead of doing what the apostles were doing, relying on Jesus and the prophets words. All this did was make people unsettled. We all remember the boy who cried wolf, and the effect it had on a village when the actual date arrived for the wolf's appearance. No one was interested anymore! Much like today, we have *"prophets"* who make their words *"as if from"* the word of God, yet they have no comprehensive understanding of biblical prophecy.

So some perspective is needed here. What I find helpful is

by studying why false predictions fail we can possibly learn from their estimations. What they strongly believed on to make predictions helps us see they weren't all far off the truth but they were working from either a bad vantage point or missing a detail. Remember from our vantage point we discover they just didn't have what we have in our vantage point. Great men starting with the Apostles themselves have tried to give their estimation of nearness by calculating ideas spoken by Christ. Even **Daniel 9** followed carefully would have given you a year to find the start of Jesus ministry. Who was to say His second coming wouldn't be the same!

The initial prediction after the early church was a man we just mentioned, Hippolytus. Following the Septuagint manuscripts for his chronology He looked for the year **6000**. Which only shows again their strong belief in the Prophetic Day code given by Peter, for the only manuscripts available and thought reliable dated Creation **5500BC**. So the thought of the six days for human history was the basis but the source for counting was corrupted by boasting of Jewish translators alongside Egypt's boasts in the Septuagint.

Bede was the first to use the right source in **800AD** as the Masoretic transcripts were first being assembled by the rabbinical order, however he was called a heretic for this change in calling out Creation in **3952**. From this point on those who predicted used the Masoretic texts primarily. Some notables during the Reformation period were Martin Luther, Christopher Columbus and Sir Isaac Newton.

Then I just jump to my generation, who due to the rise of Israel as a nation came alive with multiple prognostications. Both Hal Lindsey and Chuck Smith from Calvary Chapel became popular with their predictions using **1948** as a date for the Fig Tree **[cf. Matthew 24:32]** without regarding its maturity as the start time for counting off a final generation. Adding only **40 years** which is the turning of a generation not a passing of one, they landed on **1988**. Backing it up **7 years** for their Pre Tribulation Theorist position on another unbiblical idea of *"a seven year Tribulation Period"* it became **1981**, the year after I got saved. Edgar Whisenant then came and said you got it wrong its really **1988** and I'll give you *"88 Reasons Why ..."*.

2000AD was a popular date as far back as Sir Isaac Newton who thought Jesus was born on the year 1BC and used the correct 2 Days to equal the year 2000. Along with Jonathon Edwards they both were seeing significance in the two days mentioned by Hosea. However, the wrong starting date is used for the two days. As this book shows it should be His death. For this same reason others thought **1996 or 7**, or even **8** trying to determine Christ actual birthdate as more evidence came forth for Herod's death in **4BC**. Yet you see the trend is to use the correct prophecies and codes but incorrectly apply them.

F. Kenton Beshore predicted **2021**, which is next year based on the right period of time for a generation passing (70 years) but the wrong starting date for the Fig tree mature in its formation as a nation in **1948**. Being a pre-tribulation theorist, he used the seven years again and backs up from **2028** to get his date. So many more but the general idea is the two signs used to calculate a date are what I use "The Fig Tree Parable & "the Today & Tomorrow" prophecies. Yet what isn't being calculated is the correct starting points, duration and context.

Many can mock at this process of our estimating as a church but God has called us to this place of staying alert.

5

Discovering:

The Dawning Shadows

THE WORD

PAST PRECEDENCE

"For when they maintain this it escapes their notice that **by the word of God** *heavens existed long ago and the earth was formed out of water and by water... through which the world was destroyed being flooded with water."*

2 Peter 3:5-6

FUTURE

"But **by His word** *the present heavens and earth Are being reserved for fire, kept for a day of judgment and destruction of ungodly men."*

2 Peter 3:7

Peter tells us plainly what we should be *"paying attention"* 2 **Peter1:19** to when it comes to understanding prophecy and our future - *"THE WORD OF GOD"* **3:5,7**. Peter having narrowed the field of sources in a few verses earlier in **v2** to *"holy prophets"* not just any prophets. Now he seems to be doubling down on the definition for what is *"His Word"* **v7**. Remember the church hadn't a clear acceptable list for what was accepted at that time. This brings up a compelling insight into the coordination of two letters, **Jude & 2 Peter**, which have sections literally a copy of the other. Were they not affirming the churches doctrine with two or more witnesses? Again we see evidence of the importance of harmony!

In both epistles, they acknowledge ideas that come primarily from the most respected outside source at the time, **1 Enoch**, yet they point us back to the **"holy prophets"**. Whether it is **Jude 14** quoting of **1 Enoch 1:8** that is backed up by **Deuteronomy 33:2** or Peter's **"one day is as a thousand years"** could be affirming **1 Enoch**'s 10 week prophecy, but instead we find the concept in **Psalms 90:4** from Moses. Everything the apostles affirmed can be found in scripture traced back to the age of the Torah. Yet what the Apostles did was clever. They used portions of **1 Enoch** that were scripturally sound to expose false teachers misuse of these popular questionable writings. Peter is using this method of types and shadows himself contrasting the flood to the future fire judgments. Twice focusing our attention on the source, **"... by the word of God"** 3:5 and **"His Word"** 3:7, Peter emphasizes the authority of God's most reliable testimonies past as building blocks for future clarity!

Jesus makes no less an appeal for the certainty of God's indestructible word when in the middle of His discourse on the end times when He inserts, **"Heaven and earth will pass away, but My words will not pass away."** Matthew 24:35 Declaring His words were on the highest level of certainty to all other prophetic visions and interpretations that both preceded Him or would follow. For the testimony of Jesus is the spirit of prophesy or central to it! **[Cf. Revelation 19:10]**

That is why I will show you in the next chapter the key piece belongs to Jesus Himself declaring the finish line for the big picture and the details as well! Even His first coming came foreshadowed by examples drawn out in the Old Testament yet Jesus Himself waits four days to raise Lazarus as an example for us of God's **"right time"** Romans 5:6b. The bible comes loaded with confirming signs and parallels. God really wants us to know and be certain.

You would think we would not give up on the bible to be the key source for our understanding of the future. However starting with the interest in the year **2000**, I witnessed so many believers running to ideas of the end coming based on peripheral signs and not the scriptures themselves. Whether it was the significance they put on the end of the millennium, or astrological positioning, conspiracy theories, Nostradamus prophesies, some mysterious X planets approach to earth, etc. It was this then that with the constant fear of the end portrayed by *"doom and gloom teachers"* that drove me to go back to the bible and question all that we thought we knew.

I did not give up that the Bible had all the answers needed

but like so many I was questioning the popular opinions. They didn't harmonize with all scriptures. This led me to see that some of my own opinions were wrong by holding to nothing unless than what would harmonize with the rest of scripture. With all our fear of the end, I was convinced that we were looking through the wrong reading lens.

God confirmed this in separate glorious visions. The first was of the coming final move of God upon the earth to prepare the harvest, and the second was of Jesus crucified with me on the cross taking me up in a gathering with other saints above the earth. This began to open my eyes to truth's in His word. Remember God is not the author of confusion, only of concealment. **[cf. 1 Corinthians 14:33]** He is asking us to remain faithful to the hope even though we don't have all the answers yet. We are commended to seek, knock, and ask Him who gives generously. If we persist, He will show us things we couldn't understand in the natural.

In the Apostles time they were facing a similar potential crisis for understanding the words *"spoken beforehand"* 3:2 versus the danger false teachers posed with their *"private interpretations"* 1:20. Paul himself being clear, *"even Satan disguises himself as an angel of light."* 2 Corinthians 11:14 and *"even if we or an angel from heaven should preach to you a gospel contrary ...be accursed!"* Galatians 1:8 So how committed are we to get this straight? Enough to go where the Word leads us even if it isn't the popular teachings of our day or what we previously thought? We might want to lay down our doctrinal glasses in which we interpret the word through our lenses of what we expect to see.

So here Peter is clear, *"By the word of God"* history is and continues to be defined by what God spoke into existence and left for us to interpret! Time (kairos= appointed times) are occurring in symphonic harmony with God's intended plan. In referring to *"the heavens existing long ago"* 3:5 he seems to point not just to the flood judgment but before the earth was formed in **Genesis 1:1**. Peter clearly intends for us to consider there is much more going on than within our history itself. By suggesting of a drama being played out before even the creation account in **Genesis,** Peter is determined to display how ignorant we are to the bigger picture.

For now Peter is pointing to the floodgates that opened either in **Genesis 1 or 7** to be sure. Just as Jesus used the flood to parallel His second coming, Peter uses it to give a precedence for God judging the earth a second time for its sin, thus the phrase, *"yet once more"* **Hebrews 12:26** which comes from **Haggai 2:6**. For God has already visited the earth before. Knowing this rich history Peter declares *"the world at that time was destroyed being flooded with water but by His word ... being preserved for fire"* **3:6-7**. What the Leader of the Christian faith is doing is showing how events in time reveal patterns of God's plan. Notice *"at that time"* would be to what was previously mentioned when the earth *"was formed"* however the flood took place over **1656** years later. Is Peter speaking an age being the first **2000** years in which God judged in this manner? So that during *"that time"* or age, the floods occurred. I will let you ponder that one.

Thus during that time period when God dealt with human beings a certain way, like our current age since Pentecost where it has been declared on this age that He would pour out His grace and *"Spirit on all mankind"* **Joel 2:28,** baptizing men with fire internally and judging ultimately the wicked with fire eternally. As to the Spirit's fire, this doesn't refer to the Millennium when that will be seen in full, but now without prejudice, Jews and gentiles, bond and Free, women and Men are experiencing God's Spirit.

So one thing is for sure Peter is thinking of the big picture here and pointing us to past events. This is important to tie together with his *"one fact"* **3:8** he will introduce. Namely just as God built upon each day of creation, God is building upon each prophetic day of human history equal to *"thousand years"* **3:8** For example, **Hebrews 4** brilliantly displays this truth of both God's seventh day of Creation as ongoing for it is said, *"God rested on the seventh day from all His works ... for the one who has entered that rest has Himself rested from His works as God did from His."* **Hebrews 4:4,11** Well that means God is still on His rest! We are only now being invited to it, and then invited to it at the rapture to a greater extent, and then after the Reign of Christ invited to it into eternity to even greater extent.

The **Book of Revelation 20:4** had not been written yet when **Hebrews** was penned. However now that we have the completed Canon of scripture this certainly underscores the meaning implied by, *"therefore since it remains for some to enter it... there remains a Sabbath rest for the people of God"* **Hebrews 4:6,9** as not only experienced partially now in, *"we who have believed enter that rest"* **4:3,** but permanently on the last prophetic day of human history for a thousand years I.e. **Revelation 20:4** when death is swallowed up in victory!

So the concept of a Prophetic Week for human history is

deeply ingrained by God's established storyline with the Jewish culture; from the seven days of Creation to His institution for framing time in periods of seven days for a week with a Sabbath day of rest on the seventh to the Sabbatical year to give the land rest on the seventh year to the year of Jubilee on the fiftieth year. These Hebrew traditions passed on in the wilderness are now symbolically passed onto the Believer's as scripture in **Hebrews**.

God was laying out for the Jewish people His plan, and now it is being realized through Christ. So let's journey through the Old Testament to find these hidden gems that point us to the truth of God's ages and perfect timing for His return.

THE EXAMPLES

*"Now these things happened to them as an example, and they were written **for our instruction**, upon whom the ends of the ages have come."*

1 Corinthians 10:11

In any court of law, much is made of when a similar case was first ruled on. The pattern then is followed in future cases like the one previous. Same could be said for God's types and shadows concerning His second coming. For the argument at hand in **2 Peter 3:4** concerns this very principle. The mockers objection is that they know of no such judgment of the earth, saying, *"all continues as it was..."* and in Peter's defense, *"by the Word of God"* or by God's creative Sovereignty He has created examples and patterns for us.

Jesus using this line of argument in **Matthew 11:21-24**; explains God's consistency in judgement will doom generations better suited to know the truth, like the one in His conversation who saw His miracles. This demonstration of precedence in God's judgement should put the fear of God in our hearts, being that we are the generation given insight like no other, the final one who has a greater measure of history to consider!

So here are many examples from God's word ...

First Word in Genesis 1:1 ...

We see God declaring the end from the beginning. For **Isaiah** prophesies, *"declaring the end from the beginning, and from ancient times things which have not been done"* **46:10** The word in Hebrew is *berisheet.* For when one follows the symbols of each letter and their individual meanings, one could surmise a prophesy being read of how God would bring the cross after 4000 years and finish after 3 more days.

At the time of this writing much can be seen concerning this revelation on YOUTUBE or read from *C. J. Lovik's* book *"The Berisheet Passover Prophecy"*. Again like other sources I have encouraged, this one is awe inspiring. Whereas I statistically averaged all the expertise of men over centuries for how exact 4000 years comes to the cross, Lovik a different line of thinking. Suggest Adam spent the same lifetime, **33** years approximately, in the garden as *"the first Adam"* as Jesus spent on earth being *"the last Adam"* **1 Corinthians 15:45** to coordinate **4004 BC** the popular date from Usser [see last chapter] as the correct calculation.

Needless to say, we now have multiple signs that Jesus died at the *"right time"* **Romans 5:6** as the Passover Lamb on the fourth day, pointing to *"a day is a thousand years"* in God's strategy and plan. The details of Christ's central role in this in *chapter 6*, but for now don't miss how God is using by this the Passion week as a pattern of the big picture.

First Man, Adam ...

would have lived forever and in fact been glorified if he ate of the tree of Life. However we all know the story, which is the very first indication that a day is really a thousand years. *"For **in the day** that you eat from it you will surely die"* **Genesis 2:17** Again our first false prophesy from scripture, if in fact *"a day"* was meant to be interpreted as 24 hours. How reliable is the Word of God? For in fact Adam lives **930 years** just short of a prophetic day. This is our very first clue that even Creation *"days"* may have not been literal 24 hour periods, that God's time references are not ours. So right away God is giving us indication of a prophetic day.

First Rapture...

> *"About these men, Enoch, the seventh from Adam* [1 Enoch 60:8], *prophesied saying, 'Behold, the Lord came with many thousands of His holy ones, to execute judgment upon all, and to convict all the ungodly of all their ungodly deeds...* [1 Enoch 1:9]'"
> **Jude 14-15**

Jude makes it clear he is quoting **1 Enoch** by giving us not just one but two references. For after the one above connected to **Deuteronomy 33:2**, Jude throws in a purely **1 Enoch** expression found a few verses later saying, *"waiting anxiously for __THE MERCY__ of our Lord Jesus Christ to eternal life."* **Jude 21** Compare with *"protecting the elect and showing the righteous __THE MERCY__... when they see Him."* **1 Enoch 1:8** for the rapture. Yes, the rapture was introduced before Jesus as THE MERCY! While talking about this did you notice Enoch was *"the seventh from Adam"* and the famous verse, *"walked with God and he was not for God took him."* **Genesis 5:24**

So Enoch represents the first rapture. He was **365** years old the **seventh** generation! **[Cf. Genesis 5:23]**, signifying on the seventh day when the earth is rotating **365** days a year we will be taken. Of this amazing parallel type and shadow, God uses this man to be the first to declare the image of Christ second coming. Don't take lightly the significance either of **365** years when this occurs; for **1 Enoch** reveals Enoch's concern for the counting of time and that the earth would not always rotate the same as it did then - **360** days a year.

However much debate surrounds how much of **1 Enoch** is actually Enoch? Although we will never know what the Apostles themselves really thought about its place in the influence of the prophetic truths it shaped the Jewish culture around them. Whether Peter and Jude had to deal with it per its popularity or were acknowledging it had a place in the prophetic landscape of their day. All we know is these Apostles use it to reveal the hypocrisy of false teachers and point back to Moses. This we do know, the word of God had not been formed as accepted as Canon when **2 Peter & Jude** are written. **1 Enoch** was accepted for decades by the certain churches as Canon until it was finally rejected. This was a Jewish world in transition in which Peter Paul and Jude formed a circle of doctrinal unity to protect the legacy.

So at the very least **1 Enoch** wasn't to be ignored, for we see they just couldn't. It was neither clearly rejected or accepted for its contents. From this we see how careful the Apostles were in laying their heads of approval on anything, even with evidence today from the Dead Sea Scrolls of its popularity they held their helm of their ship firm, always pointing back to the most solid reliable sources from the Torah.

Much like a best selling Christian novel would be found next to the bible today in a bookstore so was **1 Enoch**, at a time when Messianic hope was very high. Stored away by a religious group of conservative purest & separatist called the Essenes, we can gather many felt it was genuine who were very critical of fakes. The oldest version of **1 Enoch** was found first by James Bruce in **1773AD** in an Ethiopian church. The original Enoch was credible enough to be worth the effort to plagiarize and popular enough to be found in different languages spread around the world.

What is amazing about the oldest version found also in the Dead Sea Scrolls is it dates back to **200 BC**, before the birth of Christianity. Before its existence, the term *"Son of Man"* was used once in the Old Testament in **Daniel**, yet in **1 Enoch** the term is used multiple times. Truth is **1 Enoch** sounds more Christian than anything written previous to it. Gospel subject matter of Demons, afterlife and hell even the Book of Revelation's themes of Christ's reign, apocalyptic similarities, and a Messianic kingdom are found within its pages.

Of course the chicken and the egg debate follows. Did Daniel get inspired by a genuine Enoch writing that survived the flood only to finally make its way to print after or vice versa? Did Jesus use of this expression upon Himself of *"the Son of Man"* due to the influence of these writings? Did the writer of **1 Enoch** copy an older manuscripts and if so how much was added to make a great story versus is the genuine artifacts? How genuine or reliable is this? Was it just a pure invention of a **200 BC** fictional writer inspired by the prophet Daniel and other scriptural sources? Ask God in heaven but then it won't matter. What does is that it is another source credible enough to suggest human history being only **7000 years [cf. 1 Enoch 93]**.

Since Paul warned Titus of *"Jewish myths"* **Titus 1:14**, we certainly must assume Peter wasn't gullible but a Berean in his use of it. Certainly, Jude & Peter had the opportunity to expose this writing as a fraud if indeed it was purely fictional writing. Instead, Jude & Peter pick biblically sound portions of its contents to expose the false teachers use of it for a cover of their ungodly display of behavior and *"private interpretations"*. The argument goes *"if"* **2 Peter 2:4** *"then"* **vs9.** If angels sinned and are bound for judgment from God and the same for men, then God is able to judge angels and men without the assistance of Angels and Men. Which was a suspected teaching in **1 Enoch**, saying, Enoch and angels were left to judge which I don't see.

Even in Peter's first letter we see ideas found primarily from **1 Enoch**. Due to elements and themes being drawn out and treated with respect by the Apostles, **1 Enoch** found itself widely accepted by second Century writings such as the Letter of Barnabas, and church leaders from Origen, Athenagoras, Clement of Alexandria, Ireneaus and Tertullian. The Ethiopian church went as far as accepting it as part of their bible. However over time the acceptance of this book faded and it ended up not canonized by the general church and completely vanished by **700BC**. Mostly due to negative opinions of the existence at that time of the Demonic Realm spoken of much in **1 Enoch**.

All this only to point your attention to **1 Enoch**'s big picture prophesy of **10 weeks**, which is quite telling. Each week consisting of **700 years** tells a prophetic story of human history. Pinpointing the first coming and second around the right periods. **[Cf. 1 Enoch 93]** The first of 10 weeks ends on Enoch departure on year 700 making the whole 7000 years. Again this matches what we are seeing in the biblical code. The question then becomes how much of this opened Peter's eyes to what the bible had to say about the big picture to write **[2 Peter 3:8]**? What I am drawing attention to is any connection of influence that might have existed at the time of Peter's writing. Although **1 Enoch** lurks in the background, the Apostles constantly are pointing us back to the word of God.

The First Judgment, Noah & the flood...

... is used as a parallel to His second coming by Christ Himself so there should be no surprise that Peter does as well in His defense of a timely return. **[Cf. 2 Peter 3:5-7]** Adding the story of Lot to that of Noah's, Jesus is giving us two or three witnesses to confirm a fact consistent with the rules of engaging prophecy.

Considering the days of Noah! Genesis reveals an amazing fact! Noah knew the flood was coming and preached the flood. Something that never ever happened before. Yet seven days before the flood, God tells Him exactly when! We will talk about the significance of this in later chapters. *"For after seven more days, I will send rain on the earth..."* **Genesis 7:4**

Here we are again! The last generation before God judges always knows when! In fact, God gives a seven day warning which is not only symbolic of the period it represents **[cf. "know accurately" Matthew 24:15]** but also represents a mathematical equivalent ratio to its counterparts which I will show chapter 8. Noah was told to begin loading the ark seven days prior but didn't enter Himself permanently until the **seventh day** indicating a shadow of the rapture on the year **6000**. *"Noah was six hundred years old* (indicating 6000 years of human history) *when the flood of water came upon the earth. Then Noah ... entered the ark because of the water of the flood"* **Genesis 7:6-7** Jesus will come on the beginning of the seventh day of human history. **6000** years and that is approaching very fast in approximately **2031**!

The First Purge of King Joash ...

"When Athaliah [victim of Yahweh] [daughter of cruel leader Jezebel] *the mother of Ahaziah* [meaning: God has taken] *saw that her son was dead, she rose and destroyed all the royal offspring* [her grandchildren]. *But Jehosheba the daughter of King Joram sister to Ahaziah took Joash* [fire of Yahweh] *the son of Ahaziah and stole him from among the king's sons who were being put to death and placed him and his nurse in the bedroom. So they hid him from Athaliah, and he was not put to death."*

2 Kings 11:1-2

Is an amazing story amongst the period of the divided nations of Israel revealing God's prophetic future. This real life drama plays out with so much thick parallelism to the second coming of King Jesus. Without question one of the most bizarre and complicated stories if you are trying to keep up with the whose who.

So to keep this simple. Jezebel was a wicked Queen who begat another child just like her in Athaliah who killed her grandkids just to be the Queen and rule. This manipulative Jezebel spirit passed down to Athaliah is spoken of by Jesus in the book of **Revelation** to the church of Thyatira. What is interesting to note that Jesus declares those who have this spirit of manipulation & murder who *"... commit adultery* [serving the idol of power] *with her into the great Tribulation..."* **Revelation 2:22**

Stop wait did you catch that! So before we get to the good stuff of this story we can already see its implications for those who choose the wrong side of this story symbolically. Remember we are told we endure some of the Great Tribulation **[cf. Matthew 24:23-24]** and are taken from it **[cf. Revelation 7:14]** but these people are sentenced to it for the long haul. This is a proof text if I ever saw one that we do not go through all of the great tribulation.

Next we see a type and shadow of Christ in this story. *"So he* [Joash] *was hidden with her* [Jehosheba "Jehovah has promised"] *in the house of the Lord six years, while Athaliah was reigning over the land."* **2 Kings 11:3** Satan carries man into bondage with the title reigning over man of "afflicted of God" for six years = **6000 years**. That is until a rightful heir can be found!

> *"Now in the seventh year Jehoiada* [Jehovah knows, type of Holy Spirit] *sent and brought the captains of hundreds* [elect] *...and brought them into the house of the Lord. Then he made a covenant with them... and showed them the king's son...* [King Jesus revealed at rapture]*"*   **11:4**

So we see God gathers His elect and arms them with swords and spears found from King David. **[V10]** These are the weapons of our warfare given by the Holy Spirit are passed down from a worshipping King David, who held the keys to open doors over spiritual realms. **[Cf. Isaiah 22:22]**

The king's son Joash is then presented to the people in front of the temple. In fact, it is thought that the ark of the covenant was made a throne for him to sit on. **[V12]** The story continues with Athaliah being aroused by the noice of celebration. Storming into the scene she comes to the house of God only to see trumpets blowing and all the rank and circumstance of coronation. All her followers are killed along with her. This is a beautiful imagery of what the **Book of Revelation** chapter 12 speaks of. Satan is thrown down in the midst of a joyous occasion, the rapture. Furious he tries to reach up to the Ark/tabernacle above the earth **[cf. 12:16, 13:7]** but he can't touch us. Inhabiting the beast he goes after everything else but is destroyed in the end.

In fact, Athaliah is killed at the entrance to the king's house arriving on a horse. **[V16]** This is a parallel to the Anti-Christ who heads to Jerusalem but is drawn into battle at Armageddon. The next words we hear are, **"*Jehoiada* [the Holy Spirit] *made a covenant between the Lord* [Father] *and the king* [Jesus, the Groom] *and the people* [Bride]*, that they would be the Lord's people.* [Married]"** **[V17]** Everyone said, '*Amen*', as we see the symbolism of Christ earthly reign declaring the two one. Remember Joash name means *"fire of Yahweh"* and represents Christ in His fire judgments.

Following this stories chronological parallels closely, we see something very telling. Notice before Joash is enthroned, we see His people celebrating and the enemies bewilderment which would be Jesus at the start of His coming when we enter into our honeymoon ark celebrating before He is revealed physically to the world!

Elijah's prayer ...

... **6 times** and **on the seventh time** God sends rain. Not all of a sudden but slowly until it is the fiercest rain ever. Revealing the coming of the Lord starts as a trap, not as sudden Armageddon much like the flood waters increased slowly until death occurred.

This is a wonderful picture as well as prayers have been going forth since the beginning of time for God to restorer all things.

Jacob's 2 brides ...

...are examples of God's two companies. He redeems the first after **seven years [on the last 1000, 6000]** the one he had "not" loved [Leah = Gentiles]. So he agrees to work another **7 years** [the day of the Lord & seven trumpets] to redeem the women He loved Rachel [Israel].

As the story bears out, God allows him to be married to both from the first day showing Jesus gathers us and immediately goes to work sealing & protecting the remnant of Israel. However it also displays how Israel was always God's desire to be redeemed first.

122

Origin of the Covenant begins ...

... At the time of Isaac's coming of age, according to the Book of Jubilees, was around **2000-2003**. [Ancient Book of Jubilees, Ken Johnson Th.D., Biblefacts.org, ISBN 149036854X, p72-75] Although chronology is not an exact science, this Jewish manuscript is mentioned in the bible and discovered in the Dead Sea Scrolls. For our purpose of dating the Abrahamic covenant, this source pays careful attention to dating jubilees from Creation to Exodus.

My point will not be to declare when and what exactly occurred on the year **2000**. However it is important to note our faith in this plan of God that displays patterns. It is not without reason to think God would do something significant every 2000 years given Jewish oral tradition declares it an age. For Abraham thought to have lived between the years **2100-1800 BC**, sees God make His covenant with Him around **2000**. Could God be making a covenant on the year **2000**, establishing that covenant with the lamb provided on the cross on year **4000**, to return to make firm His covenant as **Daniel 9:27** declares. A lamb in the thickets sacrificed on the year 2000, the Lamb of God on a cross year 4000, and the lamb opening the seals on the year 6000!

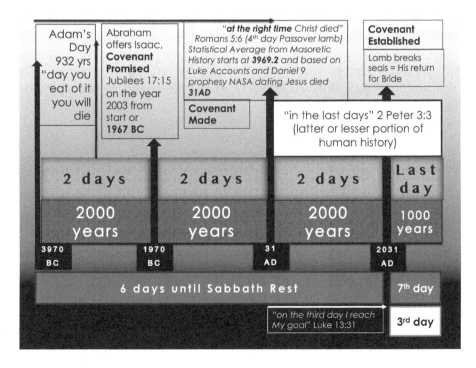

For Hebrew history and heritage started around this event in the year 2000. The promise for them should have come with Jesus first coming on their third day, but as we have seen they missed it! History now repeats or is looping back around a second time. This time God will use the Gentiles bride to awaken His Jewish Bride, As in Jacob's two wives.

The word for 2000 in Hebrew is *"alpayim"* which finds itself in the Jewish National Anthem. *"The hope that is two-thousand years old."* Again there's something deeply significant that occurs to the Jewish world every 2000 years!

As early as the writing of **Numbers** the fifth book of the bible we are introduced to the concept these *"days"* being periods of time. Balaam saying, *"what this people will do to your people at the end of days"* **24:14**

First battle in the promised land ...

Jericho reveals a consistent pattern. The Lord instructs Joshua to marches **6 days** around Jericho **[cf. Joshua 6:3]** and **on the seventh day** they were to march around **seven times** then blow a trumpet and celebrate. Again another example of 7 on a 7, and the walls came tumbling down! Signifying we are raptured and with Jesus celebrating while the walls of darkness are being dismantled. All this after **6000 years** at the beginning of the seventh day! Notice just like the equivalent third day example **[cf. Exodus 19:11]** God comes at the beginning of the day. *"On the seventh day they rose early at the dawning of the day and marched..."* **Joshua 6:15**

First fire judgements ...

Jesus not only uses Noah and the flood as a parallel but the story of the destruction of Sodom and Lot's rescue as a direct parallel. This event comes in sequential order directly before the expulsion of the false sons and the birth of His promise in Isaac. The same will be true of the rapture occurring at the beginning of God's judgment that then will rid the earth of false sons and raise up His true sons/daughter.

Then the Ultimate FIRST!

Calling attention to God's track record for all of known human history, in which we visited some of the most remarkable types and shadows, there still is one that comes with such credibility the Apostles signed off on it. **[Cf. Hebrews 12:18-28]**

The legal precedence in God's visitation on Mount Sinai **[cf. Exodus 19]** as an example of His return as well for a people is solid. For this was the first time God visited a people! All of the key events come with time signatures worth considering.

THE PRECEDENCE

"For you have not come to a mountain that cannot be touched ... but you have come to Mount Zion and to the city of the living God ..."   **Hebrews 12:18,22**

First Visitation of God for a people ...

And the Apostles gave direct credence to this being a direct parallel to Jesus Second Coming in **Hebrews 12:18-28**! Remember the importance of a precedence has in a court of law as well, for this is a first. This is the very first time God visits a people. An event so big that the fear of this *"god"* spread to all the surrounding world in dealing with this nomadic tribe of Israel from that point on. Moses a type of Christ, tries to mediate between a people God wants to choose and the Almighty Himself. To say the first visit was a success, underscores the immense failure of man to believe in God's intentions as a benefit when the visual looks anything like a beneficial visit.

Like the garden of Eden, Satan plays with the minds of humans replacing faith with fear & doubt concerning God's nature and intentions. Although God, in His defense, had already shown them great mighty things, unbelief crept into their hearts. Much like today's eschatological belief systems do in placing the emphasis on our fear of death not an opportunity for GLORY. The people shrunk back from God! However the Apostle that wrote the masterpiece we call The **Epistle to Hebrews** warns from making the same mistake again in the future rapture.

> *"For **you have not come** to a mountain that can be touched and to a blazing fire and to darkness... so terrible was the sight that Moses said, 'I am full of fear...'* **but you have come to Mount Zion** *... heavenly Jerusalem ...* **church** *... do not refuse Him who is speaking. For His voice shook the earth then, but now* **He has promised "Yet once more"**
>
> **Hebrews 12:18**

In this storyline, the New testament author of **Hebrews** picks up on its significant place in history as a parallel to the future return of God to earth through a better mediator Jesus Christ. This not only gives this type and shadow a further green light to be directly used to understand the nature of the better covenant and its fulfillment at the second coming of Christ, but it's timing as well. We will later discuss the immense importance it places on being ready for the rapture but for now we are only concerned with the timing of His return in the big picture.

What most don't know is in this event Moses will go up the Mountain **three times**. On the first ascension, God commands Moses to prepare the people **2 days**. These trips foreshadow Christ work of redemption! First at the resurrection, Jesus ascends then later to gather His people and finally to display her before the world, found in Moses three ascensions. Each ascent of Moses is surrounded with foreshadowings of what God knew of the future. Starting with the first ascension Moses is told to prepare His bride **two days**!

> *"The Lord also said to Moses, "Go to the people and consecrate them **TODAY and TOMORROW** and let them wash their garments; and let them be **ready for the third day, for on the THIRD DAY the Lord will come down** on Mount Sinai in the sight of all the people... On the third day **in the morning** there was thunder...and a sound of a very loud horn... Moses brought the people out of the camp to meet God."*
>
> **Exodus 19:10-11,16**

Notice God tells Moses exactly when He will be there for the people who He just called *"a kingdom of priests and a holy nation"* **v6**, on the beginning of the third day. Notice, this parallel is connected to the foreshadowing of preparing His bride whom He declares **"you shall be My own possession ..." v5** in the same chapter! This is significant. When should we start the **2000 years** that represents the **2 days**? After what? Notice God is speaking to Moses in His first ascent up the mountain. Moses representing Jesus first ascension after His death is told to prepare a people two days! Jesus death on the fourth day makes for a perfect seven for human history adding the 2 and a third day. Then it shouldn't surprise us Jesus refers to this timetable in **Luke 13:31**!

At the start of the third day means the end of the sixth day adding **2** to **4**. How do I know this **three days** are after Jesus **fourth day** crucifixion? Hosea will confirm the third day arrival in **Hosea 6;1-3** but not until after God has visited Israel and had to tear away and *"return to My place"* **5:15** signifying the start of a period, *"until they acknowledge their guilt"* **Hosea 5:15**. Jesus then confirms this prophecy with similar statements of *"house left to you desolate until"* **Luke 13:35**

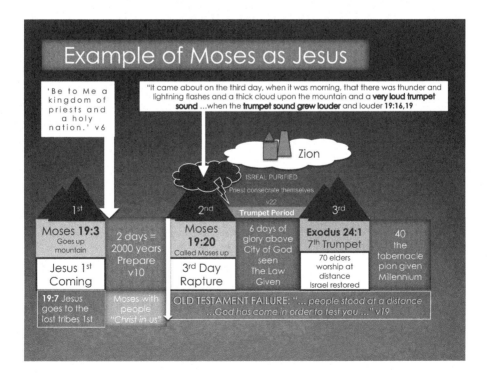

What makes this a beautiful parallel is God wants a people who are His possession. **Exodus 19** is the first revelation of the mystery of the church, His bride, I have found in scripture. Stating that this preparing and gathering a bride would be an age of **2000 years** in the words, *"Consecrate them today and tomorrow and let them wash their garments, let them be ready"* **Exodus 19:10** In the end the people became afraid of God rejecting His direct invitation and God took up **Aaron** instead with His brother Moses. Let's be very careful to overcome our fears with living faith in His loving offer before the rapture challenges us all.

It is from this contexts, I believe the Author of **Hebrews** was convinced of the truth that He would *"appear the second time ... to those who eagerly await Him"* **9:28**, and finally have Himself a bride. So He parallels these two events past and future.

THE ASCENSIONS

3 Ascensions of Moses on Mt. Sinai

Foundations to First Coming

1. *"Moses went up to God"* **Exodus 19:3**1. Jesus message & mission starts in heaven birthed from the foundations of the world.
2. Invitation to be His bride plan from the start *"My own possession"* **Exodus 19:5**
3. The End reveals the fulfillment of this plan during Jesus Reign

    "Kingdom of priest, holy nation" **v6** parallel **Revelation 20:5**
4. 1st coming went to the tribes lost. *"So Moses came and called the elders of the people and set before them all these words... to the sons of Israel"* **v7**
5. Resurrection Jesus returns to the Father *"Moses brought back the words of the people to the Lord"* **v8**

Between Ascensions

"Go to the people consecrate them
today and tomorrow"
Exodus 19:10

128

1. Moses (Jesus) now ascended is instructed to descend (form of the Holy Spirit) with a message. [Cf. *"He will disclose to you what is to come"* **John 16:13**]

2. *"Behold I will come to you in a thick cloud ..."* **Exodus 19:9** Hebrews 12:18 gives this same description for parallel to second coming. Many Old Testament prophets as well describe the day of the Lord this way. So this is a clear parallel

3. *"The Lord said to Moses, "Go to the people* (through the Holy Spirit during church age) *and consecrate them today and tomorrow ..."* **v10** (2 prophetic days) So Jesus did come and spoke those words exactly *"today and tomorrow and the third day ..."* **Luke 13:32**

4. *"Let them wash their garments"* **v10** Moses will later instruct them *"not go near a women."* **V15** which parallel the only other group non gender group told or spoken this way. [cf. 144,000 in *"not defiled with women"* **Revelation 14:4**] All this are bridal examples.

5. *"Let them be READY For the third day, for on the third day the Lord will come down ... in the sight of all the people"* **Exodus 19:11** and when on the third day did God come ... *"on the third day when it <u>was morning</u> ... lighting flashes ...a very loud trumpet sound."* **V16** and so Jesus says *"on the third day I reach my goal"* **Luke 13:32**

The 2nd Coming / 2nd Ascension

"The Lord came down on Mount Sinai, ...
the Lord called Moses ... And Moses went up."
Exodus 19:20

1. In this Ascension, Moses possibly represents us the faithful bride. Since the Lord is mentioned coming down so He represents Himself in this picture. This occurs is a parallel of **Hebrews 12:22-25** the voice calling us up. We are raptured just above the mountains.

2. If Moses is not the representation, then the next passage describes who goes first. *"Let the priest who come near to the Lord consecrate themselves"* **v22** and **Revelation 20:5** affirms the bride as a priesthood.

3. The Law of God is given like a covenant of marriage. **Exodus 20** yet the people give in to fear saying, *"But do*

129

not let God speak to us or we will die" 20:19 and they choose distance **v21**

4. Those Left Behind are tested for Moses says, **"God has come in order to test you, ..."** **v20**! This parallels **Revelation 3:20** **"the hour of testing"** for those not faithful.

5. God starts directing His words from the people in general to the **"the Sons of Israel"** **v22-26** as God directs His attention on redeeming Jacob during the trumpet Period.

The Days of Glory = Trumpet Period

"Come up ... you and Aaron, Nadab and Abihu
and seventy of the elders of Israel
and you shall worship at a distance"
Exodus 24:1

1. Finally **Exodus 24** Moses brings up, a select group closer. God draws near to Israel during the trumpet period. **"At the foot of the mountain with twelve pillars for the twelve tribes of Israel"** **v4**

2. Young men of Israel make sacrifices **V5-6**

3. **"They saw the God of Israel; under his feet there appeared to be pavement of sapphire as clear as the sky itself."** **v10** At this juncture, what we are seeing is the day of the Lord when Mount Zion seen above earth, the city Abraham sought.

4. How long? **"The glory of the Lord rested on Mount Sinai ...<u>for six days</u> and <u>on the seventh day</u> He called Moses from the midst of the cloud."** **V16** On the seventh day could be that for the Jewish people this occurs on their seventh day, or on the seventh trumpet of the Trumpet period much like the example of Jericho. We have already seen much examples of an early rapture before the Days of Glory above the earth, and the example of a period of Days when God hovers over earth.

5. To the world at this point the final 3.5 years will be like this:
   "And to the eyes of the sons of Israel the appearance of the glory of the Lord was like a consuming fire on the mountain top. Moses entered the midst of the cloud as he went up to the mountain..." **Exodus 24:17**

6. The final time Moses goes up for 40 days is symbolic of a perfect complete time which parallel's the Millennium, when at the end God must judge those who made a golden calf.

6

Decoding:
The Resurrection Code

THE FACT

*"**This one fact** ... one day **is like** a thousand years and a thousand years **like** one day."*   **[NASB]**

*"**This one thing** that one day with the Lord **as** a thousand years ..."*   **[KJV]**

*"**Don't overlook** this one fact ..."*   **[CSB]**

2 Peter 3:8

Does God have a schedule to conclude the matter of His promise? The sarcasm on the other side can be heard, *"**Where is the hope of His promise?**"* **v3**. With that in mind, we hear a very strong statement come out next, *"**ONE FACT**"* **3:8**. Notice, not two or a series of facts but a culminating factor that changes everything previously thought as the next verse so clearly states the context is God's timing. The question of the day, why the delay as *"**some count**ed **slowness**"* **3:9**.

Remembering our previous chapters that this context was dealing with God's plan *"**from the beginning of creation**"* **v4,** let us not do what they where doing and get tunnel vision. For Peter using the term, *"**It** **escapes their notice** ..."* in **verse 5** repeats it here saying, *"**Do not let this ONE FACT** **escape your notice**"* **v8** translated elsewhere means simply, *"**chosen ignorance**"* **[KJV]**. So what Peter is really stating is; *'Don't play stupid'!* I would say, consider the context for the greek word *"hos"* has room for interpreting its meaning within the context written as *"as"* or *"like"*. This comparative adverb with alternatives ranging from being *"just as"* or *"similar to"* is translated in most cases as *"equal to"* rather than one of a relative comparison. The difference is major, *"one day* is equivalent to *a thousand years"* **3:8** versus *"like"*.

One must weigh the reality that Peter wouldn't be writing right back to the same churches with new insights as his letter suggest if there wasn't something just relative to say. For Moses the source of this truth from his encounters on Mt Sinai with the living God sings, *"For a thousand years in Your sight are like yesterday when it passes by or a watch in the night"* **Psalms 90:4** In this passage, the statement *"are like"* is inserted for clarity of speech. There is no word given in the Hebrew manuscript for *"are like"*. So the passage should read *"a thousand years yesterday"*. The Hebrew word used *"yowm"* which translate as "*day*", also translates as a period of *"time"*. What Moses is revealing? Does every thousand years of our time represent a period of significant time to God? Just a day is to us for its pattern of the sun rising and setting.

If we take this seriously as a standard for accounting for all of human history *"from the beginning of creation"* **3:4** as Peter puts it, we find ourselves walking into this beauty of God's perfect timing. However, many believe Peter is making a relative statement of how things appear different for us versus God in **2 Peter 3:8**, but again watch how he uses the greek word *"heis"* with means *"a cardinal numeral"* in opposition to many, simply stated "ONE THING THAT MATTERS ABOVE ALL ELSE". How is this making a relative statement?

THE FACTS

Daniel 9:24-27 & Hosea 5:18-6:3
The two prophetic timetables merge

Only two prophetic time codes where given in the Old Testament for the timing of the Messiah revealed in Jesus Christ; the **70 WEEKS** of **Daniel 9** pertaining to true Israel's restoration; *"for your people and your holy city"* **9:24** and **Hosea 5:14-6:3**'s **2 DAYS** pertaining to the length of time God will leave their house desolate from Israel's rejection of their Messiah found in the **70 weeks** prophecy. For Daniel is told, He will be *"cut off and have nothing"* **Daniel 9:26**. So these two timetables explain each other, for God didn't want one simple easy to follow answer for the future. He desires for His own to search, compare and weigh.

What we know at the time of Peter's second letter is the **70 weeks** should have been fulfilled already no matter which decree you thought was the correct one. The six items of **Daniel 9:24** were not completed in the **490 years** *(1 week = 7 years)* after the decrees to *"rebuild Jerusalem"* **9:25** yet the Messiah came right on schedule in **verse 25-26**. I hear a lot of chatter that the **70 weeks** was fulfilled at Stephen's stoning, because from this point God moves on from reaching the Jews to the Gentiles, or so it seems. However none of that completes the six items of **Daniel 9:24**?

Next all indications from wikipedia to all that is written on Stephen's stoning is that no one knows for sure if it occurred 3.5 years from the crucifixion of Christ to honor the prophetic timetable needing 3.5 years more. These are just estimations to fit one's viewpoint, whereas it is clear Jesus ministry was only 3.5 years from passovers mentioned. So the Apostles were struggling to piece together God's master plan. However Paul nails the plan in his treaty on the relationship of the Jews and Gentile to God's master plan in **Romans 9-11**.

Here is where most Eschatological views differ and fail to connect the two time tables of **Hosea & Daniel** together as pieces of a whole. Why? They have failed to see God's storyline, His ability to pause a promised timetable based on giving Israel a choice. If could see choice was involved, they might be able to see the star witnesses testimony as unlocking everything in **Luke 13;31-35**! Instead human nature focuses on *"the stumbling blocks"* of carnal things. Who is the Anti-Christ? What is the mark of the beast? When will the temple be rebuilt? Instead of what drives God's plan to begin with His relationship with man being healed through the atoning sacrifice of His Son. Ultimately the fulfillment of the final item in **Daniel**'s list *"anoint the holy"* **9:24**!

For back to Peter's *"one fact"* which gives a hard count to Jesus use of the phrase *"today and tomorrow I do ..."* **Luke 13:32** which beautifully links itself to the **two days** being mentioned in **Hosea 6 & Exodus 19** as the Bridal Preparatory Time/Israel Timeout! Here God shows us the pathway of restoring the true tabernacle of God in Himself. Concluded by bringing a people with Him while restoring Israel on earth. The prophets seeing this culmination in events both negative and glorious refer to it as, *"on that day"*, *"the Day of the Lord"* both as *"great" and terrible"* **Malachi 4:5** So we discover we have 24 hour *"days"*, thousand year ages *"days"* and finally a period of time at the end of this age called *"The Day"*.

So without further delay, let us dive into Jesus words that tie together **Daniel & Hosea** and the grand plan of **"days"** as ages.

> "'Go away, leave here, for Herod wants to kill You.' And He said to them, 'Go and tell that fox, Behold, I cast out demons and perform cures **today and tomorrow, and the third day I reach My goal**.'
> **'Nevertheless** I must journey on today and tomorrow **and the next day**; for it cannot be that a prophet would perish outside of Jerusalem ..."
>
> **Luke 13:31-33**

Being challenged by a king, Jesus gives a KINGLY answer! "*No, you cannot effect what I do! In fact I will tell you exactly what I'm going to do.*" So Jesus hits us right away with a massive contrast between real time and prophetic time. Starting with the prophetic code of reaching a big picture goal, He then turns His focus upon the issue at hand, the present day. The whole context is addressing the timing of the expected arrival of the Kingdom of God, from the threats of the pharisees & their boss King Herod.

In doing so He attaches Himself to the drama being playing out in real time with the expectations upon **Daniel 9:24-27** fulfillment of the **70 weeks** but bringing in **Hosea 6**'s **two day** completion for Israel to be restored. In other words, the context is perfect given you have an understanding of the storylines driving these two timelines toward His coming that where very much on the minds of the Jewish people of His day.

THE CODE

32 "'... _the third day I reach My goal_'

33 '**Nevertheless** I must journey on today and tomorrow and the next day; for it cannot be that a prophet would perish outside of Jerusalem.

34 'O Jerusalem, Jerusalem, the city that kills the prophets and stones those sent to her! **How often I wanted to gather** your children together, just as a hen gathers her brood under her wings, and **you would not have it!**

35 'Behold, **your house is left to you desolate**; and I say to you, you will not see Me **until the time comes** when you say, 'BLESSED IS HE WHO COMES IN THE NAME OF THE LORD!'" **Luke 13:31-35**

Understanding what Jesus had in mind for this mysterious goal on **the third day [v32]** must be important to us. Why would we discount such a impactful declaration? For it begins with a threat from an earthly king to the King of all kings! The answer was nothing less than the fulfillment of everything that this generation both feared and hoped for; the Kingdom of God! Jesus putting Himself at its center of all this drama of His day, concludes the context with His second coming. This is about His return! *"you will not see Me until the time comes when you say, 'Blessed is He who comes in the name of the Lord'"* Luke 13:35 The context is the second coming of Jesus Christ not His triumphal entry or resurrection on the third day!

Some question whether the context for the third day was His resurrection or triumphal, but where is that the context? These events don't seem to be the focus of the rest of His answer in the fuller context of **Luke 13:31-35**. For Jesus clearly looks further out, then those events. The main focus never strays from when He will be instituted King which is this earthly kings concern. This shouldn't be a shock since it was on most people's minds at the time in Jerusalem.

Matthew 23:37-39 mimics this reference in **Luke 13:34-35** giving us a possible placement in time for these words during the Passion week possibly Tuesday, which makes Jesus resurrection still further out then three days and the triumphal entry past. This probably makes the best sense for why the threat occurred. Herod concerned over the triumphal entry confronts Jesus through his henchmen the Pharisees. The context also gives us a bigger clue in *"your house will be left to you desolate"* **v35** which indicate in this last verse of the context that this will occur at the time of His second coming giving us a target for *"My goal"* **v32**.

This would make the context of Jesus words in this passage about His plan for Israel and Jerusalem being restored through His rule in the bigger picture of God's plan. Jesus is clear, this is a Sovereign affair unaffected by the nuisance of an earthly king but one affected by Israel's rejection of her God. Which shouldn't have happened, as seen in the way Jesus speaks. *"How often I wanted... You would not have it "* **Luke 13:34** Zechariah speaking of Him as well coming, *"humble and mounted on a donkey"* **Zechariah 9:9**, concerning His triumphal entry into Jerusalem, turns around and gives us the very words, *"Shout in Triumph"* **Zechariah 9:9**.

God choosing through Zechariah to show what a continuous fulfillment would have looked like. *"I will cut off the chariot from Ephraim and the horse from Jerusalem; and the bow of war will* *be cut off. And He will speak peace to the Nations; and <u>His dominion will be from sea to sea.</u>"* **V10** As if the second coming was to follow His entry, but here Jesus declares a *"change of plans"*. You can feel it right in the context of **Luke 13**. First by saying, *"I wished ...you wouldn't have it"* **v34** so *"Behold your house will be desolate"* **v35**

How many times do we see this possible continuous last week of **Daniel 9's 70 week** broken up in scripture for even **Isaiah 61:3** isn't fully declared by Jesus. Jesus was to fulfill all seven years continuous I believe, both declaring *"the favorable year of the Lord and the day of vengeance"*. So Jesus entry into Jerusalem brought great alarm and threats to the powers that existed at that time. Why? Because many prophecies directly connected Christ arrival in Jerusalem to judgment. Here we are at this moment, Herod is determined to undermine prophecy and Jesus is *"No, God the Father already figured a different path to fulfillment!"*

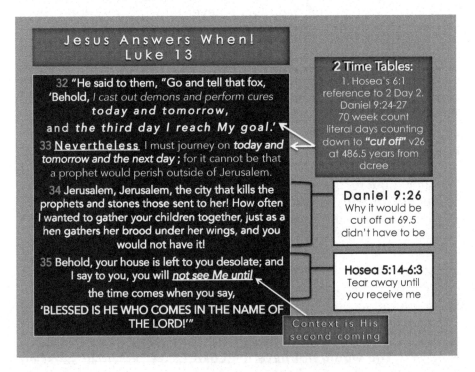

Jesus Answers When!
Luke 13

32 "He said to them, "Go and tell that fox, 'Behold, *I cast out demons and perform cures* **today and tomorrow,** and **the third day I reach My goal.'**
33 <u>**Nevertheless**</u> I must journey on **today and tomorrow and the next day** ; for it cannot be that a prophet would perish outside of Jerusalem.

34 Jerusalem, Jerusalem, the city that kills the prophets and stones those sent to her! How often I wanted to gather your children together, just as a hen gathers her brood under her wings, and you would not have it!

35 Behold, your house is left to you desolate; and I say to you, you will <u>*not see Me until*</u> the time comes when you say, 'BLESSED IS HE WHO COMES IN THE NAME OF THE LORD!'"

2 Time Tables:
1. Hosea's 6:1 reference to 2 Day 2. Daniel 9:24-27 70 week count literal days counting down to **"cut off"** v26 at 486.5 years from dcree

Daniel 9:26
Why it would be cut off at 69.5 didn't have to be

Hosea 5:14-6:3
Tear away until you receive me

Context is His second coming

Again, in giving us a prophecy reflecting how his first coming would look like, on a donkey, the prophet Zechariah then links it immediately to His second. Zechariah's prophecy though can be linked to the ending of Jesus words when it is said. *"I will pour on the house of David and on the inhabitants of Jerusalem, the spirit of grace and of supplication, so that they will look on Me whom they have pierced and they will mourn for Him, as one mourns for an only son..."* **Zechariah 12:10** For this is the same as *"time comes when you will say, 'Blessed ..."* **Luke 13:35**

From our vantage point, the first and second portion of the Zechariah's prophecy got divorced and removed in time from each other, much like **Daniel's 70 weeks** seems detached as a whole. Making what Jesus says in this passage powerful, *"How often I wished to gather your children...you wouldn't have it"* **v34** as though it could have happened. So how can we not see how God allowed for the prophecy of **Daniel 9, Zechariah and Isaiah** to be fluid according to choice?

Remember, Jesus gives two timeframes! Or at least Luke does in remembering the event to differentiate between what was said before from real time, as if to isolate the first statement as a profound prophetic truth. When Jesus speaks of real time, He says, *"I must journey on today and tomorrow <u>and the next</u>; for it cannot be that a prophet would perish outside of Jerusalem"* **V33**. This actually might be an indication that this passage is not synoptic with **Matthew 23:39** at all during the Passion week, since Jesus might be suggesting there is still a journey of more than **three days** to Jerusalem or the cross.

Whatever the pinpointed time of this dialogue, Jesus centers the prophetic fulfillment to Israel around His crucifixion. Why? Because He is answering the **Hosea 6** riddle as well as the **Daniel 9** riddle. Hosea's timetable for restoration was **two days** after an event for which they would have *"guilt"* for and cause Him to *"go away"* **Hosea 5:14-15**. The crucifixion is at the heart of God's plan, for it would have occurred anyway you look at this. Had the Jewish people received their King, He would have died for them under the hands of the Romans for the sins of mankind. For our in-depth critique of this passage, Jesus is tying His first timetable **Hosea's 2 days**, to the completion of real time when He is crucified. Then explains this break of two days must occur until the time to restore Israel occurs. **[cf. Luke 13:35]**

Either way we see the impossible connection of the third day mentioned as His goal to <u>anything connected with real time</u> like His triumphal entry, the crucifixion or resurrection! Jesus leaves the impression that real time had many more days by leaving the end open saying, *"and the next"* **v33**. Having this clear contrast made by Christ we are left with only a symbolic representation for **two days then the third**. Jesus is contrasting the two timing Prophets of the Old Testament, **Hosea 6:2-3** for the big picture of when Israel would be restored and the fulfillment of the last three items of **Daniel 9:24** mainly *"to anoint the most holy"* **Daniel 9:24** which is Zion bringing Heaven to earth would occur. Which speaks of

Himself replacing the temple with His body and blood starting at the resurrection and completing this Heavenly takeover at the end of the age to establish Himself on earth as the tabernacle of God.

The contrast is clear; in one it is said, **"I reach my goal"** **v32** and the other is a disappointing process with *"and the next"* **v33** revealing something unresolved. If Jesus first timetable was the same as the second, there would be no need to repeat or even contrast it. The first timetable is obviously the conclusion to the second, and a short summary to why Herod can't effect God's plan. Much like the logic that Christ can't suffer after being made King sounds stupid. So is the epic failure of reaching your goal only to start again on a journey that suggest crucifixion, desolation, etc. No, the first timetable is the big picture from which this real time struggle must obey! GOD CANNOT BE AFFECTED BY OUR REBELLION and frankly won't!

Be careful here, Jesus doesn't believe in speaking idle words! *"But I say to you every idle word men may speak they will give account of it in the day of judgment"* **Matthew 12:36** There is always purpose to the things He says, so we are only left with **the three days** of His death and resurrection or a prophetic timetable for a bigger picture to explain this phrase. Remember the prophet Hosea has already chimed in with, *"He will raise us up on the third day"* **Hosea 6:2** and Jesus saying here *"third day I reach my goal"* **Luke 13:32**. Hosea's context cannot be construed for Christ's resurrection either since *"His going forth is as the dawn; and He will come like the rain"* **Hosea 6:3** One is an ascension the other a descent coming down to earth, perfectly predicting the Messiah's breaking point from Israel at His resurrection and return after 2000 years or 2 days.

Next, if Christ was only speaking time codes of the present like His resurrection as the third day goal, He would not have reached so far into the future to mention something like, *"Behold your house is left to you desolate until"* **Luke 13:35** as an answer to that goal. Notice the second timeframe is a journey that seems linked with His death and Him being rejected by the Jews, *"for it cannot be that a prophet would perish outside Jerusalem"* **Luke 13:33**. For this journey *"and the next"* then becomes the context for His statement, *"you will not see Me UNTIL!"* **v35**. The context itself drives home the point that His victory is not won at the cross or His resurrection, but His goal lies further out. Is not His goal within the context itself when He says, *"I wanted to gather your children together ... you would not have it."* **Luke 13:34**?

It is a common reoccurrence also with prophecy for God to repeat patterns, to give double meaning to things both to conceal and affirm truth. Here is the way God conceals, confuses the wise in their wisdom and reveals patterns to the simple. So in this scenario, could God be revealing through His movements His plan? For Jesus moves about two full days after His death doing the Father's business. Why 2 days? Which we will see is three days and nights by the timing of His death and Resurrection. For Jesus telling His generation, *"No sign will be given to it except the sign of the prophet Jonah. For just as Jonah was in the belly of the huge fish for <u>three days and three nights</u>* (which is two full days explained later in chapter) *so the Son of Man will be in the heart of the earth for three days and three nights."* Matthew 12:39-40

Same would be true of Lazarus's resurrection after four days, declaring that Jesus was the fourth day passover Lamb, crucified in the year 4000.. Why wait if there wasn't a reason, the Father held the Son back from His own dear friend for us all to see the pattern. We find that time signatures matter to God. The Passion week then becomes a demonstration of human history. Jesus buried two days in the church, *"Christ in you"* much like He was two days in the underworld, *"casting out demons and performing cures"* Luke 13:32 which is much like what He is doing these 2000 years through the church.

Let's just take the parable of the Good Samaritan. The significance of **two days wages** cannot be overlooked as Jesus prophesying His return saying, "*He took two denarii, gave them to the innkeeper and said to him, Take care of him; and whatever more you spend, when <u>I come again I will repay you.</u>*" **Luke 10:35** *[wikipedia; denarius: classical historians often have said that in late Roman Republic and early Roman Empire the daily wage for an unskilled laborer was 1 denarius]*

So the parable acting as an overview of what is about to happen to redeem mankind from the thieves (Satanic Forces), Jesus gives us as customary a second witness to any prophetic fact. Yet as we know this **two day** period started with Moses when God declared His intention of having a people of His own and then said get the people ready **two days!** [Cf. Exodus 19:5,10-11] God choosing Hosea to marry a harlot to symbolize Israel's unfaithfulness. Then has him call his own children *"not my people".* To symbolize how one affects the other. How the unfaithfulness of the mother births *"not my people"*. Here through Jesus, He is connecting the dots. Israel's stubbornness birth's salvation to the Gentiles until the Gentiles come in bringing repentance upon the natural branch as Paul says so eloquently, **Romans 9-11** at the very end.

So we have multiple testimonies of this two days prophetically but no confirmation as to what the two days would represent until

Peter makes it abundantly clear! His reference of a time code can only be traced biblically to Moses prayer who Himself went up the Mountain and must have inquired "Why a two day wait, God when we could have purified ourselves quicker?" Why anything? God must have given him the equation that he passes on. Understand we have the Law represented in Moses **[Exodus 19]**, the prophets in the prophet Hosea **[5:14-6:1-3]** and Jesus twice pointing to Himself **[Luke 10:35,13:31]** as fulfilling this two day wait & preparation for a people. Then we find the Apostles at the very same time as **2 Peter** writing to confirm Mt Sinai as speaking of His future coming! **[Hebrews 12:18-29]** Have we missed anybody? In a court of law this would stand! No wonder Peter will say **"THE ONE CARDINAL FACT don't miss it"** 2 Peter 3:8

THE RAIN

*"He will come to us **like the rain"*** **Hosea 6:3**

So let's examine further the link that exists even in the similarity of the wording Jesus chooses to that used by the prophet Hosea. I have inserted **Luke 13** in parenthesis into the Hosea reading. So we are examining the harmony and intentionality of Jesus discourse in making a connection to Hosea's prophecy.

HOSEA 5:14 - 6:3 alongside LUKE 13:31-35
PARALLELISM DISPLAYED

*"**5:14** - For I will be like a lion to Ephraim and like a young lion to the house of Judah. I, even I, will tear to pieces and go away, [**"Behold your house is left to you desolate"** **Lk 13:35]** I will carry away ... return to My place [**after first coming]** until they acknowledge their guilt [**"you will not see Me until the time comes"** **Luke 13:35]** and seek My face [**"when you say, 'Blessed is He who comes in the name of the Lord'"** **Luke 13:35]** In their affliction they will earnestly seek Me. [**Zechariah 12:10]***

* **6:1** - Come let us return to the Lord. For He has torn us but He will heal us; He has wounded us but He will bandage us. He will revive us <u>AFTER TWO DAYS</u> [**Behold I cast out demons and perform cures today and tomorrow"***

140

Luke 13:32] He will raise us up on THE THIRD DAY **['and the third day I reach My goal" Luke 13:32]** that we may live before Him. **[Christ must be on earth from this point on]**

6:3 - So let us know, let us press on to know the Lord. His going forth is as certain as the dawn; **[not His resurrection]** and He will come **[second coming]** to us like the rain"

Hosea 5:14-15, 6:1-3

Here we see such an undeniable parallel as if Jesus is saying, *"I'm that guy, I am the Messiah you are waiting on and the answer to all prophesy yet to be fulfilled!"* So **"go tell that fox" Luke 13:31**, Herod he cannot control the outcome of something already set in motion by the Almighty Sovereign! Again we can't deny the connection to this word in Hosea and its similarity with other prophetic passages that are significant in foretelling the Messiah's time. For example **Daniel 9**, God speaks of the significance of Christ's rejection & death would have upon Israel's way of life. **"The Messiah will be cut off and have nothing ... city and sanctuary end come with flood even to the end ...desolations." 9:26** Even **Daniel 9** is tied in here by the similarities in the use of the word **"desolate" Luke 13:34** and God's wording in **"desolations are determined" Daniel 9:26** plural!

The question again of whether Christ death and resurrection is what Jesus meant by **"on the third day I reach my goal" Luke 13:32** can easily be seen as not the conclusion of God's goal by **Daniel 9:26-27** itself. To this end, we must pay attention to the context of **Hosea**. It is about the time period of Israel's **"wounding"** and final **"reviving"** at which time the Messiah **"comes to us like the rain"** which is descending not ascending. The resurrection is an ascension, whereas His return is like the rain. Next, when Jesus speaks of His **two days** He says, **"Behold I cast out demons and perform cures today and tomorrow" v32**, we must weigh is this what really happened while Christ was at the heart of the earth? We have no other place in scripture that confirms this activity except that He might have sentenced demons or preached the salvation message to saints of old. This is because Peter tells us, Jesus proclaimed the sentence of Angels imprisoned **[1 Peter 3:19]** and preaches to Old Testament saints **[1 Peter 4:6]** and that's it.

God is notorious in layering His types and shadows to speak forward to the **"restoration of all things" Acts 3:21** which is why Christ is gone, **"whom Heaven must receive until..." v21** You could say binding Angels is **"casting out demons"** and saving the

Old Testament saints is *"performing cures"* in Paradise. The scripture is still open to double meaning. Meaning God purposely stayed longer in the underworld to show us an example of when restoration would be complete.

This then gives us a shadow of the work of the church for her **two days**. For we are the hands and feet of Jesus casting out devils, for we have authority already that will be seen in full soon. A further example would be that when Christ ascended into heaven. Would this not be a type of the rapture? For it is said, *"He led captive a host of captives and gave gifts to men."* **Ephesians 4:8** Of these captives who are they? Are they not the first fruits of saints of Old who upon hearing the Good News received the word. This robbery of the grave will occur again, for the future theft of the grave when God steals from Satan's kingdom of darkness will occur at the rapture.. This *"on the third day I reach My goal"* **Luke 13:31** is so significant because God begins to gather all His kingdom people.

In examining Christ amazing statement, *"and the third day I reach My goal."* We know that Jesus reached many goals by being raised from the dead. However, this is the same argument taken into whether the **70 weeks of Daniel** have been completed. God gives 6 outcomes for the completion of the **70 weeks.** *"to 1. finish transgression, to make an 2. end of sin, to 3. make atonement for iniquity, to 4. bring in everlasting righteousness, to 5. seal up the vision and prophesy and to 6. anoint the most holy."* **Daniel 9:24** Although, Jesus resurrection fulfilled the first three items, it has yet to secure the last three items. How do I know this? Well, for one it did not seal up the vision or prophecy for Jesus will give vision after His resurrection in **the Book of Revelation [circa 95AD]**.

Consider in no time estimation does the **70 weeks of Daniel 9** complete itself at His resurrection or final ascension in **Acts 1**, or Stephen's stoning. Here many stumble over trying to make the 70 weeks continuous without break? How does something **3.5 years** later say in **34AD** fit an event that would finish such a magnificent list as **Daniel 9:24** above? The best anyone came up with is God quit the 70 weeks because of Israel's failure and moved onto the Gentiles. God does not quit and keeps His promises this we know! Sure it's an easy solution to the **70 week** conundrum but an unbiblical one.

Yet many have tried to preach replacement theology, a nullifying of God's purposes and promises yet to be fulfilled for the nation of Israel. Many act like they are already reigning with Christ, already married [as opposed to "being married" a process needing consummation], yet another mistake. This is the stuff for fools and cults, not logical within the pages of scripture, for the deeper we dive into the details of prophecy and understanding the Jewish customs God employed to demonstrate them, we see PROCESS!In Paul's writings we see God's plan working toward both an earthly and heavenly Kingdom united by Christ, not just one or the other. We see God working in different ages toward a culmination. We see God instituting patterns to reveal spiritual truths that point to His grand design.

For the moment though we are all perplexed by this idea, that God would pause the **70 weeks** or that God could do that? I mean there should be some place to at least hint of such a thing. Hello? I have been pointing to it this whole time, it's **Luke 13:31-35**. The only other alternatives are either it has been completed or its been discarded as some say by their view of Law to Grace. All these disharmonious ideas avoid the obvious from the all contexts, Israel had a choice that would affect how the prophecy would be fulfilled! The result of this choice we can see a PAUSE, *"until the time comes"* **Luke 13:35**, *"until they acknowledge their guilt"* **Hosea 5:15** and *"will be cut off and have nothing ...on the wings of abomination will come one"* **Daniel 9:26,27** In all these we can see a break in the action with Israel but then a return to deal with the nation. This is two or three witnesses.

Next we must ask where in the New Testament writings do we see an indication the 70 weeks being fulfilled? We don't! Paul never argues the **70 weeks** were fulfilled or that God had discarded His promises to true Israel. Instead Paul will defend that God hasn't discarded His promise to the physical descendants of Israel saying, *"... the gifts and calling of God are irrevocable"* **Romans 11:29 [cf. 11:1,15].** The context will conclude that God would fix the partial hardening of their nation in the end. **[Cf. Romans 11:26]** What wasn't expected was this 2 day interlude being more than 48 hours! Here we are at the mystery of His bride! There must be a paper trial right for this? There is deep in the prophets speech. Yet no greater held secret is His plan for a Bride. *"This mystery is great; but I am speaking with reference to Christ and the church."* **Ephesians 5:32** Yet this book is showing you that paper trail.

So returning to Jesus saying, I'm reaching my *"teleioo"* my perfection, my completion in mentioning His *"goal"* **Luke 13:35**. We could actually see a double meaning, for Christ referring to himself on the Road to Emmaus says that, *"Christ would suffer and rise again from the dead <u>the third day</u>"* **Luke 24:46** Christ risen reaches a goal of glorification of His human flesh. Yet the *"bigger picture"* cannot be over looked here. Jesus hasn't reached His goal of completing His body, His church, His bride as well. However, we see God is laying down an example in His death and resurrection for His work with His church buried in Him and raised on the third day rapture!

For looking at the revelation of **the 2 day *"cast out demons and perform cures"* [cf. Luke 13:31]**, we see that Christ has declared a truth to His body. *"greater works than these he will do; because I go to the Father." John 5:20* If we are His body, then He cannot be perfect without us and vice versa. This only emphasizes the issue with discarding the hope of the kingdom coming. Excuse me, why wouldn't we long for the completion of this head to body to being whole! I can also harp on this all day, but notice we are to be casting out devils and healing people! The parallel is so real that Christ died and the disciples lost hope as well and since Pentecost the Holy Spirit has been hidden in us much like the burial of Christ for these **2000 years**. There is coming a resurrection of His church just like He was resurrected gloriously!

Notice however what this does to the Passion week. It makes it a parallel to God's plan throughout human history!

The Passion Week
As an example of God's ages

MONDAY Day 1 3970-2970BC	TUESDAY Day 2 2970-1970BC	WEDNESDAY Day 3 1970-970BC	THURSDAY Day 4 970BC-31AD	FRIDAY Day 5 31AD-1031AD	SATURDAY Day 6 1031-2031AD	SUNDAY Day 7 2031-3031AD
						17th Anniversary of
						• Red Sea Deliverance
		Passover Week Nissan 10th-17th				• Noah's Ark resting back
Lamb inspected for blemishes Jesus presents Himself to the temple			4th day of Passover **Lamb killed** Crucifixion	1st day of **Unleavened Bread** Sabbath Takes the keys of death	**Regular Sabbath** Jesus preaches to the Saints	**Feast of First Fruits** Jesus Resurrection 'takes the first fruits to Heaven
Fig Tree cursed *Curse in Garden* Adam dies	Enters Temple 2nd cleansing debates Jewish Law Evening plot to kill Jesus Mt Olivet Discourse *FLOOD*	Last Supper Preparation Day for 2 back to back Sabbath's Covenant Day *Abraham/Moses Joseph to Israel's birth as a nation*	Jesus on trial= *the future prophesies of a Messiah on trial amongst the Jews, prophets killed conc;uded with Jesus actual death*			"third day I reach my goal" Luke 13:32 Christ's resurrection parallel's His 2nd coming & 1000 yr Reign
Sunday Triumphal entry Temple inspected Creation of Man				2 day parallels The ministry Jesus did in the Grave *"perform cures and cast our demons" Luke 13:32 Jesus hid within the church on earth 1st thousand church descends 2nd it rises out*		

As for Daniel's **70 weeks**, Jesus is clear it didn't have to end the way it did saying, *"O Jerusalem, Jerusalem... How often I wanted to gather your children together" Luke 13:34* And again we see this elsewhere,

*"He saw the city and **wept over it**, saying, '**If you had known** in this day, even you, **the things which make for peace!** But now they have been **hidden from your eyes.** For the days will come upon you when your enemies will throw up a barricade against you, ... they will not leave in you one stone upon another, [70AD] because you **did not recognize** the TIME of your visitation.'"*

Luke 19:42-44

For example on the surface, we might see His ministry healing, casting out demons and teaching His followers the Way. However from Caesarea Philippi during the last year of His ministry, we see another side of Christ's world show up. One of prophetic tension over God's grand plan, culminating with, Jesus wept. Repeatedly prophesying His death and resurrection until this grand moment when He says, **"YOUR GOING TO MISS YOUR TIME, YOUR VISITATION!".** So emotional was this back-story, that Jesus **"wept over it".** [Above passage]

While all the people see is a joyous celebration with an expectation of freedom from the Roman empire. Jesus weeps! Why? BECAUSE JESUS KNEW THE BIG PICTURE! He knew why He came to Jerusalem, and He knew it didn't have to be this way, God had ordained **70 weeks** but it would have to be paused. He knew **"the Messiah will be cut off and have nothing"** **Daniel 9:26.** Jesus gives us a clue, **"IF you had known"** but it was **"hidden from your eyes"** and you **"did not recognize"** **Luke 19:42-44.** All these imply they looked for the wrong thing, or failed to look at all, or better yet choose to be blind. Which is exactly what Peter is declaring here in both **2 Peter 3:5,8** a chosen ignorance when he says, **"It escapes their notice".**

The trouble starts with God's ability to conceal prophecy is really good, and the human problem wanting to control outcomes without any inner change. Clouded by agendas, we find ourselves in conflict with God's true desire and agenda. One issue is the Messianic prophesies in the Old Testament for the most part embodied Christ second coming not His first. Most people at that time where looking for a King to deliver them from their earthly troubles, the Romans. A Lamb of God to heal them spiritually wasn't acceptable to their Jewish pride. For God's redemption is a process that has steps starting with admitting our need for Him. For us those steps seem unnecessary at times, but they are unavoidable for true change.

The writing was on the wall from the beginning though. For at the start of Jesus ministry after His wilderness temptations He enters the Jewish synagogue and reads **Isaiah 61:1-2** leaving out the conclusion attached in **verse 2**. One can say the Father knew the end from the beginning, prophetically led Jesus to stop where He did. **Daniel 9's 70 weeks** would be paused. So Jesus leaves out that part that reads, *"the day of vengeance of our God"* **Isaiah 61:2b** which would have fulfilled the last verse of **Daniel 9:27's 70 weeks**. Why? Because it would not happen at that time. Jesus ministry of seven years will be cut in half as **Daniel 9** reveals.

From this verse we see a contrast given of a year versus a day. Consider the ratio of a year to a day is **.0017.** The similarities of the ratio between **2000 years** of favor versus the **1335 days** at the end symbolizing the Day of Vengeance is a remarkable **.0027** differing by **.0008!** This is less than a mere **1/100 percent** difference, or 1 percent of 1 percent. This is a mathematical equivalent not out of the reach for God to use to speak to us. For God created science, music scales and mathematics. Just think about this Jesus came proclaiming the age of grace, the next **2000 years**, *"To proclaim the favorable year of the Lord."* **Isaiah 61:2** This also would mean the Day of the Lord would be the final **1335 days** of Daniel. Ratio's can never be an exact matching science but they can point us in our faith toward amazing discoveries, for God is using the closest similarity to describe two things.

THE SEVENTY WEEKS

"Seventy weeks have been decreed for your people ...to bring in everlasting righteousness, to seal up the vision and prophecy and to anoint the most holy. So you are to know and discern from the issuing of the decree to restore and rebuild Jerusalem until the Messiah ... then after the sixty two weeks [69th week] the Messiah will be cut off and have nothing and the people of the prince who is to come will destroy the city and the sanctuary ... and He will make a firm covenant with many for one week"

Daniel 9:24-26

You have been hearing a lot about this **70 weeks prophecy** because the interpretation of it seems to lay the foundation for explaining all theories out there. What isn't surprising to me is how when I finally got the correct outlook, how that resulted in scriptural harmony with the rest of the bible. So here I am one last time, so we can conquer this mountain of prophecy. First it should be noted Daniel will never live long enough to heed the words above, *'so you are to know and discern" v25* for that is left to us! Second the whole prophecy hasn't been finished and most import the context is concerning *"the Messiah"* not an anti-Christ. Look above, notice the constant reference to *"the Messiah"* and the final item to *"anoint the holy"*.

So as we look again at the Pharisees threat from Herod **[cf. Luke 13:31-35]** and Jesus response that about covers Himself fulfilling Hosea & Daniel's timetables, we see Him saying, *'I got this'*! Giving a clear idea He will be crucified first before the *"today and tomorrow" v33,* we can easily see the **Hosea 6** part, but we might ask where in this discourse is He addressing **Daniel 9's 70 week**? Paying attention to the details, Jesus focuses on what will happen to Israel after His crucifixion as if it shouldn't have gone down this way. Christ concluding that Israel would experience a *"desolate until ...' Luke 13:35* This actually would explain the mystery of **Daniel 9:26**. For God reveals after the Messiah being *"cut off"* that bad times would come. *"The people of the prince who is to come will destroy the city and the sanctuary and its end with a flood; even to the end there will be war; desolations determined"* Daniel 9:26

This is important because the context of **Daniel 9:24-27** is not centered on an Anti-christ but the fulfillment of the Messiah to bring in the six items mentioned for Israel and the City **[cf. v24]**. When it is said, *"who is to come"*, God is connecting this prophecy as an answer to the one before in **chapter 8**. The context there was the Anti-christ spirit that finalizes itself in a man possessed by Satan. However, here we are focused on God sending a "Messiah" or deliverer connecting to conquer that spirit as suggested in the first two prophesies in **Daniel 2:44 & 7:13**. So first we must acknowledge that all the visions of Daniel have individual contexts but are tied together, explaining the last one. God is answering a prayer of concern over the last vision in **Daniel 8**.

This is also future because Jerusalem and its people, the natural descendants of Israel are not under God's rule yet. This is would seem to be the whole objective of the prophecy to be fulfilled by the words, *"decreed for your people and your city." V24* So this is still future! Next we must acknowledge that the Messiah is central to this decree in that His name is mentioned in **v25 & 26**. Even in **v26** the only other pronoun is *"the people of the prince"* not *"the prince of the people"*. So it is a huge mistake to interpret the *"he"* of **v27** to the wrong pronoun. The predicate is explaining a pronoun, then it would be *"they"* for people in **verse 27** but it is a *"he"*. Never has the interpretation of one word so shaped differing views of eschatology. Your eschatological position might just come down to *Grammar.*

Earthly bound religious people look for earthly things, a temple to be rebuilt, an Anti-Christ to recognize and so their Eschatology is driven by these storylines missing what really God driving at here. For when you choose to make the **70 weeks** about *"anointing the most holy"* which is the temple made without hands, Jesus planting His feet in Canaan to resolve the promises to Abraham then yes we are in business! Then yes you will start to see the correct timeline. For this reason, *"He"* **v27** is a stumbling block for many who spend way too much time with the negatives of the end of this age than the victory that is coming.

To attach the *"He"* to the pronoun of the preceding verse **[v26]** there is only two choices ,*"the Messiah"* or *"the people of the prince"* which is accurate description of the Roman armies who went against orders of the General Titus sent by Nero's successor destroying the temple and Jerusalem in the process. That was never the plan of the Commander of the Roman armies. The subject of the previous **verse 26** is Messiah and the whole of the **70 weeks** is concerning the Messiah. So why conclude with the negative and make the Messiah a sidetone at the very end?

Further problems occur by simply reading what is attributed to the *"He"* in **verse 27** alone. It is said that, *"He will make a firm covenant with the many for one week* [7 years]*"* yet in the middle [3.5 years into it] *"he will put a stop to sacrifices"* **v27**. If this is *"putting a stop to"* is the Abomination of Desolation spoken of in the earlier vision **[chapter 8:14]** then the Anti-Christ doesn't make anything firm for a week but for half that time. Linking the wrong predicate to *"He"* only causes us into a huge contradiction within verse itself. Does He make *"firm"* for one week [seven years] or not?

How can this narrative be correct that the Pre-Tribulation crowd has concocted of seven future years of tribulation, if the words themselves in the verse betray you? Which is my point, if the Anti-Christ betrays a covenant made for seven years, it would read differently. Especially since God is speaking. It would say, *"he will make a covenant for one week"* not *"make firm for one week"*. Are we making God a liar who is giving the word. And if I read the Pre-Tribulation Theorist correctly on there narrative, this wouldn't be a seven year Great Tribulation because the beginning half would be a time of peace. So we are in a world of contradictions!

The nonsense is real, whereas the truth is powerful. Jesus on the cross replaced the need for sacrifices, and thus established the covenant with Israel although they rejected Him for **"one week" v27**, and it still awaits them. Why is all this important? Because God doesn't contradict Himself. He is the central story. He is the **"He"** of **v27**. Only He found a way to confuse the wise man from understanding this. By doubling back in **verse 27** to the whole final week of Jesus ministry past and future, after having moving into the final week in **verse 26** with a laundry list of events explaining the pause that will connects us back to the final 3.5 years. The prophecy was meant to be layered.

How do I know I'm right? Because like I told you every vision given **Daniel** builds on the last one. There is now more coming in **chapter 11-12**. In that one God gives only **1290 days** from the Abomination and **1260** of that for Israel **[cf. 12:7]**. God cares nothing about any timing previous to the Abomination, neither does Jesus in **Matthew 24**. Fro God is answering the riddle of this **Daniel 9's 70 week** in **chapter 11-12**.

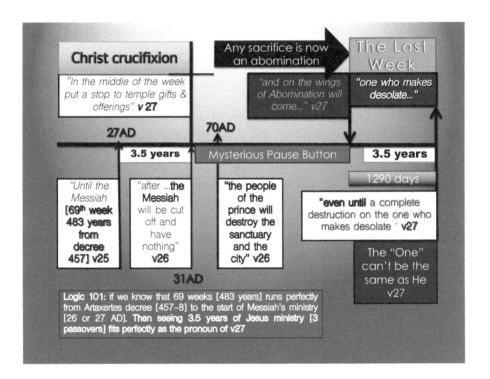

So we see the timetable is affected by attaching the beast or Anti-Christ to a false notion of *a seven year period* in which no other passage declare one involving a tribulation period exist. The upshot of it all is the Anti-Christ would make a promise to Israel that later is broken contradicting the claim of the angel speaking from heaven that it would be *"firm"* for the whole week. We make a mockery of prophecy by forcing upon it our narratives. The timing of the Abomination by this interpretation would fall at the mid-point which is created by this wrong interpretation. Instead we have no clear lead in for the Abomination scripturally.

All of a sudden many are convinced they are waiting on a covenant with Israel to prepare them with enough time to prepare. That lie will hurt many when all of a sudden the Abomination is established worldwide with only days or at most a month approximately to get ready for the rapture. Saying the Anti-Christ *"puts a stop to sacrifice"* **v27** after making a covenant establishing sacrifices which are now an abomination due to Jesus sacrifice is massively off-center. Stopping the sacrifices on a future temple would be in God's will not against it! That is not the Abomination but I don't expect the carnally minded to get it.

Next, **Daniel 11:32-35** describes how many start to understand the timing of the end and declare it to others only after the Abomination occurs in **verse 31**, not before. Yet under the umbrella of this Pre-Tribulation Theorist/Dispensationalist thinking one would know the timing of the end at the making of that covenant. One could say, *'Okay it is seven years of tribulation now'*. So why are people only waking up after the mid-point according to **Daniel 11:32-35**?

Instead another more scarier scenario awaits. No covenant no warning and all of a sudden an army invades Israel walks into the temple mount and declares *'no worship of any god will be allowed worldwide'*. This with only **30 days** until the Beast goes possessed crazy and demands He be worshiped as well, and possibly a shorter period until we the faithful are GONE!

So again, in review how can an Anti-Christ make firm **[gabar = prevail, strengthen, confirm]** a covenant with Israel that he breaks mid point when it says it is strengthened the whole week or seven years? Next how can *"the stop to sacrifice and grain offering"* be the Abomination of Desolation when an event itself would honor God having ceased such practices through the blood of Jesus. Finally, did anyone notice that an even greater evil event is about to occur, *"on the wings of abominations comes one who makes desolate"* **Daniel 9:27** There it is, one who comes is not the *"He"* of the verse and better fits the Anti-Christ, who is attached to the height of Abomination which is replacing Jesus sacrifice.

When Christ Jesus our Messiah is the subject throughout the prophecy all fits. For example of getting the details right, many read, *"From the issuing of a decree to restore...until the*

Messiah" **Daniel 9:25** as reaching to the triumphal entry. Yet notice it says, *"until the Messiah"* **v25** which is when He is anointed Messiah by His Father at His baptism. Are you telling me He wasn't Messiah until He entered Jerusalem the final week. This fudging with pronouns and time has to stop!

If we use the correct initial decree of Artaxerxes in **457BC,** and stay true to time being **365 days** a year *[duh does not God know time correctly]*, we find **69 weeks = 483 years** later ends up being **27AD**, the actual start of Jesus ministry. This stays true to the presentation of the Messiah at John's baptism, when God speaks, *"This is my beloved Son"* **Matthew 3:17** as the coronation of heaven for the Messiah and true to the words *"until the Messiah"* **Daniel 9:25**.

Next we must look at **v26** as an overview, different than the details of the Messiah's ministry for seven years in **verse 27**. Why does God do this? Remember, **v26** includes an event of **70AD** that happens after a continuous **70 week (490 years)** thus God is pointing to a bigger time period occurring until the fulfillment to help those confused later by a pause. This is another way God is concealing and revealing by giving us interludes and overlaps as He does in other places like **Revelation 12**. With that in mind, when it says, *"then after the sixty-two week the Messiah will be cut off and have nothing"* **v26**, the key word is *"after".* Which is not saying Jesus is crucified at the start of that period but *"after"* the **year 483** which **v27** clarifies was **3.5 years** later, if we link *"put a stop to sacrifice ..."* **v27** to Him being *"cut off"* **v26** as both representing His crucifixion.

God is making you piece this all together by understanding what He really did on that cross. Why? He hates the proud, loves the seekers who has spiritual insight, who looks for the right thing. So Jesus ministry is **3.5 years** taking us to **486.5 years** of the **490**. Remember **one week is 7 years**. This leaves **3.5 years** only to prepare Israel for restoration at the end of this age! This takes us into the final verse, where we can match Jesus sacrificial offering of His very life to the words, *"put a stop to sacrifice and grain offering"* **v27**. Did not His blood in the middle of the week put an end to the need for sacrifices on an altar?

The remaining half week then is left and revealed later at the end of **Daniel 12** twice **[v7,11]**. Notice Jesus came preaching the kingdom, affirming to Israel the reality of God's answer to His covenant with them, thus making it firm through His sacrifice. One could make a case for God still waiting for Israel to repent all the way up to Stephen's stoning if in fact that was **3.5 years**. My point is the prophecy was left open to a pause in the future. Notice *"at* *the height of the abomination"* **9:27** gives the idea that time has passed. Even the previous verse seems to be looking out further than **70AD** in, *"it's end will come with a flood" v26*.

The opposing argument would say **the book of Daniel** contains two other references to *"the stop of the daily sacrifices"* both in **Daniel 8:13** by the prominent Horn or **11:31** by the Armies of the King of the North. Yet in both of these texts the contexts is the enemies work not the Messiah's fulfillment. I am telling you, God is actually amazing at concealing truth from the wise by organizing history in patterns to keep people off the scent who don't know how to focus on the context, the grammar and storyline that drives prophecy. Jewish people in **167BC** saw the desecration of their second temple. The appalling thing at that event wasn't a Gentile entering declaring Himself God but Israel Rabbinical Order breaking down into corruption. They allowed it, because they opened the door to it years earlier. This brings up a point.

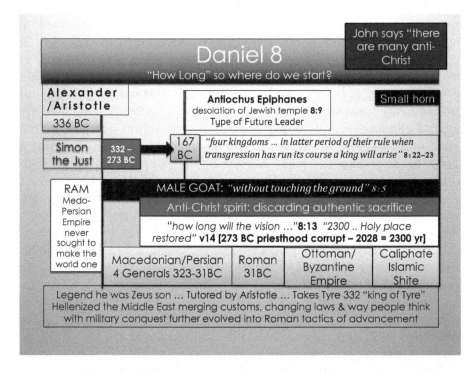

Understanding what is an abomination to God is vitally important in understanding **Daniel**. For example, there is a strong connection between *"the stop (shabath = rest, inactivating, ceasing) of sacrifices"* and what follows in the **Daniel 9:27** the statement *"on the wings of abominations"* which infers something totally separate is occurring. The first causes the second is clear, but the first event stands out separate and comparable to the second. One is good the other an evil attempt to reintroduce those sacrifices. The truth is Jesus death ripped the veil and caused the Sanhedrin building to collapse. God made it clear everything had to stop and eventually it did. However **Daniel 8** gives a clue that the sacrificial system was already corrupt before Christ, as far back as Alexander the Greats influence of Hellenizing the Jewish sacrificial system.

God showing by a temple destruction how it needed to go? Yet remember they had a choice and their acceptance of Christ could have led to the temples destruction by Roman armies sooner. The prophecy would fit either choice, but the temple had to go. Since we know a third temple is prophesied by **Jeremiah** in **7:4**, then we must ask ourselves what God is saying in this prophecy to Israel? For Jeremiah says, *"Do not trust in deceptive words" v4.* What words? *"This is the temple of the Lord"* and he says it three times. A future third attempt will fail like the rest, because Israel is missing what God desires!

Here we see Satan in the final **3.5 years**, pandering to this need of Israel for a temple, *"will come as one who makes desolate"* **v27** riding on *"the heights of"* **v27** signifying the greatest period of replacing God with earthly hope. Satan is trying to preempt Christ Jesus return by establishing Himself as God in some temple in Jerusalem is actually seen in this last verse but it is disguised. For again in **v27**, the pause can be seen in the words *"on the height of Abomination"*. In other words, after the crucifixion any other attempt at another entry point to God will be in effect an Abomination to Him, but how much more when it is Satan who tries to pretend to be Jesus and supply a false hope!

So at the height of those attempts by Israel to have a temple, *"the man of lawlessness is revealed"* **2 Thessalonians 2:3** which is in **Daniel 11**'s vision the context. The Abomination being setup first **[cf. 11:31]** leads to this demonic revelation a few verses later in **Daniel 11:36** as the King now goes *"dark"* as they say. Thus *"on the wings of abomination"* could also mean soon after this Abomination of Desolation by government forces, Satan will arrive and all hell will break loose. However this is not the focus of **Daniel 9**. For the **70 weeks** is not leading us to an EARTHLY TEMPLE but Jesus being crowned as King bringing in Heaven on earth as God's temple not made with hands, ZION!

In the end, earthly Jerusalem will be joined with Heavenly Jerusalem, as the context says, *"for your people and your holy city"* **Daniel 9:24** Notice, it reads for your people and your holy city and NOT your temple! So the prophecy ends with Christ victory over Satan, *"until a complete destruction ...is poured out on the* *one who makes desolate."* **V27** Understand from the crucifixion until Jesus shows up for the final **3.5 years**, we have the existence of an Abomination already as seen in *"on the wings of" v27* Why? **Daniel 8** reveals this spirit of Abomination, the corruption of the HOLY in the tabernacle life of the Jewish priests reaching as far back as Alexander's influence to the present day. No greater application of an offense to God would be His people's rejection of His sacrifice to reestablish the Holy in Himself. By reestablishing an old system that allows Hellenizing influences of other gods still.

For this is the constant testimony of scripture, *"Sacrifices and offerings and whole burnt offerings for sin You have not desired, nor have You taken pleasure in them. Then He said, 'Behold I have come to do Your will.' (Which is?) He takes away the first in order to establish the second."* **Hebrews 10:8-9** So by getting the context central to its theme, *"anointing the holy place" v24*, we find there is no future seven year period of tribulation. Just what Daniel prophesies later, **1290** and **45** more days **[cf. Daniel 12:11-12]** from a future Abomination of Desolation.

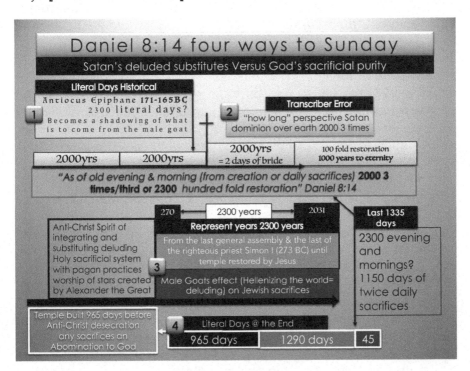

So we see this scheme of dark Spiritual forces using Alexander's influence to dilute the "holy" spanning **2300 years** in the statement, *"In the latter period of their rule, when transgression has run its course a king will rise"* Daniel 8:23.

[see chart last page] Even Jewish historians tell of of how the miraculous events in the sacrificial world stopped during Simeon the Just, around 270 BC. Understand **Daniel 9** is a response to **Daniel 8** vision of the *"holy"* being corrupted. The Messiah Jesus came to reclaim the *"holy"* and bring heaven to earth. As an answer to *"How long ...holy place ...be trampled"* **8:13**

Thus Christ comes a second time to finish His quest to restore the *"holy"* or as **Daniel 9:24** says the objective is to "*anoint the holy"*! This final period of **1335 days** includes those **1260 days** smack in the middle after the **30** and before **45** days where Jesus finally brings heaven to earth and sets up His tabernacle! Only God can give us a prophecy in **Daniel 8:14** that can be fulfilled in four different ways *[again see chart last page]*.

THE DATING

"In the latter days ye shall consider it perfectly."
Jeremiah 23:20

Even though it is a great Idea to date or romance Jesus, what I am talking about here when we say dating Jesus is the importance of finding the right year Jesus died so we can know the year he will return. You might say why not the year He was born? Well, His birth doesn't matter since scripture is clear, the **2 day** (**2000 year**) pause starts from *"go away and return to My place"* Hosea 5:15 and as just discussed the **70 weeks** is paused at a half week before its end at the cross. Even Christ indicates the two days and third day reaching of His goal had to wait until His journey to Jerusalem & the death were done. As we find this attached to the conversation, **"Nevertheless I must journey today tomorrow and the next for it cannot be that a prophet would perish outside of Jerusalem."** **Luke 13:33**

Given the advances in Astronomy, we can come pretty close to the day of the week for each of the possible years Christ may have died. At which point we can then work backwards to the beginning of His ministry to confirm with **Daniel 9's** prophecy. Again this is another reason our generation can decipher what others couldn't. For reasons of astronomy's ability to back date star formations including the moon *[see chart last page]*, we can narrow down the possible years from the time period Pontius Pilate governed in **26-34AD**. Here are the results from NASA.

YEAR	14th of Nissan	New Moon Rule: One +
26	Sunday, April 21st	Saturday - Monday
27	Friday, April 11th	Thursday - Saturday
28	Wednesday, April 28th	Tuesday - Thursday
29	Monday, April 18th	Sunday - Tuesday
30	Friday, April 7th	Thursday - Saturday
31	Wednesday, April 25th	Tuesday - Thursday
32	Monday, April 14th	Sunday - Tuesday
33	Saturday, April 4th	Friday - Saturday
34	Thursday, April 22nd	Wed - Friday

http://www.usno.navy.mil/USNO/astronomical-applications/data-services/
spring-phenom @ judaismvschristianity.com

So we have narrowed down **9** possible years to **six**, based on Jesus dying on either a Thursday or a Friday. Now we must ask did Jesus speak idle words again? NO! For we have a dilemmas to solve between Jesus words stating, *"**The Son of Man must suffer many things ...be killed and be raised up on the third day.**"* **Luke 9:22 [c.f. Matthew 17:23, 20:19]** and these words ...

*"An evil and adulterous generation craves for a sign And yet no sign will be given to it but the sign of Jonah the prophet; For just as Jonah was **three days and three nights** in ... so will the Son of Man be **three days and nights in the heart of the earth**"*
Matthew 12:39-40

You could fairly ask, how can Jesus be two full days in the grave yet be three nights and three days as well? We probably should be asking how do we even get **two days** from the pagan tradition of good Friday. Being that He died at **3pm** during what we know to be **the fourth day of Passover**, many feel it is in order to count the first day as the time when God covered the place with darkness **3-6pm** on **the fourteenth of Nissan**. Putting the body in the tomb right before the next day started was only possible because of how near the tomb of Joseph was in relation to Golgotha. The Jewish day started at Sundown. This is seen in the creation account, night then day **[Genesis 1]**.

However, when we examine both approaches to starting a day as in the Table presented below, we find only one fits an accurate description of what Jesus said if we were to take Him again *"seriously"*. Remember the premise of this book is can we take the bible seriously and find harmony? So God sent a three hour period of darkness as recorded in history over Jerusalem from **3pm - 6pm** from the moment Jesus passed away.

This prevented the Savior from being taken down until 6pm close to sundown and the next Jewish 24 hour period. We know that by the following verse which shows they followed a NIGHT/DAY order we have the following to go by.

Thursday	Friday	Saturday	Sunday	#Day & Nights
3pm died before sunset	Night/Day	Night/Day	Rose before sunrise	Jewish order 3 day/3 night
	3pm day/night	Day/night	Rose early morning	Traditional 2 night/3 days
	3pm day	Night/Day	Night/rose morning day	Jewish/ Trad 2 Night/ 3days

> *"Then the Jews because it was the day of preparation so that the bodies* ***would not remain on the cross on the Sabbath*** *[for that sabbath was a high [mega, grand] day] asked Pilate that their legs might be broken, and that they might be taken away."*   **John 19:31**

This is great indicator that Thursday was **the 14ᵗʰ of Nissan**. Most believe in Good Friday death followed by the regular Sabbath on a Saturday, which we show falls short of the allotted time. If I am splitting hairs I apologize. However because the day after His death would have been a High Sabbath on a Friday, the first day of Unleavened Bread both scenarios would explain why Mary didn't visit the Tomb until Sunday morning.

John differentiates though this Sabbath as one of the yearly ones not regular ones on Saturday with the Hebrew word for *"mega"*. Ask yourself the question why does John need to make it clear this wasn't the regular Sabbath day if in fact the Mega Sabbath fell on the regular Sabbath? All this means is we are now looking for Astronomy results for the years in question to give us a result of Thursday and not Friday to fall on the fourteenth of Nissan, with room of one day for human error since they started their months by deciphering the new moon.

We now have gone from **six** possible to **five**, eliminating **33AD** which is the most popular believe in Christianity today for the timing of His death. **33AD** is a Pre-Tribulation theorist favorite calculation based on further wrong calculations of Daniel's **70 week** prophesy. It also has been driven by the good Friday fallacy making Jesus full of erroneous statements. So far if you are adding this up they are wrong on so many accounts and seem to be responsible for fudging with time like God isn't aware of how long the sun and moon and earth rotate. It's ridiculous. This is coming from people who call themselves *"fundamentalist"* and *'experts'*.

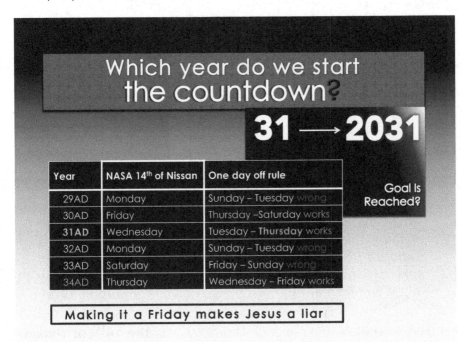

Which year do we start the countdown?

31 ⟶ 2031

Goal Is Reached?

Year	NASA 14th of Nissan	One day off rule
29AD	Monday	Sunday – Tuesday wrong
30AD	Friday	Thursday –Saturday works
31AD	Wednesday	Tuesday – **Thursday** works
32AD	Monday	Sunday – Tuesday wrong
33AD	Saturday	Friday – Sunday wrong
34AD	Thursday	Wednesday – Friday works

Making it a Friday makes Jesus a liar

For example, in calculating the time given in **Daniel 9:25** these same *"scholars"* have chosen to use a **360 day** year calendar to make their calculations work. They justified it by saying it is the Calendar of Babylon or the prophets, etc. Remember God gave the word to Daniel. God is counting the time not Daniel. If God counts time how does He count time? Does God not see the Sun, Stars and the moon accurately? Does He not know how time "flies" so to speak or has a Birdseye view of the planets? Does He not see the earth rotate daily and make its circumference around the sun? God who doesn't fudge words doesn't fudge time!

Never have I seen so much foolishness as to think the earth rotated different from how it does today without it being mentioned or indicated somewhere in scripture or history. In taking a **360 day** year and multiplying it by the **69 weeks** of the **70** which is **483 years**, they come up with **173,880 days**, which is then recalculated down to **476.38** actual years. Breaking the rules of reality for some *"biblical prophetic code"* never legitimized in anything other than this was true during the flood period is breaking God's rules for interpreting scripture. This is very creative effort to keep their narrative alive but some of us live in the real world.

They then use the wrong decree even to make matters worse to make their calculations work! Choosing Nehemiah's confirmation in **444BC** to honor Artaxerxes previous decree to rebuild Jerusalem in **458BC**, they have not chosen the one that initially granted the rebuilding process. Then to top off everything, they have chosen to interpret *"until the Messiah"* **Daniel 9:25** as His triumphal entrance instead of when the Messiah started His ministry, as if He wasn't the Messiah until the final week.

This is so they can have their *'seven year tribulation period'* which works well for the devil's plan to keep everyone asleep, for one would think they will get enough fair warning. Understand on either side untruth's have put people to sleep. For on the Pre-Tribulation Theory side, a false view of the rapture being something *you need not be ready* for, it just happens. To the other Post Tribulation Theory side, where there's this seven years to process that gives fair warning so why prepare or be alert.

More on that later, for now have you noticed by science and Jesus words we have narrowed down the years to **27,28,30,31,34CE** for the crucifixion. Of those years only **31AD** fits **Daniel 9**'s prophesy the best however let's look at some other biblical indicators. Starting with the most notable in Luke's gospel, *"Now in the fifteenth year of the reign of Tiberius Caesar ..."* **3:1** John the baptist has started His ministry **[cf. verse 2]**, and it is assumed Jesus follows in the same year. This would be easy if there wasn't a transition in Tiberius rule. For **two years** before His solo reign which started in **14 AD**, He already took over for his relative predecessor due to failing health as a *"co-princeps"*. So, we have two dates for the start of Jesus ministry adding **15 years** to **12** or **14AD**, giving us either **27AD** or **29AD** for the start of Jesus Ministry.

"Thus, according to Suetonius, these ceremonies and the declaration of his "co-princeps" took place in the year 12 AD, after Tiberius' return from Germania. "But he was at once recalled, and finding Augustus in his last illness but still alive, he spent an entire day with him in private." Augustus died in AD 14, a month before his 76th birthday" [https://en.wikipedia.org/wiki/Tiberius]

The question to ask here is what would have Luke a physician and detailed oriented man considered for the start of Tiberius's reign? The Gospel of John gives us three passovers **[Jn 2:13,6:4,11:55]** which Jesus attends including the one He dies on, and this is our very best clue as to the length of His ministry. There is no indication whether two of those passovers were the same one repeated. Maybe now you can see how **27** can end up at **30, 31 or 32 AD** and the **29** start scenario can end up at **33 or 34 AD**.

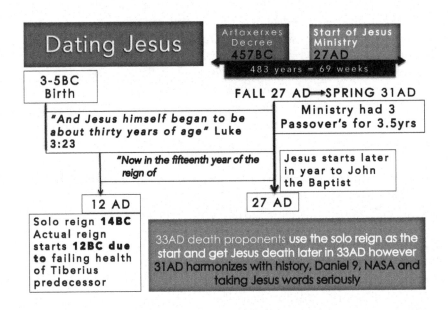

The last of the indicators is Luke's apparent guess at how old Jesus was. ***"And Jesus himself began to be about thirty years of age" Luke 3:23***. Luke a very detailed man would not have said, ***"about"***, if He knew exactly. So I am not sure this helps us at all, except one would think Luke had some indication that Jesus was close to that age to say, ***"about"*** and not the other option of *'we don't know at all'* or *'around His mid-thirties'*. Since new evidence has Herod's death further out to **4BC**, this presents a problem for those who are proponents of a ministry starting later in **29AD** instead of **27AD** which would have made him more like **33** than **30** at the start. You can see where all this is going. Remember again Luke is a doctor and very detailed, as seen in His gospel & Acts.

Next Paul's conversion is calculated backwards from dates given in **the Book of Acts**, landing around **34AD**, presenting a problem obviously for the **33AD** crowd in that this is too condensed, a virtual impossibility for year to occur from the crucifixion to Paul. Jesus dies then Pentecost then immediately Paul? This shrinks events into a narrow margin to have Paul converted so quickly even for the **33AD** proponents. What we are seeing is our years shrinking into only one possibility that actually fits everything, the year **31AD**. Remember, we already did the statistical averages for all the calculations for the Fourth Millennium start based on the Masoretic Texts and came up with the year **3969.2** for the start of Human History. That would be **31.8AD** equaling **4000** and of course within the year **31AD**!

THE HIERARCHY

*"From now on I am **telling you before it comes to pass**, so that **when it does occur, YOU MAY BELIEVE that I am He**."*
John 13:19

Understand even if we get this pinpointing thing off a bit we are still talking about completing everything by **2037** as a confirming witness. For one can fit the **3.5 years** in and still be good if any of these years **2029-2033** were correct for His return. The beautiful thing is we are seeing everything harmonize now. By taking every word Jesus spoke seriously. By respecting history, astronomy and contexts which words are written.

So why are we so sure Jesus is returning a little over a decade from now in **2031**? Because this court case is solid! Yet no one I have seen is talking about this from the angle I have just presented! Why be surprised that this is coming from Jesus own lips, because if anyone was going to indicate when He was going to return it was Jesus Himself! HE IS THE SOURCE, HE IS CENTRAL TO ALL THIS, AND HE IS THE HIERARCHY OF TESTIMONY! Notice Jesus is not giving us a *"day or hour"* but the years and season of His return!

Of course Israel as a nation didn't mature or ***"branched out or pushed forward"*** until **1967** at which time you add **70** years to make a generation passing equaling **2037**. We now have the furthest point of **2037** for everything having to wrapped up. Minus the **3.5 years** of Daniel's count in **Daniel 12:10-11 & Daniel 9:27** and you are finding yourself in **2033** as the latest time for His return.

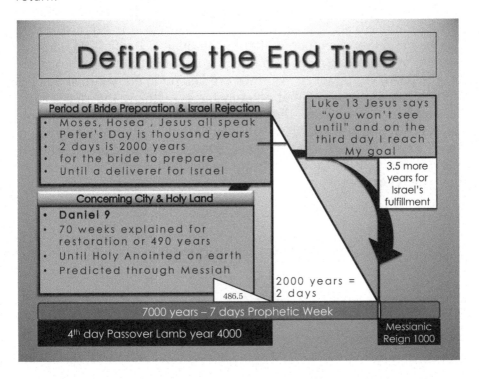

Defining the End Time

Period of Bride Preparation & Israel Rejection
- Moses, Hosea , Jesus all speak
- Peter's Day is thousand years
- 2 days is 2000 years
- for the bride to prepare
- Until a deliverer for Israel

Luke 13 Jesus says "you won't see until" and on the third day I reach My goal

3.5 more years for Israel's fulfillment

Concerning City & Holy Land
- **Daniel 9**
- 70 weeks explained for restoration or 490 years
- Until Holy Anointed on earth
- Predicted through Messiah

486.5

2000 years = 2 days

7000 years – 7 days Prophetic Week

4th day Passover Lamb year 4000

Messianic Reign 1000

AWAKENING GLORY

The Mysterious Days of the King

3 VOLUME

CJ Michaels

"You are not in darkness that the day should overtake you like a thief." 1 Thessalonians 5:4

7

Preparing:
Maturing the Harvest

THE "ALL"

*"**God is not slow** as some count slowness, **but is patient** toward you, not wishing for any to perish but **for all to come** to repentance..."*

2 Peter 3:9

Making the transition from **verse 8 to 9,** Peter shows us a vivid contrast from, ***"One fact not to escape your notice"* v8**, to the salvation of the ***"all"***. Moving us from a mathematical equation key to unlocking God's fixed order to the ages & completion of this one; to the other half of that equation that drives the timetable; souls saved! For honestly, this is not just about the fixed ages that count the quarters of the ballgame of human history or even the x's and o's drawn up before the game of life started from His Sovereign perspective, but His amazing value He places on us who believe and the patience to complete that task of delivering us from this present world. Peter exclaiming to best a few verses later, ***"regard the patience of our Lord salvation"* 2 Peter 3:15**

This verse is an admission that many are only counting time when they should be more concerned with their own finish line, their soul and that of others. As the song declares, *"I want to be in that number when the saints go marching in ..."* For included in everything I have been showing you to indicate God's masterful perfection and ability to manage time is God's Sovereign ability to save us to the uttermost or within the construct of that time. For not only does He manage time, He manages the free & often stubborn wills of men and women in coming to Him within that time. To this end, we appeal to you the reader not just to know His timely return but to use that awareness of His perfection with time to change your thinking into confidence, heart into passion and your focus to rewards of winning souls to this message of a timely and good God.

The grand mistake would be to interpret this verse **[above 2 Peter 3:9]** as saying God is waiting on us. I must remind you what Jesus said, *"If these become silent* [lose their confession of faith] *the stones will cry out* [others will be saved in their place]*!"* **Luke 19:40** The question is not going to be whether God is waiting on any but whether you choose to be one of those chosen *"all"* that He speaks of here. For though *"God so loved the world"* **John 3:16**, *"the all"* **2 Peter 3:9** He speaks of above here isn't the world He died for but His chosen *"all"* that respond to that offer. For He knows those who are His. God doesn't need to know, we do. We need to be convinced which is FAITH!

So in response to *"the Lord knows those who are His"* **2 Timothy 2:19**, we are then encouraged to prove it! *"Abstain from wickedness"* **[same verse]**. For everything in scripture repeatedly points back to defining the true salvation by its byproduct, I.e., a seed sown in good soil will grow stronger and bear much fruit. The mistake we make is misinterpreting God's choosing, which is based on His foreknowledge of the finished product, as accomplished by human effort or some entitlement achieved by a single action in time.

The issue is never anything but whether we pass the test of the early church who said, *"He made no distinction between us and them, cleansing their hearts by faith"* **Acts 15:9**. Just as the key is in the following verse, *"For by one offering He has perfected for all time those who are sanctified"* **Hebrews 10:14** The action in both verse is ongoing, the cleansing and sanctifying work is progressive by the tenses of the greek verbs. Sure it's by faith and not works **[cf. Acts 15:9]**, sure we are guaranteed the end result **[cf. Hebrews 10:14]**, BUT as long as we are in *process with Him*. As long as we abide, stay in Him.

John by defining for us *"unrighteousness is sin"* **1 John 5;17**, shows us how God looks at this. It's not the actions as it is the position of our hearts from which those actions come. We look at actions and attempt to form a resume to be approved by Him, *"Lord, Lord, did we not ..."* **Matthew 7:22**, however Jesus says a verse earlier these religious boasters aren't in line with His will saying, **"But he who does the will of My Father."** **V21** What is His will? In short Paul says, *"for this is the will of God your sanctification; ..."* **1 Thessalonians 4:3**

Maybe this is why the scriptures will declare *"lawlessness"* **2**

Thessalonians 2:7 a mystery since it can hide in white washed tombs, the unregenerate. As well the word speaks of *"godliness"* **1 Timothy 3:16** as a great mystery. Why? Because a struggling addict can enter heaven by faith quicker than someone with who takes pride in their high morals. The bible revealing that *"the heart is more deceitful than all else and desperately sick who can understand it?"* **Jeremiah 17:9** and only another *"the mystery of faith"* **1 TIMOTHY 3:9** in His sacrifice can CORRECT THIS REBELLION!

Maybe no scripture assures us how powerful placing our faith in Him not *"good things"* is when **Hebrews 7:25** says of His Sovereign ability to save us to the *"uttermost"* if we *"draw near through Him"*. The greek tense for *"draw near"* is in the continuous. Also notice it is through Him, His sacrifice and not of our own effort! Just because one is convinced it is not based on their works, does this mean they do nothing? No, the contrary, all the more we run to Him. All the more we do works worthy of repentance.

Of those who don't faithfully seek Him as their source their entire life, Jesus says, *"Every branch in Me that does not bear fruit, He takes away"* **John 15:2** No one can manipulate the salvation process, which is simply *"do not be deceived God is not mocked; for whatever a man sows, this he will also reap."* **Galatians 6:7** God is not talking about sowing actions to be approved by Him, but sowing seeds of reliance upon Him! In any case, you want to be sure you are apart of this *"ALL"*, he speaks of.

THE SOVEREIGNTY

*"**Everyone** whose name has **not** been written **from the foundation of the world** in the book of life of the Lamb."*
Revelation 13:8

However to my point, we see God tracking souls both on the inside and outs of His Kingdom when we read the above verse. The logic is clear. If God knew everyone who isn't in the Book of Life, then He knows everyone who is before time. When did God know who was not going to be saved? It was from before creation, *"from the foundation of the world"*! This means God at least saw everything before it started. He is now just waiting for the last souls to come in. In Jewish Lore, they believed there was a bowl in heaven full of every living soul when the last soul to be eternally saved (chosen) entered the world the end came.

Of course this idea doesn't originate from the scriptures but the idea of God tracking souls is deep in Jewish tradition & His word! Without an understanding and conviction from scripture defining God's action as coming from foreknowledge, we are left with very darkened understanding of a God who Himself is in the dark as to what will happen next! Some will take the middle ground and say He knows but chooses to wait on us! Or He doesn't know but can fix the chaos at anytime? The hard work versus fate argument, which often times underestimates the marriage of our proper response to God's ability to keep.

Peter doesn't keep quiet about this in His second letter *"The Lord knows how to rescue the godly from temptation, and to keep the unrighteous under punishment for the day of judgment"* **2 Peter 2:9**. This partnership of faith in His chosen destiny for us continually cleanses our hearts as we partner even when we are struggling or sinning. This relationship keeps ruling the day. A life of always seeing ourselves as the will of God on earth, instead of trying to find it in some place, person or purpose.

Peter is not vague, God isn't slow, isn't wondering, isn't sleeping neither is He delaying! *"For He is coming will come and will not delay."* **Hebrews 10:37** and *"vision for the appointed time ...it will not delay."* **Habakkuk 2:3** For He has *"fixed a day in which He will judge"* **Acts 17:31** and again *"time and epochs"* are *"fixed"* **Acts 1:7.** So true salvation likewise is not God waiting on us, but us finding His timing and responding appropriately as the prophet so elegantly says, *"Seek the Lord while he may be found; call upon Him while He is near."* **Isaiah 55:6**

Why? Because He can raise up another! Of this backwards mentality of waking God up, we see the single most intrusive element to revival today! How arrogant our movements have become to sink to this level. We weigh that if God seems to be uninvolved in our day, then why should I engage Him. I'll just take what He's offering like a buffet table and live out my own destiny! Why would He care, He isn't paying attention. For if He was bad stuff wouldn't be happening.

The scripture is clear, *"He who keeps Israel will neither slumber sleeps nor sleep."* **Psalms 121:4** No clearer do we see God working but right before the end of this age! *"Before the Great and awesome day of the Lord comes. And it will come about that whoever calls on the name of the Lord will be delivered ..."* **Joel 2:32** This great truth points us to maybe the greatest revivals ever is in NOW, at a time when majority are sleeping! All because God is merciful to reveal signs to herald His arrival is coming soon. Those who this mantra, "He is coming" is getting old will be replaced by those hungry! **[Cf. Matthew 22:1-14]**

Just to review, Peter who uses this concept of *"all"* here, is consistent in both of his letters with using the idea of God's chosen through foreknowledge. Starting with the introduction of his first letter, *"chosen according to the foreknowledge of God"* **1 Peter 1:1-2;** *"inheritance reserved in heaven"* **v4** ; *"For the eyes of the Lord are toward the righteous"* **3:12**; *"God of all grace who called you into His eternal glory in Christ will Himself perfect ... you"* **5:10**; and in his second letter, *"all more diligent to make certain about His calling and choosing you... You will never stumble"* **2 Peter 1:10**;

So we see this strong dynamic taught by Peter of God's given ability to *"rescue the godly"* or as the King James translates, *"kept by the power...through faith unto salvation revealed in the last time."* **1 Peter 1:5** When are we revealed with Him **[cf. Colossians 3:4]** but on that final period or day, the seventh day or 1000 year reign of Christ, just as Jesus said in **John 6:40**.

Peter supporting Paul's teaching in fact on this subject of the salvation of the chosen *"all"* says, *"Paul ....wrote ...speaking ...of these things in which are some things hard to understand"* **2 Peter 3:16** To this I agree, for we see that in **Romans 11**. For this subject of God gathering (harvesting) and forming His kingdom both the remnant of Israel (Jacob & 12 tribes) and Abraham's children of faith (Isaac: His Bride) making the two one is compelling and confusing at times yet so central the very gospel message! For we read *"He is our peace who has made both one and broke down the barrier of the dividing wall."* **Ephesians 2:14** Should we not expect Christ Kingdom to reflect this truth in the end!

So Paul using strong language suggests a completion of a designated amount says, *"until the fulness of the Gentiles has come in ...all Israel will be saved."* **Romans 11:25-26** This word *"fulness"* gives the idea of a final number that fills up an allotment. Paul borrowing the term from Jesus who said Jerusalem would be trampled under foot by the Gentiles until *"the times of the Gentiles are fulfilled"* **Luke 21:24** So both a number of souls followed by a time for judgment is specified, not sure anyone knows for sure how that works with God's foreknowledge but we are told it does. For instance, does God have a set number to grant salvation to or is it just He knows how many He was able to save in that time frame and that became the set number. For Paul gives a strange statement, *"branches were broken off so that I might be grafted in."* **11:21** We might from this statement assume God has a firm count of the final number, the *"all"*. We might fear God who can change the destiny of one for another. So again I reply, don't let another rock cry out for you!

So these are the two measuring sticks, time & souls, that bring us to the conclusion of this age. It can be likened to a designed amount of time for certain amount of souls to be saved under God's workmanship. I say that with confidence for Paul says earlier. *"Though the number of the sons of Israel be like the sand of the sea, it is a remnant that will be saved ..."* **Romans 9:27** The truth Paul develops from **Romans 9-11** is that God is making *"no distinction between Jews and Gentiles"* **10:12** regarding salvation, by grafting us all together into one *"olive tree"* **Romans 11:24** in this age.

However, God does make distinctions in other ways according to origin and purpose saying, they are the *"natural branch"* **11:21** and making mention of them having a separate plan later saying, *"partial hardening has happened to Israel until ..."* **v25** Until what? Until this age concludes and the next starts! So in this context of God counting Israelites saved says of that new age, *"But a third will be left in it and I will bring the third part through the fire"* **Zechariah 13:8** The prophets called this a *"surviving remnant"* [**2 Kings 19:30, Is 37:31]** and Joel linking these survivors with us into one Kingdom both heavenly and earthly still makes distinction as other prophets did saying, *"for on Mount Zion and in Jerusalem there will be those who escape ..."* **Joel 2:32** Two ages colliding into one Kingdom, thus possibly two olive trees of **Revelation 11,** your two witnesses.

Notice the order has only two companies the Heavenly Bride Jew & Gentile first and then an earthly Israel bride protected in the next age. Both are apart of what Paul reveals a bigger plan *"making the two into one new man"* **Ephesians 2:15**. Even though we are linked together in the same breath of prophecy there remains a *"distinction"* not based on salvation and kingdom but based on promise, purpose and role. For example we read, *"... but on Mount Zion [Heavenly Kingdom Hebrews 12:18-22] there will be those who escape [rapture] and it will be holy AND the house of Jacob [not Abraham or Isaac but God's promise to Israel (Jacob)] will possess their possessions then the house of Jacob will be a fire..."* **Obadiah 1:17**

So we see by this we have two promises fulfilled but ONE KINGDOM coming. Zion the promised sons of Isaac birthing Jacob the earthly portion of His kingdom, an eventual marriage of heaven with earth with Jesus ruling over all. Just to clarify the reference to *"Mount Zion"* we only need to read **Hebrews 12:23** to settle its role as *"the general assembly and the church of the firstborn [Jesus]* *who are **enrolled** in heaven... to spirits of righteous made perfect."* This is Heavenly Jerusalem! Even the idea of enrollment here is a way of God tracking a count of the all. So we see Heavenly Jerusalem exemplified in the covenant made when Isaac was supposed to be killed but God instead made covenant with Himself with Abraham laying on the altar asleep (in rest).

Next, the connection of the Book of Life to the final harvest is key. Since it contains all the names of the chosen. Central to the drama of **the book of Revelation** is the opening of it, *"who is worthy to open the book and to break its seals."* **Revelation 5:2** Well Jesus was worthy at His resurrection which may very well be the first seal. Again we have the divide of those seeing an Anti-Christ under every tree, as the first seal fulfillment. This relegates everyone in a waiting posture for where's Waldo.

What if instead the seven seals are seven wonders God accomplishes to bring Israel back into the land and establish the souls for the Kingdom above. The resurrection would start us off as the first seal until we come to the holocaust when a fourth of the Jews were killed. Why is this a seal? It opened the doors for Israel to be granted a return to her homeland. It follows the storyline of how God brought Israel back. What I am suggesting here is; often God performs double fulfillments of prophecy in order to conceal it.

Although we might be seeing the Corona Virus today as another fulfillment of the fourth seal just as the days of the Black Plague brought about a fourth of the world to die, we might want to stop looking for signs to line up and listen to this author tell you what more reliable; God's timetable! For when men are waiting for the seals fulfillment maybe we will be shocked at a sudden end! In looking for events future, we might have missed them in the past being fulfilled in the storyline of God's plan to bring His Kingdom together in Canaan!

Even the idea of *"birth pangs"* **Matthew 24:8** and the story of the women in **Revelation 12** is in synch with Isaiah's prophecies, reveal this begetting of Isaac to Jacob. The nature of the end time is one of a building jealous love for His sons and daughters to be born and revealed! From *"daughter of Zion like a women in travail"* **Micah 4:10** and **Isaiah** that declares, *"as soon as Zion travailed she brought forth her sons"* saying, *"Can a nation be brought forth all at once?"* **Isaiah 66:8** Remember, we already know when everyone written in the book will be delivered, during the time of the end. *'Everyone who is found **in the book**, will be rescued"* **Daniel 12:1 [cf. Daniel 12:7 *3.5 years*]** Again this suggests a number fixed. When will this birthing occur but at the travail of the church in the fifth seal **[cf. Revelation 6:9 and 8:1-4]** going into the rapture which has already occurred by the sixth seal **[see chapter 8 why]**. So everything future, the whole storyline of the judgments concerns birthing His promised kingdom through revealing His sons and daughters!

So this should be taken seriously how we see the church heading toward the end of the age. **Malachi 3:16-18** suggesting a crisis will occur for what is true righteousness, gives us an oracle of what it will be like right before the coming of Jesus as seen in **Malachi 4:1's** *"day is coming burning like a furnace"* reference. A revival fire separating out the imposters, for the prophet explains, *"you will again distinguish between the righteous and the wicked"* **v18** Clearing the way for God's redemption & revealing. In order to do this God is sending both a strong delusion **[cf. 2 Thessalonians 2:11]** and as the King James interprets **Isaiah 59:19** a raising of the standard! *"when the enemy comes in like a flood, the Spirit of the Lord shall lift up a standard against him."*

The standard is a wall or boundary like a dam, or a wall of fire of passion from a generation catching the ever increasing outpouring of the Spirit! No more fence sitting, the winds will blow people one way or the other. I believe in God's protection & demonstration of His power starts way before the rapture for His own, in our display of courage and faith!

THE OUTPOURING

> *"Be patient brethren **until the coming** of the Lord. The **farmer waits for** the precious produce of the soil … until it gets the early and **the latter rains**."*
>
> **James 5:7**

You have heard me say that God isn't waiting on us. However, here we see God is waiting on something else, *"the latter rains"*! For Jesus explains it this way saying, *"let them both to grow together until the harvest."* **Matthew 13:30** The idea here James gives is of a farmer who is governed by the seasons, and the best time to harvest. We find more here to suggest God governing time than subject to it.

As mentioned in the second chapter of this book, Peter wasn't the only disciple to find the need to finally explain the apparent *"delay"* in their estimations of His return. For the Apostle James is seen here above encouraging the saints that their delayed expectations could be explained by the need for the *"latter rain"* to prepare the harvest. Peter aware of the effect these estimations had on others writes, *"God is not slow as some count slowness ...regard the patience of our Lord salvation"* **2 Peter 3:9**.

Even with their persistent wrong estimation of the end, the disciples knew with God there was never a delay but a beautiful order to His timing. There's a reason to it, for although God isn't waiting on us, He is waiting for the harvest to be ripe! Here, James says the same thing, the *"rains"* must nurture our yields so be like a farmer and chill!

James, like Peter & Paul, gives a precursor to explain the delay, *"the latter rains"* as seen above. They understood well that, half of the equation was the salvation of the *"all"* **2 Peter 3:9**, while the other half was God's Sovereignty to bring it forth on schedule. Just like the Jewish harvest season had stages to its completion marked out by key feast to celebrate those stages, so God was patiently going to have His way on the earth through a process of preparing the harvest and reaping it the appointed time as revealed in scripture.

In all their estimations however, they couldn't see as we do today. For here James says there must be first *"the early ... rains"* **James 5:7** as well as the *"latter"*! We see this in the way the Spirit was outpoured on the Early church giving them such an evangelistic thrust and success even in the face of persecutions to bring in an early harvest of souls and thrusting the Gospel into all the known world at that time. The early church was assisted by the Roman roads whereas this generation has a much greater tool of spreading the outpouring live on the internet and mass media to the entire world. Our generation can now sense what the early church couldn't since they were at a disadvantage in viewing only the start of this process. Today we are looking down the barrel of what is the greatest most polarizing periods of human history globally. The wheat and tares are becoming distinct.

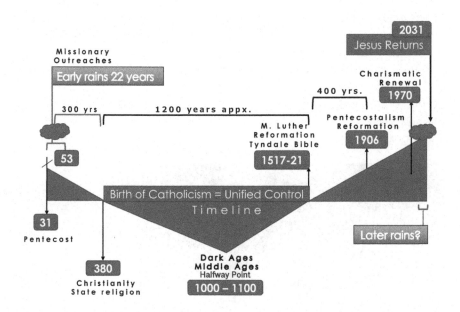

It would have been impossible to understand the concepts here for the early church since they were involved in the early rain itself. They couldn't see how the rains would eventually dissipate. As we study history, we see from our unique perspective a straight correlation of the rains dissipating due to a church no longer under persecution trying to reestablish their hopes in the ecclesiastical order and it's influence on the earth instead of a coming Lord. This abandonment of expectations of His kingdom coming to trying to establish it on earth is the key to understanding how the rains of the Spirit's outpouring diminished and how we will see it return again.

For when this trend reverses there will be a sudden wake up call for the church to evangelize and draw near to Him, I believe it is happening NOW. Movements & ecclesiastical orders and influence will pale in comparison to a desperate abandonment to prepare the way for the King's coming. May this book contribute to that wake up call! So as many will sense His return, many will not. It's always interesting to consider what will happen leading up to Christ return given the extreme views both with negative and positive Eschatological views.

Yet when we look at how God has moved His church out of the dark ages and into this place we stand today, we cannot ignore His ability to act mightily on this earth through His Spirit. Could God not be pushing forward toward one last great awakening? Regardless of what God's move ends up looking like, the bible is clear there will also be a great falling away!

For the dichotomy is most intriguing actually biblically. For on one end we have natural families betraying one another **[cf. Mark 13:12]** and yet God says, *"I am going to send you Elijah the prophet before the coming of the great and terrible day of the Lord. He will restore the hearts of the fathers to children and the hearts of the children to their fathers"* **Malachi 4:6** On one end there is *"an apostasy"* **2 Thessalonians 2:3** prophesied, which is a massive scale falling away from the faith by organized "Christianity" and on the other hand a *"latter rain"* **James 5:7** occurs suggesting the Spirit being poured out in the greatest measure before the end. Jesus gives a parable for this very thing declaring, *"a king who gave a wedding feast for His son* [bride of Christ, faithful]. *... sent out his slaves to call those who had been invited"* **Matthew 22:2-3** As the story goes they refused so the King went and invited those who knew nothing of the wedding to begin with and they came! Many rightfully explain this as an example of God pausing the Jewish hope and reaching out to the Gentiles for salvation. However I find this true of the days of the end. God will raise up stones if He has to.

So the question we must ask is what does the later rain accomplish, what will it look like? Rain is the stimulus and medium by which the nutrients in the soil are drawn into the root system of the produce. The spiritual equivalent is the Holy Spirit. Are the rains that come with storms of persecution meant to mature the wheat so it's ready for harvest? Yes! Jesus called this wheat the *"sons of the kingdom"* **Matthew 13:39**. These two elements cause a maturity amongst true believer's which causes the wheat to be identifiable from the tares. It happened in the early church as James makes mention to *"the early rain"* and it will happen before the end. Frankly that is NOW! This distinction between the wheat and the tares is necessary before harvesting begins. It's this distinction between the two sides that is noticeable in prophecy before the end! An apostate "church" and church on fire will co-exist on earth but be violently separated right before the end.

This maturing of the Harvest is the key in the timing of the end. Notice Jesus words that everyone on earth will have heard the gospel **[cf. Matthew 24:14]** and made up their minds to such a degree as to leave no one on the fence. This literally brings the end! It is in these polarizing times that we see God setting up His harvest. The prophet **Malachi** saw this when he said, *"those who feared the Lord spoke to one another and the Lord gave attention... and a Book of Remembrance was written before Him for those... so you will again distinguish between the righteous and the wicked..."* **Malachi 3:16-18**

Here we see *"a book"* recording and keeping track of the number, which is the *"all"* **2 Peter 3:9** Jesus tells us as well this will happen before the end, explaining *"the wheat sprouted and bore grain THEN the tares became evident also."* **Matthew 13:26** that both will *"grow together until the harvest"* **13:30** or become locked into their respective destinies as the prophet **Malachi** shows happens right before the end. **[Cf. Malachi 4:1]**

Joel our source for the term *"latter rain"* **Joel 2:23** seems to separate Israel's outpouring from our own. Using two distinctive terms *"on Mount Zion"* and *"in Jerusalem"* as Isaiah does as well, he speaks of separately what is accomplished in the world from what he is doing in the land of Canaan. Saying before the Day of the Lord he would, *"pour out My Spirit in those days"* **2:29** and *"on all mankind"* **v28** then shifts specifically in **chapter 3** *"to restore (ing) the fortunes of Judah and Jerusalem ... at that time"* **3:1** when He *"gathers all nations ...into judgment"* **3:2** which is at the end of the Day of the Lord.

My point is the churches later rain is coming before Israel's latter rain prophesied in **Joel 2,** one then the other. **Hosea** is the clearest as to when this occurs for the natural branch of Israel saying, *"His going forth is as certain as the dawn; He shall come unto us as the rain, as the latter rain..."* **6:3** Revealing when Jesus comes for us at the beginning of the Harvest after the 2 days or 2000 years. *"Harvest is appointed to you when I restore your fortunes of My people"* **Hosea 6:11**. I believe this seen in Jewish festivals celebrating the Barley, Wheat and finally Fruit harvest periods.

Paul describing it this way saying, *"until the fulness of the Gentiles has come in and so all Israel will be saved"* **Romans 11:26** One harvest then the other occurs, everything having order. Notice, Israel's awakening is during the fruit harvest after the general harvest of the wheat while its being gleaned.

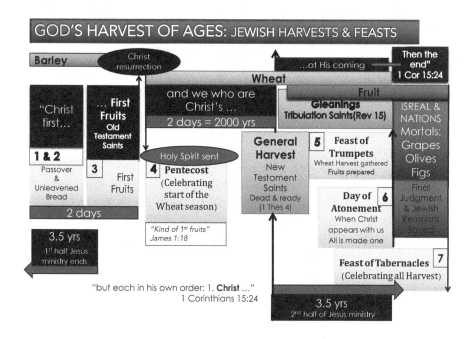

This suggests that, *"in this manner"* *"all Israel will be saved"* takes on deeper meaning of how this occurs, by our entrance or acceptance above the earth at the end. As one age concludes suddenly, another erupts suddenly. For how else will Paul's words make any sense since the context was a *"partial hardening had occurred"* with the natural branch only to be resolved after the Gentiles *"come in"* which is the rapture of the faithful. This causing a revival in Israel, we are talking about a remnant born again sealed by God and the only survivors in Jerusalem when all is said and done.

THE DUALITY

*"And it will come about that whoever calls on the name of the Lord **will be delivered** [raptured]... **the survivors whom the Lord calls** [at the end of His Day]."*

Joel 2:32

*"partial hardening has happened to Israel **until the fulness of the Gentiles comes in** [at the rapture]; And so (in this manner) **all Israel will be saved**; Just as it is written, 'The Deliverer will **come from Zion** [Heavenly Jerusalem above earth], He will **remove ungodliness from Jacob**."*

Romans 11:25-26

So key in comprehending the mysteries of the Day of the Lord [next two chapters topic] found in John's vision, **the Revelation of Jesus Christ**, is this storyline of God's promise to Abraham. One that He would be *"father of a multitude of nations"* **Genesis 17:6** and two *"I will give to you and to your descendants after you, the land of your sojourning, all the land of Canaan."* **v8** The question then is are we not seeing how both of these promises will be fulfilled and played out in this time of the harvest/Day of the Lord/Trumpet period with these two companies mentioned; the *"144,000"* **Revelation 7:1-7** of each tribe of Israel and *"the great multitude"* **Revelation 7:10-14** of every nation? Or are there two companies representing a separation in His Kingdom between the Bride from the rest of the attendants of heaven?

Paul links **Isaiah 59** as the conclusion of his discussion to **Romans 9-11** on whether God is still fulfilling His promise to Abraham/Isaac and Jacob that included the Gentile nations being grafted in. However notice the conclusion returns to the natural descendants who will finally inherit Canaan. In so doing one thing is clear, this is a new covenant thing start to finish! The prophet Isaiah tying this work of the Redeemer starting with Zion, *"A redeemer will come to Zion, ..."* **59:20** and concluding with the natural branch *"and to those who turn from transgression in Jacob"* **v20** agreeing with Joel's order & Paul's of a subsequent coming *"from Zion"* **Romans 11:26 & Joel 3:16**. Of this conclusion, Isaiah declares in the next verse of his chronology, *"this is My covenant with them ...My Spirit which is upon you ..."* **v21**. This leads me towards both being symbolically being bridal and made into one new man.

So in any discussion of God's plan moving from this age to the next, the covenant of a new heart remains the same start to finish. I do not want you to mistaken my faith as some Dispensational mumbo-jumbo, where God finished with grace and returns to some form of law for righteousness. God never saw the Law as a means toward righteousness. From Abel to the end, faith through the proper sacrifice has been the means of being right with God. However as we have mentioned God is fulfilling two different promises one to the Isaacs, the sons of promise and two to the Jacob's who are physical descendants, yet both must be *"born again"*!

Make no mistake about this, we are raptured in **Isaiah 59:19** which is a parallel to the **Matthew 24:27** event when Jesus comes with Zion mentioned in the next verse **Isaiah 59:20** which is also harmonious with **Hebrews 12:22-25** before the shaking of the day of the Lord **[cf. Hebrews 12:26-28]**. So Paul will explain this deep mystery in the prophetic picture of how the fulfillment of the one promise springboards the next fulfillment saying, they *"come in"* and *"so"* or in this manner *"all Israel is saved."* **Romans 11:25** Isaiah being crystal clear that the end of everything will be *"in the Lord ALL the offspring of Israel will be justified and will glory"* **45:25**, which in the context is the time that every knee bows at the end of the Day of the Lord **v23**. Neither is Paul unclear here in **Romans 11**, for he is differentiating in his speech the role of the Gentiles and the Jewish believer's along with how they are linked together.

In showing how they are connected, God seems to be using the one to influence the outcome of the other. When the Gentiles are raptured this will bring the end to a partial hardening with Israel. How? Paul gives us how. *"He will remove ungodliness from Jacob"* **Romans 11:26** Think about this, does the last gentile salvation bring an end to Israel's opportunity and thus *"all Israel"* is saved in the same day? Or does God know those who are His, and these are those who because of the rapture fall on their knees so God seals them before entering that Day? The duality we should never question in God's plan but how it unfolds is a great mystery indeed. However, I believe all is in order from the start of the new age, God seals and knows who He will protect.

Could not God drive the Jewish people to brokenness and repentance over seeing the mystery of the rapture? YES! So that at the point of entering this Harvest period the remnant is sealed and protected to fulfill the promise of an earthly surviving remnant? Or is the 144,000 something bigger more symbolic of the bride taken above the earth, but still in the atmosphere needing protection? Whereas the surviving Israelite mortals are not the 144,000? All this head room I believe was left in scriptures. God doing a fabulous work of concealing the mystery of His bride both in this age and the next.

This idea of a sudden work has roots in Isaiah's visions. For He says, *"Before she travailed, she brought forth; before her pain came she gave birth to a boy. Who has heard of such a thing? Who has seen such things? Can a land be born in one day?"* **Isaiah 66:7-8** So this first part represents how the women [the righteous seed, Mary] in **Revelation 12:5** gives birth to *"a male child ...who is to rule all the nations with a rod of iron"* Who we should attribute to Jesus who then becomes the cornerstone. the template stone placed for this holy nation & priesthood both Heavenly and in Jerusalem through His resurrection to be raised up. One women births one man who births one new race both Jew & Gentile, one Kingdom of Heaven linked to earth.

Now the women plural is unveiled as Zion [the dead in Christ coming with Jesus] who is in travail. [Seen in the **1/2 hour** of silence **Revelation 8:1**]. After she has given birth it is said, *'Can a nation be brought forth all at once?'* <u>*As soon as Zion*</u> *travailed, she also* <u>*brought forth her sons*</u>*. Shall I bring to the point of birth and not give delivery?" says the Lord"* Isaiah 66:8-9 Now the Zion company births a nation and the two cannot be one and the same identity but they are connected together by relations. As a mother is connected in the deepest way possible to her child so are we one in that way but separate companies? Some see this as expressed in the two companies of **Revelation 7, or 11.**

Yet remember the 144,000 are on top of Mount Zion with Jesus towards the end of the Trumpet Period not earth, with solid Bridal overtures given for descriptions **[cf. Revelation 14:4]**. The likelihood is that the Great Multitude is *"the general assembly"* **Hebrews 12:23** of Zion, and the 144,000 is the Bride of Christ or *"church of the first born ...spirits of righteous made perfect"* **v23** also mentioned as coming with Christ at His arrival. The kingdom of God having rank and order, we see the Great Multitude *"washed their robes ...in the blood"* **Revelation 7:14** but His bridal army are those *"clothed in fine linen"* **Revelation 19:14** later on defined as *"the righteous acts of the saints"* **19:7**. If I seem to bounce between two possibilities for how this plays out, I am. I am simply showing you what is possible because God didn't define this in a concrete way.

In **Revelation 12**, we see this same *"women"* taken to a safe place for **3.5 years** while Satan enraged goes after *"her offspring"* **Revelation 12:17.** Here the term "offspring" is linking the origin of their faith to the women's faith. We see the evidence of her travail has produced salvation for many in the start of new age! Consider Daniel even speaks of this **3.5 years** as time of God's threshing and removing wickedness from His people, *"For a time times and half ... as soon as they finish shattering the power of the holy people all these events will be completed."* **Daniel 12:7** So what we have in total is three companies really at the finish of Revelation. **Revelation 12** revealing one women fleeing **[v6]**, one women flying **[v14]** and her offspring left on earth **[v17]**. More and more this looks like the 144,000 flee sealed by God, the great Multitude raptured and raised and finally those left behind unready.

So returning to Isaiah's description of a nation being born all at once **[cf. Isaiah 66:8]** through new sons and daughters; he explains how he will remove all others from the land saying, *"For the Lord will come in fire and His chariots like whirlwind ...the Lord will execute judgment by fire"* **Isaiah 66:15-16** Showing as well a harvest separation at this time, *"those who sanctify and purify themselves to the garden"* but the others *"will come to an end altogether"* **v17**. When? Before Armageddon mentioned in **v18.**

As for there being differing groups separated amongst His kingdom, Jesus says that He *"gathered good fish into containers [plural]"* **Matthew 13:48** One thing we should keep in mind, the difference from what is absolutely proven by two or three witnesses or the process of elimination from what is speculative. This area has room for clarity to be sure.

THE FIRST FRUIT(S)

"Kind of first fruits" **James 1:18**

James gets this concept of *"early and latter rains"* straight from **the book of Joel,** the prophet concerning God's promise to the sons of Zion **[cf. Joel 2:23]** both Jew & Gentiles. This very context of Joel, Peter uses at Pentecost concerning the Holy Spirit age arriving which had just been announced from heaven by tongues of fire, which Joel states five verse later will eventually be worldwide *"on all mankind"* **Joel 2:28.** Revealing the early church was lit up over Joel's imagery and wording revealing what was a mystery to many. Here in **2 Peter**, we see a firm defense that those *"last days"* **Acts 2:17 [cf. Joel 2:28]** had begun.

James picking up on this harvest theme that was displayed on the actual *Feast of Weeks*, *Pentecost* to the Greeks, a time to celebrate first fruits of the wheat harvest, saying they, the apostles generation, were *"a kind of first fruits"* **James 1:18** having uniquely been given the Spirit at the beginning. Pentecost however was only a first fruits celebration of the wheat season as opposed to the Barley season celebrated earlier which had its own first fruits celebration on Christ's resurrection day.

Of the Barley, Jesus being called Himself *"the first fruits of those who are asleep ... each in its own order: Christ the first fruits, after that those who are Christ's at His coming, then the end ..."* **1 Corinthians 15:20,23** Reveal a purposeful plan for gathering His own. For until Christ death was finished the price hadn't been payed for any Old Testament saint. However now we see the harvest has begun already with the Old testament saints.

Upon Jesus death alone it is said, *"The tombs were opened and many bodies of the saints who has fallen asleep were raised; and coming out of the tombs after His resurrection they entered the holy city and appeared to many."* **Matthew 27:52** Not only this but Paul puts it this way, *"Therefore it says, "When He ascended on high. He led captive a host of captives, and gave gifts to men."* **Ephesians 4:8** Since He told the other person on the cross, *"Today you will be with me in Paradise."* **Luke 23:43**; we can understand that His victory on the cross was so complete that that very moment could have been when Jesus released those awaiting Him! Others surmise He took them on the third day when He became glorified and took His body as well.

You may say what's going on here? If Jesus is the first born then did others precede Him? No, they certainly did not. Understand Jesus is the first to be raised with a glorified body [eternal imperishable one] on the third day. This is my point. Resurrection is a process! Enoch and Elijah had been translated ahead of Christ's resurrection, yet they are not *"first-born"*. For Jesus body itself was laid in the tomb while it is said He was in Paradise.

My point will be profound. Jesus victory on the cross was so complete, His divinity so real that he could go wherever He wished. Yet His physical body was required to stay on earth three days to fulfill and pattern prophecy. Maybe our clues are in the scriptural text and Jewish feast? For one, Paul declaring Jesus ascension brought with Him those captive. He first states an argument possibly in the daily life of the church, "Where actually did Jesus go after He died?" Paul saying that He not only ascended but descended. **[Cf. Romans 10:6-8]**

So where is Paradise? Cross references suggest where God is! Could not Jesus before His body was raised and ascended on the third day, go where He wished? And again He was not ever held in captivity or needed no further punishment for our sins as the prosperity movement suggests! But tells the man on the cross *"TODAY!"* Many think Paradise is a place where the Old Testament saints were held. Regardless of where we believe God held them, their penalty was not paid until Jesus paid it all! They still were held to the same standard to receive Jesus Himself so He had to go where they were to release them.

This deliverance from death that Paul speaks of in saying, *"captives"* occurred during the feast which symbolized the removal of death and decay or *"leaven"*, which is what Jesus did *"in the heart of the earth"* **Matthew 12:40** when *"he went and made* *proclamation to spirits in prison."* **1 Peter 3:19** Paul speaking on God's order mentions Christ then "the first fruit" and then us as if he is making a list for the grocery store. **[1 Corinthians 15:23].** I believe Paul is declaring Jesus **v20** and then the Old Testament saints **v23** here were both first fruits. God removed the Old Testament saints sin at the cross and allowed them access into heaven not permitted before legally as a kind of harvest of the Barley not the wheat. In this Jewish perspective, there is an order to the harvests. First Barley, then wheat and finally the fruit harvest which I find separated spiritually by the ages they come from..

The order is important though, Christ is *"the firstborn of every creation"* **Colossians 1:18** preceding the Old Testament saints in being glorified by the Father with an imperishable body. **Hebrews 11** speaks of the Old Testament saints faith being rewarded at a later date, saying, *"God provided something better for us, so that apart from us they would not be made perfect."* **V40** Admitting they had to wait for Jesus finished work on Calvary for the *"something better"* and they are awaiting the *"all"* at the very end on the seventh trumpet to be glorified or made perfect together.

So these faithful men and women of the Old are spoken of as a *"cloud of witnesses surrounding us"* **Hebrews 12:1** awaiting for us to be made perfect with them. Which is a firm declaration of their entrance into Heaven but not yet changed in a twinkling as will be mentioned at the end of Paul's declaration on the Resurrection process in **1 Corinthians 15:52**. This barley harvest clearly a different harvest than the wheat which started at Pentecost.

All that's left to the wheat harvest after the first fruits of that harvest will be the General Harvest at the rapture and the Gleanings that follow. The three stages of the Jewish wheat harvest. This then brings to light why there are already **24 elders** seated in **Revelation 4** before the rapture. For the first fruits of the Wheat harvest have seemed to have gone ahead of the rest of us, the **12 disciples** plus possibly another select group of 12 from the Old Testament. So James was right, they were a kind of first fruits.

Paul tells us, He *"will bring with Him those who have fallen asleep."* **1 Thessalonians 4:14** suggesting the rest of us are being prepared for one moment in time to be raised together from sleep! As heaven jumps dimensions to the upper atmosphere of the earth and Zion is formed above with the dead in Christ. Consider even before Christ's death at His transfiguration, we see Moses and Elijah in Heaven. Even before the rapture we see 24 elders in Heaven in **Revelation 4**. Jesus declaring His Kingdom was at hand was the truth, it was present in Himself and already being assembled once He was crucified with the first fruits.

THE PREGNANCY

"All these things are merely the beginning of birth-pangs"
Matthew 24:8

The whole perspective of the end times could be summed up in this concept of a women about to give birth. As we have already seen in Isaiah, Jesus makes this the focus of His end times dialogue. Paul very attentive to this says, **"For the anxious longing of the creation waits eagerly _for the revealing of the sons of God... for we know that the whole creation groans and _suffers pains of childbirth_ together until now."_ Romans 8:19,22** Many have pondered just how this manifestation would occur and when? Doctrines where created especially in the **1940s**, under the Latter Rain Movement, called the Manifest Sons of God Doctrine. The whole interpretation of the verse we just read was this revelation would occur before Christ return and be the reason He returns. Then came the idea a new Apostolic renewal would usher it in as part of it.

Yet if one follows the teachings of Christ in **Matthew 24** where this concept is introduced of **"the beginning of the birth pangs"** **Matthew 24:8**, there's no mention throughout the context of organizational movements or triumph of the organized church, not even a hint. Jesus concept of the labor that pushes forward the drama of the end times is more in alignment with Paul's notion that the context is one of the mature growth of the wheat revealing true sons and daughters who find no more place for them in this world, and not some ecclesiastical triumph. So yes I believe the manifestation becomes real right during this final period before the Abomination mentioned but through the organic expression of the true church. This manifestation also does not become as evident as when Christ is revealed with us by His side already.

Much speculation revolves around locating the time length and duration of this period of these labor pains that occur previous to the Abomination. This is where typically the Pre Tribulation Theorist place the first half of their seven year theory that I find unbiblical. Others say, *'Oh we've always have had wars, famines and earthquakes.'* Which is what I might think if I saw a women complaining of abdominal pains. Instead if it were my wife I'm not going to say, *'Stop your belly aching you just ate something bad.'* You don't because you have watched her belly enlarge, you know what is behind the surface, what is being born. You are deeply attached to the storyline if you are the husband if you are a child of God! In this case you are tracking the nine months for natural birth. You and I should not be *"in darkness"* **1 Thessalonians 5:4** as Paul proclaims.

Yet even here at this earliest point in His discourse we have our first clue of something very unique beyond the occurrence found in general so far. *"You will be hearing of wars and **rumors of**"* **v6** Which if I turn on the news, I am certain to know about any war going on via the Internet and satellites via Cable TV. Is this a sign that Satellites will not be functioning in the world? This could be caused by a meteor or tampering between nations, or solar flare but definitely the idea is multiple nations using this lack of eyesight to take advantage on other nations. Consider in **2029**, such a meteor will fly between the moon and earth possibly interfering with satellites called *Apophis* by NASA. Just the other day Russia was reported following our spy satellites closely. Have we entered the time of Space Wars? Soon very soon the world could go dark, and as they say, *'let the games begin.'*

In Luke's account, Jesus gives us the idea of many nations will grow in power during Israel's rise to power. **[Cf. Luke 21:29, Matthew 24:32]** As we see today the earth's RISK playing board is loaded with armies and nukes all over the world. Japan, China, N. Korea, America, France, Turkey, Russia, Iran, Israel having this ability to dominate in regions of the world given the advantage of surprise.

Another *key word* comes a verse later, when Jesus describes *"**all** nations"* **Matthew 24:9** hating Christians, this is another clear sign of something unique. The whole world will be unified around the Christians being an issue or the problem for world peace! The United States must join the world in hating Christians as an outward statement of policy; or the United States must collapse and align itself to the world's agenda. This hasn't occurred yet but we are closing in on it. Just consider what we are witnessing already in the last four years in our nation with the unprecedented hatred toward conservatives, President Trump and the police. By associating a *"evil is good and good is evil"* mentality, by twisting the laws of our land, by hypocrisy this can occur in the near future. The mystery of lawlessness will have its final sway on earth! **[Cf. 2 Thessalonians 2:7]** God will reject all those who pretend faith but follow its lawlessness. **[Cf. Matthew 7:23]**

Never before have we seen the unveiling of a deep state in coalition with Media moguls to move money fraudulently to our politicians and build alliances globally forsaking our constitutional laws, sovereignty and true justice. No longer is America *"for the people"* but the agenda underlying in our nation has surfaced for world trade profit and power over our constitution, Babylon is being born before our eyes. How long until Satan's agenda takes full power, could it not occur in a day or a season?

The next step would then be the apostasy, but now unfortunately as I am editing the book I believe we are there! Many will forsake Christianity to be apart of this coalition of Nations message, once laws are changed to make it dangerous to defy the deep State; then another acceptable form of "Christianity" will emerge in step with the deep state. On the heels of that many enlightened New Age Prophets will lead people astray with alternatives and acceptable watered down versions of "christianity". **[Cf. Matthew 24:10-11]** At this point, this lust for moral freedom will lead to the betrayal of human life in the name of the New Age leading to the mark of the beast.

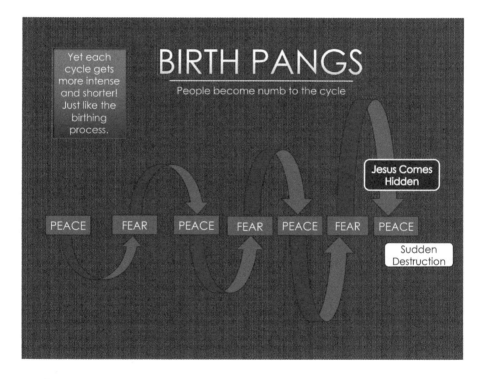

One bright spot occurs in Jesus description of this lead-in period. They will ***"Bring you before kings and governors for My name sake. It will lead to opportunity for your testimony. So make up your minds ...for I will give you utterance and wisdom that none of your opponents will be able to resist or refute."*** **Luke 21:12-15** The world is still hungry for answers they know we have! Like what the heck is going on? People will want answers and those who understand these things will win many **[cf. Daniel 12:3]**.

Luke's account gives us why this might be occurring. Jesus says, *"There will be terrors and great signs from the heavens"* **Luke 21:11** and this is before we ever get to those signs being in our own solar system when later it is spoken, *"there will be signs in sun, moon and stars ..."* **Luke 21:25a.** Where do we find these *"signs in the heaven"* but alongside the Birth-pangs **[cf. Luke 21:10-11, Matthew 24:6-8]**.

Jesus will then go on to finish His description of the sky reflecting what we know is the Day of the Lord/Trumpet Period by declaring it a time when, *"the powers of the heavens will be shaken" v25b* **[cf. Hebrews 12:26-28]** Whereas the seals 1-5 in Revelation **chapter 5-6** read more like a history lesson from the resurrection of this present age; and the birth pangs in Jesus gospel accounts is definitely the period right before the Abomination in which signs start to occur in the heavens gradually.

THE WARNINGS

"Whoever seeks to save his life will lose it and whoever loses his life will preserve it."

Luke 17:33

When Jesus first brings with Him heaven above the earth, Zion **[cf. Hebrews 12:18-25]** without warning, suddenly or as He says, *"I come quickly [suddenly]"* **Revelation 3:1**, He promises the faithful church of Philadelphia they *"will be kept from it"* **Revelation 3:10** From what? *"I will keep you from the <u>hour of testing</u>, which is about to <u>come upon the whole world</u> to test those who dwell on the earth."* **Revelation 3:10** Now here is the debate that follows that passage. Jesus comes before the hour of testing for the faithful however in Jesus account the great tribulation occurs in **Matthew 24:21** before He comes in **v27** which is followed by another tribulation *"in those days <u>after that</u> tribulation"* **Mark 13:24** which is the judgment portion of the Day of the Lord **Matthew 24:29**. So we learn from this that the start of the Great Tribulation is just a test for us the righteous not the whole world.

The relationship also is one of more regional that quickly escalates to global, from the wrath of man regionally to the wrath of Satan globally. The beginning part which is the start of the Great Tribulation period is man's doing not God's and is focused regionally near Israel and grows quickly to be a ONE WORLD GOVERNMENT conspiracy against the Holy. In the Heavens at this time, **Revelation**

12 reveals *a domino effect* has begun. Satan being thrust to earth **[cf. 12:8]** comes the pronouncement of the soon arrival of Jesus! **"kingdom of our God ...have come" 12:10** Satan having little time tries to heavily persecutes the bride of Christ who is quickly taken **[cf. 12:14]** to up with the dead in Christ who are already celebrating **[cf. V10-12].**

This then begins the judgement sequences as found in **Revelation**. Try to keep this in order because it will greatly help you see all scripture begin to align and harmonize; the great Tribulation starts immediately after the Abomination and continues all the way to the very end. During this time the order is great deception, betrayal and confusion followed by the arrival of Christ hidden and then our departure within the first month. When we depart the fire judgments begin for 3.5 years ending with Christ appearance with us. Again there is no seven year tribulation period.

Let us not make the assumption, we are being removed from the start of the great tribulation itself for **Revelation** is clear we come out of that larger period **[cf. 7:14]** and Jesus again makes this clear positioning His coming after it in **Matthew 24 [cf. Verses 22,27]**. Again this should concern most who aren't prepared to overcome by *"eagerly awaiting Him."* **Hebrews 9:28** or think you'll have obvious signs or opportunity given them. Since we have refuted the false narrative of a seven year covenant made with Israel by an Anti-Christ from **Daniel 9:27** and given that the Abomination is set up by Government forces not the crazy phase of the Anti-Christ, the end is very deceptive and a trap!

Consider Jesus strong words once the Abomination is mentioned in **Matthew 24:15**, saying, *"those in Judea flee to the mountains"* **v16**. This occurs during a time of peace because Jesus has to tell you to *"flee"*! Daniel reveals this period as one where people have to inform others of its significance because of its deceptive start **[cf. Daniel 11:32]**. Why? Because it will go unnoticed by many. This is the first of two warnings Jesus gives for this final period in which He arrives in. Regionally *"to flee"* **v16** and globally to look up for His sign will not be on earth but *"as the lightning flashes"* **v27**. What is simply amazing is that **Revelation 12** gives a parallel to these two warnings saying first, *"the women <u>fled</u> (flees) into the wilderness"* **v6** and in the second reference saying she *"fly (looks upwards and is taken) into the wilderness to her place"* **v14**

One at the time of the Abomination when Armies surround Jerusalem *"to flee"* **Luke 21:21** and the other when the glory appears in the sky when Jesus warns us *"not seek to save your life"* **Luke 17:33**. In other words, DON'T FLEE but show forth faith, *"to lift your heads"* **Luke 21:28**, to stand before your God! In the first case we are staying alive from the wrath of Satan regionally, in the second we are standing by our faith in God looking upwards when He appears to us globally! And He is able *"to make us stand in His presence of His glory"* **Jude 24** The distinction between these two is plain.

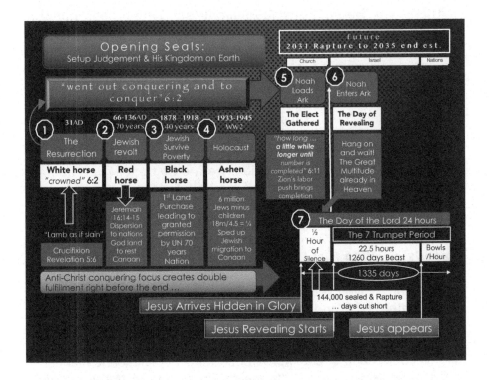

Due to this warning Jesus gave, in **66AD** right after this second letter of Peter was written, Jewish believer's fled Jerusalem due to Roman armies surrounding Jerusalem. This was directly due to Daniel's prophesy in **9:26**, and Jesus words in the Gospels. Due to this, the Partial Preterit Theorist today, surmise an Abomination of some sort occurred in **66AD** according to Jesus warning ushering in the end of the age of the Law. The attempt is to make all the judgments past which builds a popular message that the church just needs to be triumphant to usher Christ in next.

Notice though how Daniel's prophecy continues *'even to the end there will be war; desolations are determined ..."* **v26** pointing to returning to this same place of being surrounded by armies in the future as spoken in **Luke 21:20**. Of course this wouldn't be the first time God concealed the future by allowing similar events past, as in, Antiochus Epiphane's desecration of the Jewish temple in **135BC** which occurred before Jesus words and the **70 AD** demolishment of the temple.

Yet here we are in **30AD** with Jesus pointing us back specifically to *"Daniel"* **Matthew 24:15** as if the Abomination was still future and then in **Revelation (circa 95AD)** points us forward yet again after the destruction of the city and temple in its the rear view mirror as if the end of the age is still upon us. Pre Tribulation Theorist will argue as they should, that the Abomination in **Daniel 11:31** is a past event whether that it happened in **135BC**, or **70AD**, for how else can Jesus coming be mentioned in **Matthew 24:27** after the tribulation starts in connection to the Abomination **[cf. 24:15]?** Instead they say that is all past and at a different time far removed in the future we pick up with **Matthew 24:27**. Understand they must separate the second coming from the rapture or remove the words prior to His coming to another time.

These aren't the only ones trying to find a smooth sailing into His return. For the Partial Preterit Theorist claim that all the bad stuff is past can be lumped into the same motivating factor that drives Pre Tribulation theorist. These arguments usually go hand in hand into the goodness of God who wouldn't allow certain things upon His own. The logic would be incredibly blind to all of historic atrocities or the early churches persecutions and martyrdoms. Even to confuse Paul's revelation that, *"God has not destined us for wrath"* **1 Thessalonians 5:9** with not receiving tribulation is contradictory to Paul Himself. The overwhelming revelation that tribulation is both something prophesied for us and necessary for us is real. **[cf. 1 Peter 1:6, Acts 14:22]** For Paul is not shy to say, affliction was a true sign of the wrath coming. **[Cf. 2 Thessalonians 1:4-5]** .

Last, much is written on how one can see history unfold from the beginning of **Daniel 11:1** to this placement of the Abomination in **verse 31**, leading us to believe the event was the Abomination in the Jewish Temple in **135BC**. This gives Pre Tribulation Theorist & Partial Preterit Theorist room to say the next thing will be the coming of the Lord immediately before **Daniel 11:36** when the King of the North/ Anti-Christ exalts Himself. So again I went to town searching for answers. I found another timeline that fits historically perfect that is currently leading us up to a **verse 31** Abomination. This is done by seeing a different focal point for advancement and placement of prophetic revelation from verse **11:4**. The focal point is the history of the occupation of Canaan until now. This is too deep to make apart of this book but points to how amazing God is in working history into a dual fulfillment of both an 167 BC Abomination and a future one.

So going back to Jesus warnings, I believe both are for this short period between the Abomination and His arrival. One is a warning regionally and the other globally. Connecting them again to Jesus descriptions in **Revelation 12:6,14**, the question we now can raise is, is this what we are seeing in **Revelation 7**. First an earthly remnant sealed **[cf. 7:1-8]** that flees with God's protection followed by a great multitude suddenly before the Lamb. Jesus would then be giving instructions for both them, one to flee to survive and the other the hope of flying away in the rapture. Instructions for two different ages, one for mortals and the other for immortality.

The realms of possibilities exist here with many surmising where God will hide His remnant on the earth versus what happens when the rest *"fly into the wilderness"* **v14**. As to the timing being **3.5 years** for both, the proponents of a seven year period chime in here wanting this to speak to two 3.5 year periods back to back. However looking first at **Matthew 24** context, the seven years would then occur after the Abomination **[cf. 24:15-27]** not at the mid point of Daniel's seventieth week **[cf. Daniel 9:27]**. **Revelation 12** closely viewed we actually see two themes being woven together. The first **v1-6,** focuses on the women being the righteous seed that brings Jesus into the world thus birthing the bride, sons and daughters of the Kingdom, Zion. She then being regional as the physical descendants are spoken of as fleeing 3.5 years. This is seen in the direct link from **v5,** the resurrection, jumping immediately to her **3.5 years v6** displaying God's pause at the **sixty-ninth week** and **half** mark of the **70 weeks**.

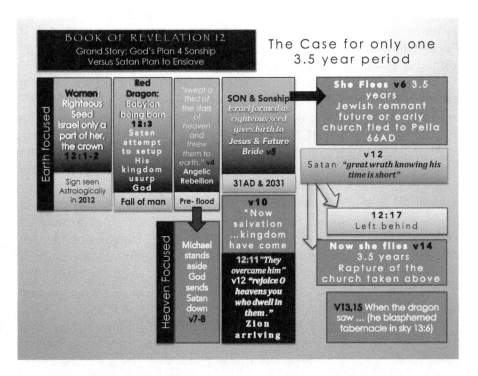

Next from **verse 7-14**, we shift focus from the war on earth to the heavenly war. Angelic warfare finally is resolved by the restrainer Michael standing aside or expelling Satan to earth. Satan is allowed to go to earth but what this really is at same time is a trap. For the immediate response is *"Now salvation and the power and the kingdom of our God and the authority of His Christ have come for the accuser   ...has been thrown down..."* Revelation 12:10 Much is made of the seventh trumpet revelation that Christ kingdom has finally taken over. Yet even here **3.5 years** from the finish, the Kingdom has entered earth's dominion and begun to rule over all mysteriously hidden by trapping Satan on earth. Notice both Satan is on earth and Jesus has arrived and we haven't been taken yet! This is why the Day of the Lord is a mystery, trap and comes during declarations of Peace & Safety before we are taken.

Carefully looking at Jesus warnings in **Luke 21:20-24**; we see a fit could be made for the destruction in **70 AD** and the dispersion of the Jews as a result. The key words though is *"Jerusalem will be trampled under foot by the Gentiles until the times of the Gentiles are fulfilled."* **Luke 21:24** which seem particular interesting in our day. Both with the rise of Israel and her possession of most of the city, the growing trend is towards retaking all the holy sites. Could this be a telling sign when the Jews push out the Muslim Mosque and restore her sacred places?

Yet when we get into the trumpet period we read, *"outside the temple ...given to the nations and they will tread underfoot the holy city for FORTY TWO MONTHS."* **Revelation 11:1** which isn't for seven years just **3.5 again**. Understand again **the Book of Revelation** was written after **70AD**, this is still future. When Jesus spoke, **Luke 21** Jerusalem wasn't trampled by Gentiles and in **70 AD** Jerusalem wasn't trampled or occupied for a period but destroyed in a day.

In reviewing, **Luke 21** chronology Jesus does attach this drama in Jerusalem to the next statement, *"There will be signs in sun and moon and stars and on the earth dismay among nations in perplexity at the roaring of the sea and the waves, men fainting from fear and expectation of the things which are coming upon the world; for the powers of the heavens will be shaken."* **Luke 21:26** This throws out any possibility of past fulfillment and points us to the whole period from the Abomination to His arrival.

So the nature of the fire judgments are like the water judgments. When Noah was loading the ark, clouds were forming, maybe fog, dew on the ground, humidity all never experienced before. Maybe even a drop of rain, then the floods came slowly increasing until it was too late. Much like boiling a frog, it never knows wiser until it is cooked, so people will see this as the *"new normal"*.

This makes Jesus words very important, **"On the day that Lot went out from Sodom it rained fire"** Luke **17:29** More and more Noah preached the more they mocked. Until that final seven days when Noah stopped preaching and loaded the Ark. So when we see the events regionally for which Jesus is saying, **"flee"** go down, we should all be getting ready to take flight like eagles! The warning is to flee Satan and face our Redeemer!

THE YOU

*"Not wishing for **any to perish** but for all*
to come to repentance" **2 Peter 3:9**

Simply put, a directors viewpoint of putting it "all" together is different from the actors role of playing his part in the movie or even the audiences in watching it play out with all the drama attached. We are the actors and the unsaved are the audience and God is producing an Academy Award Winning drama! Peter here is just telling us, God planned the script with you and I in mind and this movie will not be finished until **"all"** the actors play their roles and are accounted for. So the flip side of this is Peter's encouragement, for them **"to make certain about His calling and choosing you"** 2 **Peter 1:10.** How? By evidence of growth which comes from heart repentance! Another words do not give God a reason to choose another in your place.

God is sitting patiently in His directors seat for you to respond to Him and His cues! Peter will leave his audience with two references in **2 Peter 3:9,15** concerning God's patience to our **"salvation"** 3:15 encouraging us to **"repentance"** 3:9. Which is I was living for myself, what I saw best for me; now I surrender to what God tells me is best for me. One does not need tears for this **"for the sorrow of the world produces death"** 2 **Corinthians 7:10** just the knowledge of God to change your heart. Are we sorry that our sin is offensive and violates God's will, and is marked for judgment? All this is relational not transactional.

If we view salvation in our easy step methods and modern apostate teachings on grace we will find no context or appreciation for these passages showing the labor of love God takes to save us! For repentance is deemed necessary for salvation, repentance is not works of the law but a change of direction, a surrendering over to Him our own works of being right by submitting to His grace to empower us to live godly! Remember Peter in His first letter said, **"If** *it is with difficulty that the righteous is saved then what will become of ..."* **1 Peter 4:18**

Many want to content that, repentance is not necessary under grace. This is foolishness since, *"the beginning of the gospel of Jesus Christ"* **Mark 1:1** had commenced and then John' the baptist preaches three verse later, *"a baptism of repentance for the forgiveness of sins."* **v4** This is very harmonious everywhere you look in the New Testament.

Peter answering the cries of *"what must we do"* at Pentecost declares first, *"Repent"* **Acts 2:38** Paul later leaving no room for error saying, *"now commands all men everywhere to repent."* **Acts 17:30 [NKJV]** and elsewhere, *"all must repent of their sins and turn to God, performing deeds appropriate to repentance"* **Acts 26:20 [NLT]** Jesus sends out His disciples preaching, *"that men should repent."* **Mark 6:12** and even out of hell Jesus tells the story how a tormented soul hopes his friends will *"repent"* **Luke 16:30.**

All this leads us to the concepts of being *"born"* into the kind of life that is eternal. This reality is organic not mechanical. This is relational not religious. God should expect growth from something that is alive! So the standard is, if *"He who began a good work will perfect it"* **Philippians 1:6** then *"work out your salvation with fear and trembling"* **2:12**. This is to say you repented of your own works to replace it with His work, so now let Him have His way and partner with Him. *"For it is God at work in you, both to will and to work for His good pleasure."* **v13**

The unshakable truth is found in Jesus words of building on a firm foundation. *"Everyone who hears these words of Mine and (doesn't) acts on them"* **Matthew 7:24,26** Remember Jesus isn't telling the last days churches in **Revelation 3** *"I know your heart"* but *"I know your works"* **v15.** In which His conclusion is for them to *"Repent"* **v19** by opening the door of your heart and falling in love with Him again so your good works can return.

One doctrine is so unshakable with multiple witnesses, that endurance is needed! *"That after you have done the will of God you may receive ..."* **Hebrews 10:36**

"...if we hold fast our confidence and boast of our hope firm until the end"   **Hebrews 3:6**

"For we have become partakers of Christ, if we hold fast the beginning of our assurance firm until the end." **Hebrews3:14**

*"The full assurance of hope **until the end"*** **Hebrews 6:11**
*"Let us hold fast the confession of our hope **without wavering**, for He who promised is faithful ..."* **Hebrews 10:23**

So it should be understandable God is only coming for those who *"eagerly await Him"* **Hebrews 9:28** The author of Hebrews then concluding his relentless drive for faithfulness as necessary describes God's displeasure if we shrink away from our faith even at His coming itself! *"For yet in a little while He who is coming will come and will not delay. But my righteous one shall live by faith and if He shrinks back My soul has no pleasure in him. But we are not of those who shrink back "* **Hebrews 10:37-39**

8

Calculating:
Awaiting the Arrival

THE NUMBERING

*"So teach us to **number our days** that we present to You a **heart of wisdom**"*

Psalms 90:12

We live in a day when many would question whether it's even healthy or biblical to have any precise expectation for the return of Christ. Yet in **Psalms**, from the only song attributed to Moses, comes this famous quote above. Moses has already by **verse 12** given God's prescribed way of calculating an age **[cf. V4]** and a lifetime **[cf. V10]**. Why? One would say Moses ain't playing around here with anything relative given this **verse 12** is apart of the context. He is serious about the numbering part! Why? Maybe because God met Moses on Mount Sinai and explained that Her ain't playing round either with time.

What is so apropos about this verse is: we are in this book being careful to rightly divide God's concealed truth of how many days we have left. We found to do this we had to weigh terms used with prophetic value attached to them, such as, *"**last days**"*, *"**last day**"*, *"**on the final day**"*, *"**third day**"* differently due to the context it is written in. In each case the context suggested something beyond real time to a larger grand scale measured by Prophetic code of equivalency. As opposed to the context where natural days are implied within a certain specific period mentioned, such as from *"those days"* **Matthew 24:22** plural comes a *"day and hour ... no one knows"* **Matthew 24:34.** Understand, we are not choosing when to interpret time differently, the context is telling us along with the harmony of scripture.

As we examine His plan as it pertains to these big picture days winding down toward the end of this age; we are introduced to an entirely new set of terms for *"day"*. This group neither falls in the category of the big picture days or a literal day. Instead we find they are descriptive of the short period at the end of this age. These terms will be covered in this chapter are *"the Day of the Lord"*, *"His day"*, *"the days of the Son of Man"* and the *"day of His revealing"*.

However in getting back to the importance of numbering our days, as mentioned in Moses's **90th Psalm**, we can very well ask the question of why did He make a song to remember this? Did the mathematical equations for time written in this **Psalm 90** and this concern to consider them come from the heights of Mount Sinai visitation? If so we have a wonderful circle of connection. Hear me out, Moses writes a song to remember God's words describing His timetable for an age and for the period of a generation passing, because God has possibly told Him atop Mount Sinai the grand plan is hidden in the symbolic nature of His request for a two day purification of the people.

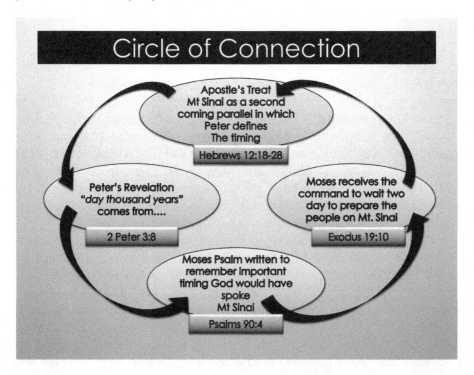

Circle of Connection

Apostle's Treat Mt Sinai as a second coming parallel in which Peter defines The timing

Hebrews 12:18-28

Peter's Revelation "day thousand years" comes from....

2 Peter 3:8

Moses receives the command to wait two day to prepare the people on Mt. Sinai

Exodus 19:10

Moses Psalm written to remember important timing God would have spoke Mt Sinai

Psalms 90:4

Peter realizing the significance of this **Psalm** echos Moses' declaration. *"A day is as a thousand years"* **2 Peter 3:8 [cf. Psalms 90:4]** During this period **Hebrews** is written showing the Apostles also saw the connection of **Mount Sinai** had as an example for the second coming. **[cf. 12:18-28]**

So the Mount Sinai experience for Moses was a watershed moment for the prophetic timetable of God. Giving us everything from the big picture 2 days and the third to prepare the people, to the picture of the Day of the Lord on that third day. The measuring sticks for unlocking this, **Psalms 90.** Enter Jesus who says, *"This generation will not pass away until"* **Matthew 24:34** which is connected to the *"fig tree mature"* **v32** governing the final period from Israel's independence as a nation to her true independence with her Messiah, **1967 - 2037**. Again we are back to **Psalms 90** for the length of that time. *"As for the days of our life they contain seventy years"* **Psalms 90:10** So at the very time when God was displaying the timetable on Mount Sinai, He was also giving the ruler to measure it!

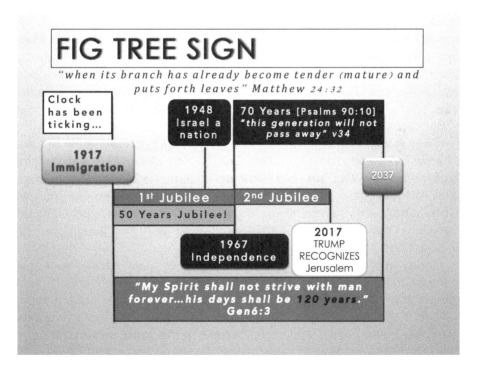

So here we are **2020**. I was born in **1965**, maybe this is why God choose me for this task, for I am literally the last generation. God saying you will not get to your seventieth birthday! Yet some of you are younger than I am and the thought of not "finishing" your life is a bit troubling I'm sure. Yet we read these words, *"**NUMBER YOUR DAYS!**"* Why? Because logic tells us someone is the last generation and God wants them to know! Why? Because He's going to reward His servants for caring about this **Amos 3:7.**

Peter was clear, we should have reason to look forward to the worst period in human history, *"looking for and desiring the coming of the day ..." 3:12* Why, because that seems strange thing to desire a day *"thick darkness"* **Joel 2:2**? Remember it is called *"great and very awesome"* **Joel 2:11,31; Zephaniah 1:14** and *"great and terrible"* **Malachi 4:5** because it is both positive and negative depending where you sit going into that day! For Amos was given an entirely different picture!

> *"Alas you **who are longing for the day** of the Lord. **For what purpose** will the day of the Lord be to you? **It will be darkness and not light;** ... "*
>
> **Amos 5:18-19**

So which is it? Notice in saying for some they will go through the ultimate disappointment, it also saying for others it will be *"light"* **Isaiah 60**? The difference is key! Amos received a negative word for those who in God's word here seem to do everything right! God hated their *"festivals"* and their *"solemn assemblies"* **5:21** which pretty much covers every type of event. It didn't matter what extreme they took. Next He says, He won't even look at their *"peace offerings"* **v22**. Which is when we do the right thing to just check that off of our conscience. God says I hate that!

They sang beautiful worship *"songs"* **v23** played well on the *"harps"* **v23** but God says, *"let justice roll down like waters and righteousness like an ever-flowing stream"* **v24**. Why? Because God reminds them they did the same thing in the wilderness, paying God respect and then they would go home (tent) to their idols. Sound familiar? They took an entitled approach to God and it reflected on their actions preventing justice.

Today the question is where are you in your heart? A whole generation can be singing beautiful worship songs, identifying with movements, participating in great meetings and even leading them yet what are the gods or interest that are governing our decisions when we go home? God asks us *"where is the justice in this?"* Why don't you long for Him to return, why don't you bring Him home with you and make Him your very life! **[Cf. Colossians 3:4]** Jesus is life not an extra alternative thing to do!

> *"**When He appears we shall be like Him**, because we shall see Him as He is. Everyone who has **this HOPE fixed on Him purifies himself** just as He is pure."* **1 John 3:2-3**

My point is it is easy to replace a personal love for Him with other pursuits and end up instead giving Him lip service, or song service. I'm here to say Jesus is seriously real and returning! Let's be on the anticipating side of His return not the surprised side. Let God birth in your heart a love and longing for Him.

THE SUDDENLY

*"I come **suddenly**"* **Revelation 3:11**

*"But the day of the Lord **will come like a thief** in which the heavens will pass away ..."*
2 Peter 3:10

Our letter writer, the apostle Peter, seamlessly connects God's grand achievement of getting His *"all"* **2 Peter 3:9** with the sudden arrival of *"the Day of the Lord"* **v10** with one word *"but"* and one description *"like a thief"*. As if nothing else determined this date but the fulfillment of the *"all saved"* that ushers in a sudden mysterious end to this age by His second coming! Peter borrowing the idea from Christ words, *"the Gospel of the Kingdom will be preached in every nation ... then the end"* **Matthew 24:14**.

Again we find this concept of a chosen number being a focal point occurring in the fifth seal leading up to the Day of His revealing in the Sixth seal in these words, *"they should rest a little while longer until **the number** ... would be **completed**."* **Revelation 6:11** With so many before the altar on the fifth seal, and the sixth seal exceeding Jesus sign of a mere *"lighting flashes"* **Matthew 24:27** for His coming **[cf. *"so will the coming of the Son of Man be"* v27]**, one can either surmise the fifth seal when the dead in Christ are gathered or it is the rapture. For by the sixth seal apocalyptic event we have arrived at the fire judgments, the Day of His revealing.

Carefully follow me here, when it says *"the souls who had been slain because fo the word of God"* **Revelation 6:9** on the fifth seal, they suddenly appear in heaven as a group! This is identical to **Revelation 20:4** and most likely a symbolic representation of what occurs in the resurrection process. We first die to ourselves and receive the Spirit's indwelling mind. We have given up our minds (beheaded) for the mind of Christ during our lives and if you have followed my harmony of scripture on the rapture itself you would know it is a slaying as well to enter heaven. This might be one of the greatest revelations to understand the book of **Revelation**! Flesh and blood cannot enter heaven, we die first and leave our bodies as we go up. This changes how we see many things spoken in **Revelation.**

Returning to *"the number to be completed"*, we can surmise a period might exist for either of two senerios. This depends on the identity of those at the altar on the fifth seal. If the fifth seal is the rapture, then the prudent virgins awaking from sleep to be loaded after the faithful makes sense. If the fifth seal is describing the dead in Christ going first then those who are still alive hadn't been caught up yet to complete the number for the Bride. In both senerios, the parallel exist of the loading period for the ark. This is a critical time, for once the sixth seal occurs, we are moving from 30 days to the 1260 of the beast authority and Jesus final ministry to Israel. The ages will have changed! The door will have closed to being apart of this age, this dispensation of grace.

So we come to this sixth seal where glory flashes are not the order of the day! It is here we see the distinction Jesus made between the longer period of *"the days of the Son ..."* **Luke 17:26** from the event that follows, *"the day of His revealing"* **v30**! For by the time we get to *"the great day of their wrath has come"* **Revelation 6:17**, we can be certain that Jesus has already arrived and what is ahead is not for the faithful **[cf. 1 Thessalonians 5:9]**! Understand Jesus sheds light into this in **Luke 17**, differentiating the start of His *"days"* plural to *"just as"* when Noah loaded the ark **[cf. Luke 17:26-28]** from *"day of His revealing"* **v30** when Noah finally entered for the ark for good and God sealed up the door **[cf. Luke 29-37]**.

Notice the obvious, *"the sky was split apart like a scroll when it is rolled up"* **6:14,** Jesus could have easily told us that was the sign of His coming. The only other logical order is very illogical, that the deceptive lightning flashes of His coming occur after this Apocalyptic event. Post Tribulation Theorist are yelling from their perch right now, *'Can't you see that the Sixth seal is the end of the day of the Lord on the seventh Trumpet, they are the same'.* Okay, consider this, the moon is blood at the start of this unveiling in the sixth seal. *"And the whole moon became like blood"* **Revelation 6:12** Later we will observe the moon is darkened in the trumpet period **[cf. Revelation 8:12]** as it should be, because the Trumpet Period is the Day of the Lord! Why? Well Joel differentiates the Day being when *"moon grows dark"* **Joel 2:10** versus the *"moon into blood before the Day of the Lord"* **Joel 2:31**

This is also my problem with those who relegate the Day of the Lord to the timing of the Seventh seal, for it has already begun *"half an hour"* **Revelation 8:1** before the Trumpet Period begins.

Notice the Day (or period) of destruction commences on the Sixth seal **[cf. Revelation 6:14-17]** at the time when heavenly Jerusalem

[Zion] tears into our atmosphere in full. So it makes sense that now John sees the Great Multitude in the vision with Jesus **[cf. Revelation 7:9-14].** No where else in **Revelation**'s chronology do we find a clearer marker for the rapture but just prior to the commencement of the fire judgments shown in the sixth seal. The next part is just an estimation of what is really happening, but since we know that *"the dead in Christ will rise first"* **1 Thessalonians 4:16** this could explain the initial lighting flashes across the globe, as Angels retrieve the dead. This then leaves those who remain faithful and ready to be caught up right before the sixth seal.

As to the confirmation at the beginning that Day of Revealing **[cf. Luke 17:30]**, Jesus makes sure we know who and where these have come from. *"These ... from the great tribulation, ...have washed their robes and made them white in the blood of the Lamb"* **Revelation 7:14** We see the harvest/the Day of the Lord had begun secretly now revealed to the world during this larger period called the Great Tribulation. When did the Great tribulation begin? Before we are taken. When is it done? After we are taken from it. The fifth seal as well has all the elements of Jesus description *"of those days"* **Matthew 24:22,** but **Revelation** doesn't gives us absolute clear markers of when it actually starts or when we are taken. The mystery of the bride being one of the deepest in scripture, makes us dig for it.

Similarities exist though from Jesus description of right before the end, *"who cry out to Him day and night ...bring justice quickly"* **Luke 18:7** and the fifth seal statement *"How long O' Lord ...little while longer"* **Revelation 6:10.** Time between the fifth and sixth seal is not long. Here's where I must mention how important sticking to the bible for definitions is vitally important in finding harmony. For the Post Tribulation/Pre-Wrath will most likely agree with me on the placement of the rapture right before the sixth seal. However the big issue I have with them is on keeping the seven year interpretation of **Daniel 9** and the semantics involved with propping up that false notion. The Great Tribulation does not end here at the sixth seal, you cannot make it entirely separate from the day of the Lord as some suppose.

Jesus divides the Great Tribulation into two parts; one we experience **[cf. Matthew 24:15-27]** and the one we shouldn't, *"in those days after that tribulation ... the moon will not give its light"* **Mark 13:24**. This second part clearly is being defined as the Day of the Lord by the moon becoming dark. **[cf. Joel 2:31, Revelation 6:12]**. Jesus leaving behind any personal conversation and instruction such as *"I tell you in advance"* **Mathew 24:25** for the impersonal *"they"* in **Mathew 25:30-31** shows we are gone now. The reason many can't see clearly is they haven't imagined that Jesus will come to earth before the end and hide above the earth creating an ark for His people to be gathered too. Many can't see this as happening while **Revelation 8-19** pours out details of what is taking place on earth as such a polar opposite. It's just inconceivable to many. For many, the day of the Lord is not defined by Jesus being present on the earth. For many the Great Tribulation is synonymous with the day of the Lord and it is not.

The assumption we can observe from Jesus teaching on the harvest **[cf. Matthew 13]** is at the beginning salvation is completed! The wheat would then be fully grown and the only difference from the start to its finish is the stages of gathering the wheat into the barn which Jesus gives indication of plurality or process, **"good into containers"** **Matthew 13:48**. From what the Jewish process teaches us there is first fruits, a general harvest and finally a gleaning phase. Many argue over **Matthew 25** parable revealing such a process since **"virgins"** are not the Bride and the focal destination is not the Chuppah tent but "**the wedding feast**" that occurs later.

Although one spot for the gleaning process could be this period parallel to Noah's loading the ark between the fifth and sixth seal, others believe God is using the **3.5 years** of the trumpet period/day of revealing to finish that process. **Daniel 12:1** says, **"... everyone found written in the book, will be rescued."** When? During this time frame I believe is spoken of for the seven trumpets **[cf. Revelation 11:2]** defined verses later in **Daniel 12:7** as 3.5 years. This would push the rapture very close to the sixth seal for the faithful, **"those who eagerly await Him"** **Hebrews 9:28** Consider, no one else is being included in this initial gathering!

Many can play the games in order to catch the last train out, I have to warn you, you are playing with fire. The realm of speculation does not help us when **"the Lord knows how to rescue the godly ...and keep the unrighteous under ..."** **2 Peter 2:9**. Key word there is righteous. No where can you be right with God by playing games with your odds. You are exposing your hearts true love is somewhere else. What is significant about the trumpet period is no one changes allegiances from the start, **"The rest of mankind ... they did not repent"** **Revelation 9:21** Concerning those left behind the statement, **"Here is the perseverance and faith of the Saints ... Blessed are the dead who die in the Lord from now on"** **Revelation 14:12-13 (cf. 13:10)** which reveals not salvations starting but finishing!

The number would be unchanged from the start of that Day. The number is completed but the harvest has started. This is why I believe the age changes during this gleaning process/harvest/Day of the Lord/Trumpet Period. The last **3.5 years** of the **70 weeks** is the start of the new age and Jesus reign hidden above. Who upon arrival has had Satan thrown to earth, and is now hidden reigning above! Why is this important? Because Jesus made the end the goal! *"One who endures to the end will be saved"* **Mark 13:13**, **Matthew 24:13** *"by your endurance you will gain your lives."* **Luke 21:19**

Paul is giving us the clearest link to the timing of our departure, *"After that those who are Christ's at His coming, then the end."* **1 Corinthians 15:23b** The end in this context isn't the end of the age but instead of everything, the Seventh Trumpet *"when He hands over the kingdom ... Abolishes all rule ..."* **v24.** Jesus being clear that, *"His day"* **Luke 17:24** was plural *"the days of the Son of Man"* **Luke 17:26** that starts when the world is unaware **Luke 17:27-28** and He is already present above the earth hidden in the coming glory. Paralleling Noah's seven days loading the ark and his time above the flood Jesus made it clear, *"just as the days of Noah"* **Luke 17:26**

The logic should be plain to us. Christ won't be recognized by the world first as having arrived. Notice at the very end they see Him physically **[cf. Matthew 24:30-31]** yet at the sixth seal they merely feel His presence. **[Cf. Revelation 6:16-17]** The revealing has just started. Yet we are not on the same level as this world, if indeed we are His own. We'll have both recognized He has arrived and been taken before Him as His bride.

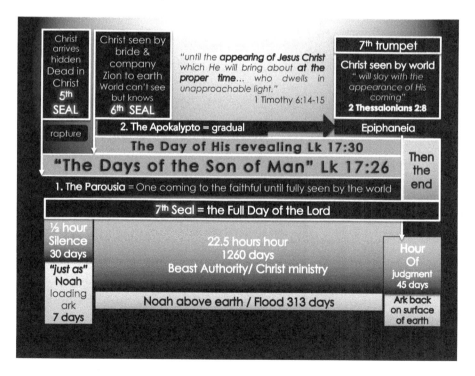

For **Luke 17** is the clearest on this separation between the whole time Christ is on earth hidden then revealed as *"the days of the Son of Man"* **v26** versus what occurs from the start of the fire judgments, called the **"day of His revealing" v30**. Jesus in describing the difference between these two uses Noah's as an example. Which calls to mind that Noah loaded the ark for a period of time when signs were increasing of a coming flood. Saying the world was still making plans until, **"Noah entered the ark ...Lot went out" v27,29**. Judgment started immediately as we see on the sixth seal. Yet the idea was that the Day of the Lord/Christ presence in the earth's atmosphere had already begun unsuspected. In Paul's words, **"the day of the Lord will come ... while they are saying, Peace & safety"** 1 **Thessalonians 5:3**

So we see the day of the Lord (Jesus arrival) begins before the **"day of His revealing,"** which parallel's Noah's entrance into the ark and God sealing the door, **"the same on the day that the Son of Man is revealed" Luke 17:30**. So the deduction should be that before that point He is not revealed or evident to the world but to us. So this is one of the greatest mystery and revelation of the Bible! There's a short period before that that no one has an idea that heaven has already invaded earth! Even when Christ has begun to be **"revealed"** used in **Luke 17:30**, the word **"revealed"** is in the passive indicative and translates as a process of understanding **[cf. Romans 1:17]**.

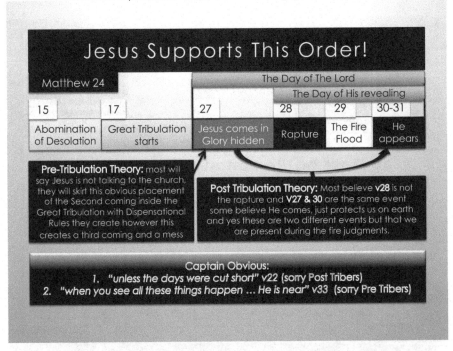

So backing up Jesus gives us a sign that precedes the obvious one the world wakes up to in the sixth seal, in the revelation of His glory in the sky. Most don't quite get how this occurs by reading the **Matthew 24** discourse from **verse 27-29**. Most read the Glory **v27**

then bam judgment **v29**, skipping the significance of **verse 28**. We will talk about these Eagles and dead bodies further along as a description of the rapture itself! But for now ... when we see the description in the sixth Seal, we may be only seeing what happens after we have left and the world now knows something for sure is up! Even here it starts with only *"the presence of Him"* **Revelation 6:16** only later saying He has come to reign **[11:15]** seen from Mount Zion **[14:1]** and coming with His armies **[19:11-16].** Jesus making clear at the onset He would only be discerned by signs in the sky *"just as lightning comes from the east and flashes to the west so will the coming of the Son of Man be"* **Matthew 24:27** but later after the description of the judgment portion of the Day of the Lord saying, *"then the sign of the Son of Man will appear in the sky... they will see"* **Matthew 24:30-31**

This concept of Days is hard for the church to comprehend since we have the extreme popular views making His coming an individual event on a single day in time. Pre-Tribulation Theorist seeing Him coming leaving and coming a third time creating license to change the word "coming" from its context of singular to multiple comings! Post Tribulation Theorist attempts to condense everything down to one single event at the very end. Tell me how can the church be so far removed from harmonizing prophecy and scriptures?

In Peter's description of this period of Christ arrival to His physical manifestation to the world, called the Day of the Lord, *"in which the heaven's will pass away ... the elements will be destroyed with intense heat"* **2 Peter 3:10a** would make you think this must be the very end of everything. God is wiping out the heavens with intense fire of His presence! Notice though, Peter says this actually happens before, *"the earth and its works <u>will be</u> burned up."* **v10b.** This means it is still future! Only after the elements of the universe have been wiped away, does God's plan on judging the earth. How is this possible with **3.5 years** still to go? Could not the heavens easily destroy the earth itself? Well, for starters all things are possible for God.

The only way for the sixth seal signs to occur without completely and immediately damaging the earth is God's protective canopy around the earth. To have the affect of *"stars fell to the earth"* **Revelation 6:13** or *"the sky split apart like a scroll"* **v14,** suggest a rip in our dimension as heaven comes to earth. Peter hints as to what is happening in the verses that follow his discourse, *"heavens will be destroyed by burning ... we are looking for a new heavens".* **2 Peter 10,12** For when we lineup all the chronological events of Revelation, we find their is an unseen war in heaven with angels and Satan is cast down to earth for 3.5 years in order to test men's hearts.

The distinct possibility is Satan was trying to destroy the earth while God is protecting it. However, what results is God gets to recreate the heavens before judging the earth for His bride to see.

In protecting the earth from complete oblivion, He then becomes the fire in our mist instead! This turns out badly for Satan. So why desire it this day? Peter's whole point *"desiring the coming of the day of God" 3:12* would only be because Jesus is present and has created a *"new heavens and a new earth in which righteousness dwells" 2 Peter 3:13* in the process of coming. Hidden behind His canopy of fire & clouds, Jesus has a surprise for is bride. Otherwise we might tell Peter, what are you smoking, why look forward? Yet Peter is adamant about what's in store for us, a honeymoon or "Huppah tent" in the sky, followed by inheriting with Christ a glorious *"new earth"* in which we triumph with Christ.

Backing up though before the great tribulation or even the Abomination occurs, we see this gradual sign occur in the sky afar mentioned included in **Luke's** account of Jesus words **[Luke 21:11]** giving insight into this heavenly drama being played. Tracking this ever increasing drama in the days leading up to the end of this age, **Luke 21:26** now brings these signs into our own solar system, suggesting a cataclysmic event starts over time from afar finally reaching our part of the galaxy. Could this be why we are dragged into court for questioning? Like, *"what is going on, is this what you been saying the bible has been saying?"*

Moving forward we see how the intensity of these celestial signs grow to cause this, *"men fainting for fear and the expectation of the things coming ... for the heavens will be shaken" v26b* Just when all seemed doomed to destruction, God is seen as interceding by jumping in the way, *"the stars of the sky fell to the earth ... the sky split apart like a scroll when rolled up" Revelation 6:13-14* Notice the effect of peeling aside this dimension and entering this one with Heaven's tabernacle, New Jerusalem! At this point you have got to believe the only reason the earth still stands is because of GOD! For Heaven must have caused the tear in the fabric of our dimensions in order for the sky to be split open! Suddenly the King has arrived in full. In the **book of Hebrew** this terrifying moment is just the start of a period of shaking, *"Yet once more I will shake not only the earth but also the heaven." 12:26-27*.

So powerful is this Mt Sinai parallel of the coming Heavenly Zion in **Hebrews 12:18-28** that it puts the origin visit to shame. In the case of Mt. Sinai, God desired a bride **[Exodus 19:6]**, so He leaves for two prophetic days **(2000 years)** with the instructions for her to prepare herself **[Exodus 19:10]**. On the third day instead of seeing faith out of His expected bride *(the wandering Jewish people)*, he sees rejection and fear. So God uses Moses with Aaron going up the side of the Mountain part way as a type of the future rapture. Thus the author(s) of Hebrews attempts to point out the hope for a better outcome when Christ returns for His bride the church, and admonition to not fear!

Paul shows us this part way when he describes our departure, we will *"meet the Lord in the (lower atmosphere) air"* **1 Thessalonians 4:17**. **[Cf. Exodus 24;1]** Previous to this *"Mount Sinai was all in smoke because the Lord descended upon it in fire ...like the smoke of a furnace and the whole mountain quaked violently."* **Exodus 19:18** which is equivalent to Paul's description of His coming in **2 Thessalonians 1:9**. Since there isn't just one vision that is consistent for His coming, this should suggest a gradual event over days that increasingly becomes undeniable. Just as Paul give a single point in time as apart of the whole in *"the appearance of His coming"* **2 Thessalonians 2:8**

Yet after the terrifying opener it is said they *"saw the God of Israel; and under His feet there appeared to be pavement of sapphire as clear as the sky itself."* **Exodus 24:9-10** Then it is said that the next six days *"the glory of the Lord rested on Mount Sinai and the cloud covered it."* And *"to the eyes of the sons of Israel the appearance of the glory ... was like a consuming fire"* **Exodus 24:17** Only on the seven days later, does God call up Moses again from the clouds where the elders were part way up as a sign of the conclusion of the Day of the Lord, when we are gathered from the sky itself and the world sees Him. **[Cf. Matthew 24:30-31]** I know I got you confused because yes its a process. Many of you were looking for easy answers. Hang in there though, a puzzle can start out bewildering until a greater percentage of the pieces are put together.

Okay so this is God's chosen parallels, when God visited Noah & Moses. So don't miss that the author of **Hebrews** identifies this period, starting at our departure, as equivalent to the seven days of His glory between Moses second and third ascension; as *"yet once more I will shake"* **12:27**. For just as God found those faithful in the seventy elders (faithful) to go up in the sky, He will remove the faithful above the earth during the beginning of the Day of His revealing. However He doesn't stop there, God has just started to harvest and judge the earth.

THE LINKS

*"... With regard to **the coming** of our Lord Jesus Christ and **our gathering** together to Him, that you not be quickly shaken...**to the effect that the day of the Lord has come.**"* **2 Thessalonians 2:1**

From this context one might think that Paul is linking our gathering directly to His arrival and the Day of the Lord as a threesome. Instead he doesn't object to their concerns that the Day of the Lord could sneak up on people, which is their fear here concerning a letter written. Instead He uses precursory events to locate its start. **'Let no one deceive you, for it (the day of the Lord) will not come unless ...'' 2 Thessalonians 2:3** The objective being the awareness of the start of **the Day** because it comes **"like a thief" 2 Peter 3:10** while people are unaware. Understand this concern by the church comes from the first letters revelation that it starts very deceptively **"while they are saying" 1 Thessalonians 5:3**.

Remember, Paul had singles out who doesn't escape that Day saying, **"they will not escape" 1 Thessalonians 5:3** never mentioning that we won't enter that day but instead we would not be in darkness that the day would **"overtake us like a "thief" 1 Thessalonians 5:4** meaning unaware. The assumption all enter but we are in the *"know"* and not sleeping *"as others do"* but *"sober and alert"* ready for God's divine exit strategy. For the start of the day is mysterious full of deception and a test. If we are looking for His kingdom here on earth, we will be enticed by signs in the sky and a man doing miracles? If we are paying attention to Jesus words then we are looking up for the Glory?

If you were to get anything from this complex chapter full of puzzle pieces, this one should be a lock. The Day starts mysteriously before the suddenly of our departure connected to the immediate sudden judgment. Read it right there in print! **"For you know full well the day of the Lord will come just like a thief in the night. While they are saying, "Peace & Safety" then destruction will come suddenly ..." 1 Thessalonians 5:2-3** The order is plainly seen here, the Day of the Lord starts with signs and wonders in the sky and people actually celebrating 'Peace & Safety' and Paul is saying the whole thing is the **Day of the Lord**. How can it be *His Day* without Him being present for it? Thus my conclusion is the only one possible, Jesus is hidden in earth's upper atmosphere.

In fact, Jesus words are most disturbing. Explaining that not only will people be doing life as usual in Noah's case **[cf. Luke 17:27]** but making plans for the future in Lot's case. **[Cf. Luke 17:28]** All this when Jesus first arrives shrouded in His glory. **"Just as it happened ... so it will be also in the days of the Son of Man" Luke 17:26** Paul's point will be **"God has not destined us for wrath, but for obtaining salvation through our Lord Jesus Christ" 1 Thessalonians 5:9**; thus we will escape that Day's trap before the commencement of judgment, because it does not start with His wrath, instead it starts with His arrival.

The idea is *the Day of the Lord* is synonymous with judgments misses the point of why we call it *His Day*. Its *His day* because He is present for it! The Day doesn't begin with judgments it starts with His arrival. Nor does it immediately start with our departure. His coming being **"days" Luke 17:26** gives room for our departure during this period not necessarily at its very beginning.

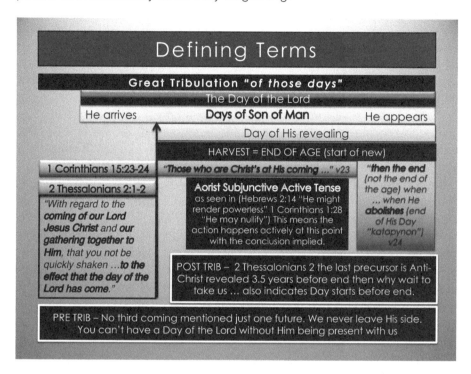

For example even in the opening of the sixth seal **Revelation 6:12-17**; we aren't given an indication that the Great Multitude was removed then, only that John can now see them and now it is exclaimed **"they have come out of" 7:14** past tense. This is where my analytical side kicked in, because a time code seemed to be attached to the beginning of the Seventh Seal or the Day of the Lord when it says, **"The Lamb broke the seventh seal there was a silence in heaven for about a half hour" Revelation 8:1**. This is before the judgment portion starts which seems to be announced by the sixth seal. As if Jesus was giving us the prelude timeframe when the gathering occurred from His arrival until the obvious happens in the sixth seal.

So we are backing up from the sixth seal to include the whole of the Day of the Lord because Jesus arrived 1/2 hour earlier and took us out of the world, this coincides with the context of the Fifth Seal prayers and the prayers at the altar **"which was before His throne" Revelation 8:3**. The idea is His throne is now entered the earth's upper atmosphere and we are there with Him. The whole of the Day of the Lord then would be revealed from the *"silence for about half an hour"* **Revelation 8:1** starting it and finished by *"the hour of His judgment has come"* **14:7** and *"For in one hour your judgment has come"* **18:10** as a symbolic 24 hour period left to us to figure this out by ratio comparisons to other parallels.

Did you get that, **a half hour** is declared before the judgment portion of the Day and **an hour** for the final judgment at the end. Could God be that obvious in **Revelation** to give us an example of a **24 hour period** to represent something he calls *"the Day"*? This then would give us **22.5 hours** in-between, for the **1260 days or 3.5 years** of the Beast authority/Trumpet Period, to complete the time.

Believing that all time codes have meaning in scripture either as symbolic prophetic codes or real time, I stumbled upon this. The first **half hour** would have a ratio of **.0208** divided into **24 hours** of a single day. When compared to Noah's example, our *"just as"* parallel, **Luke 17:26**, Noah spent 7 days aware of when the flood would occur which we can directly linked to how at *"the abomination of Desolation"* **Matthew 24:15** we should have a hard count. So counting the ark **313 days** above the earth as the **3.5 years** we have equivalents for both periods. For these seven days I have a ratio to the whole of **.0218** this is a difference of a mere **.001**. One percent of one percent, giving us a very high probability God is pointing towards this comparison. So I kept comparing.

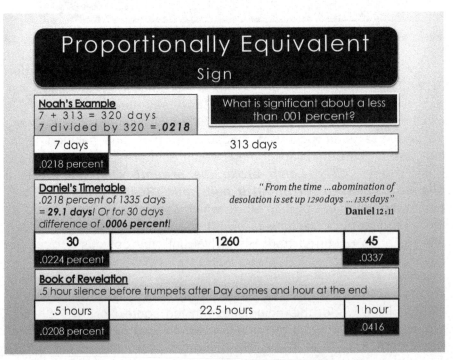

Proportionally Equivalent
Sign

Noah's Example 7 + 313 = 320 days 7 divided by 320 =.0218	What is significant about a less than .001 percent?	
7 days	313 days	
.0218 percent		
Daniel's Timetable .0218 percent of 1335 days = **29.1 days!** Or for 30 days difference of **.0006 percent!**	*" From the time ...abomination of desolation is set up 1290 days ...1335 days"* **Daniel 12:11**	
30	1260	45
.0224 percent		.0337
Book of Revelation .5 hour silence before trumpets after Day comes and hour at the end		
.5 hours	22.5 hours	1 hour
.0208 percent		.0416

Next I took Daniel's time table of **1290 days & 1335 days** from when the Abomination of Desolation would be setup until Christ triumph over the Anti-Christ King and resultant Kingdom rest **[cf. Daniel 12:11]** as a parallel as well. The ratio of **30** into the total amount of days of **1335** in **Daniel 12:12** was **.0224**. Again the difference was **.0016** from the largest of the three and only **.0006** from the smallest difference. That's two or three witnesses showing the same amazing coincidental equivalency.

In making this comparison, I took the **.0218** ratio for Noah's loading period directly into the 1335 days [Daniel 12:12] we would get **29.1** days, these parallel's are that similar. Knowing that **30 day's** from the Abomination the beast authority begins gives us a deeper view into these critical days and revelation into other scriptures. For when we are removed in **Revelation 12:14**, we are rescued right after Satan is thrown down **[v13]** and right before he goes crazy **[v15]**!

Even the bulk of *the Day of the Lord* should be **1260 days** which matches the Trumpet period/Beast Authority and most importantly **Daniel 12:7** timespan for how long until wonders seize from Satan's beast by Jesus finally physically appearing in the Sky resolving the greatest mystery of the ages. Again minus the half hour and hour at the end we take **22.5** into a day equaling **.9375** then times it by the full **1335 days** and we get **1251** days, **9 days** short of the **1260**. The ratios are that close. It is amazing to me to see clearly *the Day of the Lord* in **Revelation** in terms of a **24 hour** period confirmed. God is using the closest relevant terms, to help those who truly seek answers.

When we see slight variances, we can understand that "**no one knows the** *literal* **day**" because God has taken the liberty to **"cut short"** **Matthew 24:22** any expected count. All because God is usurping the usurper Satan by keeping this one secret.

THE UNTIMELINESS

*"For this reason you also must be ready; For the Son of man is **coming at an hour you do not think** He will."*
Matthew 24:44

As stated before Jesus cannot leave and take us to heaven and then return again! This presents a real problem! Parousia, the greek word for **"coming"** is singular always with the definite article **"the"**, so there is no indication anywhere of a third. Well, no mention of one exist in the bible only different events that are apart of His coming that are perceived to be the whole. The point is we can never leave Him once gathered. ***"So we shall always be with the Lord"* 1 Thessalonians 4:17**. We cannot go to heaven while He remains here either, neither can he leave with us and *the Day of the Lord* start since He must be present for that.

Thus then' predicates a removal from the surface of the earth but not the earth itself. During this period Jesus must be with us the whole time and connected to earth in some way. Just our blessing that the bible is harmonious and what I just described is the actual description of the prophets for what is ahead. Jesus takes us to a solitary wilderness "chuppa" tent canopy above the earth. This is the honeymoon portion of the Jewish Wedding for where else are we fitting that in. For anyone who knows the traditions of the Jewish wedding must acknowledge it comes before the feast **[cf. Revelation 19]**.

Remember the only other options are unfortunately very disharmonious to scripture. The Post Tribulation position for example, we go to heaven with Jesus when He is revealed to the world. The Day of the Lord would begin at this point in time at the seventh trumpet. This creates massive problems for Paul taught that, ***"When Christ ... is revealed then you will be revealed with Him"* Colossians 3:4** Yet **Matthew 24:31** the Post tribulation Theorist rapture has us gathered after the world has seen Him. This is odd and not in keeping with common sense. We are revealed in anti-climatic fashion. Yet **Revelation 19:14** is clear, ***"were following Him on white horses".*** So many why's to consider because this is not the the biblical representation of what really happens. Why are we going through the Trumpet period which is similar to the "flood"? Why would God answer our prayers by sending judgment where we are during that Trumpet period? Did not God use Lot as an example who was tormented by being around the ungodly **[cf. 2 Peter 2:8]**.

Why? Why would God reward the faithful with "sealing"? This makes no sense! Why would the Groom delay? No God forbid, as Paul spoke so well! The groom comes directly for His bride, first with the best man (Holy Spirit) heralding Him then He knocks. For the Seventh Trumpet involves us already suited up as an army with Jesus. Like why is the entire Trumpet Period after ***"the great day of their wrath has come."* Revelation 6:17** when God hasn't destined us to that!

Why does Satan try to reach for the Raptured saints from the surface of the earth if we are still on the earth sealed? **[cf. Revelation 12:15-16]** So Jesus finally appears to the world we are said to be with Him as ***"His bride who has made herself ready"* Revelation 19:7**, who has already had time to prepare herself! For ***"When He comes to be glorified in His saints on that day"* 2 Thessalonians 1:10** it is as if we are His bride by His side at this moment.

The only way to solve the Post Tribulation puzzle would be to make the sixth seal and the seventh trumpet the same event. Jesus shows up in **Revelation 6:16** with the moon blood though. So the Day of the Lord then wouldn't occur until the hour of judgment. Yet during the Trumpet period **Revelation 8-11** the moon is darkened which is a Day of the Lord marker from **Joel 2:10** and seen a verse before **[cf. Matthew 24:29]** Jesus is revealed from the clouds **[cf. V30-31].** Everything feels out of order in this scenario, because it is. Does God need **3.5 years** to bring His wrath? I don't believe so, instead He is testing the earth to harvest the remaining souls?

For the Pre-Tribulation crowd, why didn't God take Noah and the eight to heaven, but revealed an Ark above the surface of earth? Why can't we just admit we are wrong in our estimation of how all this goes down? Is it not scriptural harmony what we hunger for? For if we go off to some far away heaven then *the Day of the Lord* must start at the Seventh Trumpet, because Jesus is gone that whole time with us! So why is the Trumpet period celestial markers in sync with Joel's Day of the Lord markers **[cf. Joel 2:10, Revelation 8:12]?** Again so many inconsistencies when you believe you can make the Word of God say what you want it to say.

For Jesus to leave earth with us as the Pre-Tribulation theory suggest to start the Day of the Lord is ridiculous as well. The Day can't be His while He is away! It is *His day* because He is present for it! I figure if I say it enough times it will dawn on you how ridiculous it is to believe otherwise. If Noah **[**a type of Christ **cf. 1 Peter 3:20]** saved His family through an ark that was above the earth why are we saying we will saved alongside the unrighteous on earth sealed or some far away place in the heavens?

If you can hear me out, God made everything about this a mystery for a reason! ***"This mystery is great but I am speaking with reference to Christ and the church"* Ephesians 5:32** So should we not expect to have to dig for this revelation or expand our thinking or imagination, for He does things above our imagination **[cf. Ephesians 3:20]**. God isn't going to put it in plain speech, For He is creating a new reality never seen before, a cinema for the ages! Could not the Lambs throne, His tabernacle come with Him to earth in the form of Zion, and park it above the earth hidden?

Finally for you Mid Tribulation Theorist, there can't be a mid-point without a seven year duration for the Great Tribulation. **Daniel 12:11-12** gives only **1335 days** from the Abomination and **Matthew's** account uses ***"then"* 24:16,21** twice making it impossible to place the Great Tribulation before the Abomination. For example, even if you took the main support for a seven year theory from **Daniel 9:27** and attributed *"He"* of the verse incorrectly to a future Anti-Christ. You would have an Abomination at the mid point but not the rapture. For Jesus chronology is clear, the Abomination *"then"* **Matthew 24:21**, *"those days cut short"* **v22**, *"then"* **v23** and finally *"so will the coming of the Son of man be"* **v27**. Jesus clearly places our departure at a later time then the Abomination. So to be true to scripture there is only Jesus forewarning us *"at an hour you do not think"* **Luke 24:44** indicating the truth will be very unpopular or not as simple as we are making it out to be.

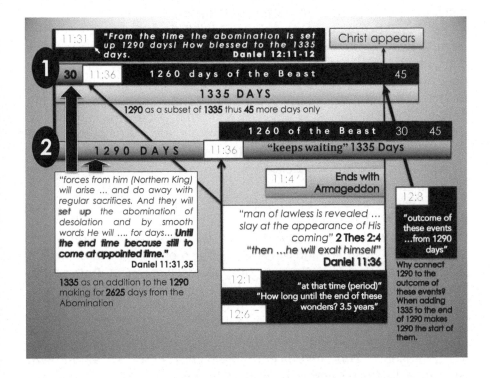

To view how messed up our scholarly estimations are, we need only look at Daniel's chronology alongside the best minds of the last century! After the Abomination is setup one would have to recognize a **thirty day period** precedes the **1260 days** of the Trumpet period/ Beast Authority by reading **Daniel 11**. Yet all I have read make it after. The Abomination occurs in **Daniel 11:31** followed by a period represented in **Daniel 11:32-35** before the Anti-Christ King goes crazy in **v36** which would be the start of the **1260** days. This puts a period between the two, which even the prophecy has to tell us this is NOT the final period or THE END **v35**. This is key because the Angelic messenger will conclude by giving the count of time from the Abomination being setup until the wonders of the **3.5 years** mentioned in **Daniel 12:7** are done thus *"1290 days"* **12:11**. [See above chart for 2 options available and why I decided on #1]

This leaves no other placement for the **30 days** but before the **1260**, however all the scholars I have seen place it after the 1260. This is so they can support their interpretation of Daniel's **70 weeks**. Yet careful study of the context of the **1290 days [cf. Daniel 12:7-11]** points to it's completion after the **1260 (3.5 years)** not the before that portion. Next, the wonders that must cease **[cf. 12:8]** at the end of the 3.5 years **[12:7]** are then connected to the outcome of those events in the 1290 count **[cf. 12:10]**. Nothing fits this concept like Paul's words that, *"the Lawless One ...Lord will slay ...and bring to an end at the appearance of His coming"* **2 Thessalonians 2:8**. This makes no sense then to have 1335 days after Christ is seen by the world.

Due to this fixed duration of 1260 days that can be counted that leads into His appearance to the world, this event of Matthew 24:30-31 can no longer be His arrival or gathering of the Saints since it can be counted and known. Remember Jesus tell us, *"the days will be cut short"* **Matthew 24:22** and two, it will occur on a day unknown **[cf. Matthew 24:36]**. This is why the gospel writers inserted *"let the reader understand (know accurately)"* **Matthew 24:15** from this point in time that the Abomination occurs because there is a hard count. Notice Jesus mentions Daniel by name to connect the context of **Daniel 12** to **Matthew 24**. You can't cut short something without first there being a count! So even in this short period of one month between the abomination and the beast Authority over the world, God is choosing a secret *"no-one knows the day"* **24:36** to take us!

Not the month, not the year but no one knows the day! Some say well there's really **1290 days** and then **1335 days**, so more like a seven year period from the Abomination. Quoting the next verse where we are encouraged to reach the blessing of the **1335 days**. [cf. **Daniel12:12**] So some see this as an option that we aren't just adding **45 more days** which would easily include the hour of judgment and cleanup but a whole **1335 days** added on. The issue here becomes real. Remember only one period is between the Abomination being set up and the Beast authority starting. The question over time was when does the wonders of the **3.5 years** end. What wonders? The ones the Beast incurs. I see this period as **Daniel 11:36-45** in the wording *"at that time"* in **12:1** referring back to the end of the **chapter 11** with what is said next in **12:1-7**.

However those who see this **1290 and 1335** adding up after the Abomination here are the problems. So in making the **1260 days** apart of the last **1335** avoids the original question of when the wonders stop which was at the end of the **1290 days** not the **1335 mark [cf. Daniel 12:11]**. The **1290 days** resolves the *"outcome of these events"* **12:8**, only Jesus appearance slaying the Beast resolves these events. This then creates **1335 days** of God's wrath? It even sounds ridiculous.

The **1260** then should follow the **30** logically, maybe the easiest deduction from scripture ever. Since the **1260** ends with the beast being slain and Jesus return, it makes sense this resolves the wonders **[Daniel 12:8]**. **30 days** that exist between the Abomination and the Beast Authority, then explain Jesus chronology of the time period of the Great Tribulation following the Abomination setup in **Matthew 24:15-27** and why there is a count that is shortened for our exit.

Yet many pushing for a seven year theory trying to add **1290 & 1335** forgetting that that is seven years after the Abomination. Even **Daniel 8:14** *"2,300 evening mornings"* are not equal to the *2625 days* if you combined **1290 & 1335**. My chart exhaust all possibilities for what that passage could mean, but none suggest seven years of great tribulation. The closest period mentioned in scriptures of **2300 days** would suggest a third temple period of only **6.3 years** with the Abomination & the Great Tribulation occurring only at the final **1335 days** of that period.

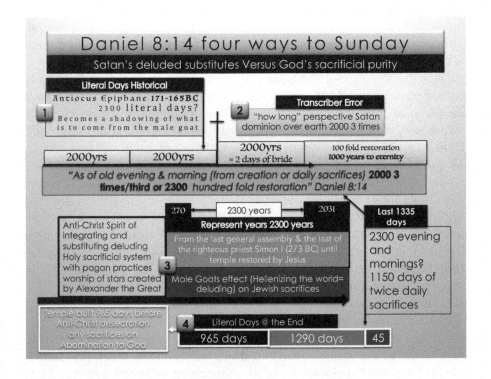

Notice though the passage in **8:14** *never mentions* **2300** as representing days. Whereas later God does refer to days in **Daniel 12:11-12**. Instead **"evenings and mornings"** is used which is relate to sacrifice times or creation days in that, **"as of old"** precedes it. Some make this 2300 years and I even have suggested it was mistakenly retranslated wrong and its 2000 year ages three times and then hundred fold restoration.

However the most logical explanation for **8:14** comes from the context of all of **chapter 8's** vision of the Abomination in question starting with the Hellenization of the Jewish priests to the end of this current age. One could see this as a vision of the epic story and struggle from heaven's perspective against the forces of Satan for **2300 years.** From the documented last time God was present in the temple sacrifices performing miracles was around **270AD** with Simon the Just. If Jesus comes as the anointed **"holy"** in the future in **2031,** we have just found out why this drama in chapter 8 goes from Alexander to the Future.

I encourage you to read wikipedia and its footnotes on Simon the Just. Many have written of this departure from the Shekinah showing up in the temple, Josephus, Sirasch, 2nd Book of Maccubees & the Talmud. Do your own study and make your own decisions on this. Consider this, Daniel visions are threaded together changing themes but related as answers to the previous one. In the next vision God will help answer this very question of **chapter 8** left us with. When will God **"anoint the holy"** **Daniel 9:24** again.

Next moving from precise to general revelation, Jesus says, **"when these things begin to take place"** **Luke 21:28**. However this means the Pre & Post Tribulation theories are wrong! It doesn't start before the things mentioned in the previous section of thought **Luke 21:20-26** or at the very end of them. This context seems to starts right before the Abomination of Desolation and ends with His appearing to the world. Which shouldn't shake us since Paul supported **"the revelation of the lawless one"** as the last precursor to our departure and the fire judgment portion of His coming. **[Cf. 2 Thessalonians 2:3-8]** which occurs at the Abomination revealing who is the Anti-Christ.

This brings us to Paul's use of a restrainer that gives the context as to when the lawless one will be revealed. This is popular for the Pre Tribulation Theorist to argue that when the church is raptured, this releases the fury of the Anti-Christ, given my placement for the rapture that may very well be true. The Lawless One is restrained and according to Paul's argument until He finally goes crazy. Well, according to what I see the rapture is where it belongs then and where Pre Tribulation Theorist don't want it. After the Abomination within **30 day** period before the beast goes crazy for **1260 days** finishing the **1290** when Jesus appears and ends the Beast. **[Cf. 1 Thessalonians 2:8, Daniel 11-12]**.

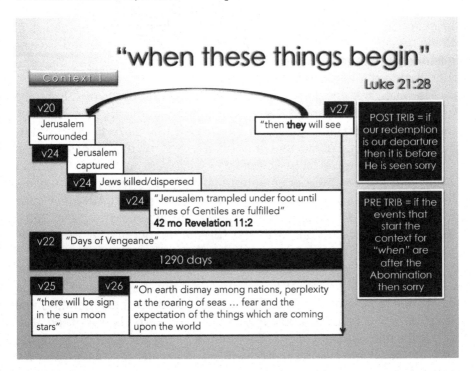

As for the restrainer of Paul's dialogue, *"you know what restrains him now"* **1 Thessalonians 2:6** from what was spoken previously *"exalts himself ... as being God"* **v4,** which is the last precursor to God's judgments & our departure, Paul doesn't say, *"you are restraining him"*. Notice the church was taught what restrained him as if it was well known. If it was the church that would be a new teaching. No, this isn't difficult to understand. For Daniel tells us who. *"Now at that time [referring back to the last section from that starts with the King going crazy] Michael the great prince who stands over the sons of your people, will arise [stand up or step aside] and there will be a time of distress such as never occurred since ... everyone who is found written in the book will be rescued."* **12:1** Even after Paul's letter Jesus gives us a further witness to this affect in **Revelation 12**. *"Michael and his angels waging war with the dragon ...not strong enough and there was no longer a place found for them in heaven. And the great dragon was thrown down"* **v7-8**

In this domino effect, Satan seems to come to the earth before the final **1260** while the faithful are still present in the first **30 day** period. For he immediately *"persecutes the women ... But the two wings of an eagle were given to the woman so that she could fly into the* *wilderness (secluded place)"* **Revelation 12:13-14** which is the rapture 3.5 years from the end. The idea is we are not on earth alongside Satan for long at all! Then what happens? The dragon *"was enraged with"* the rapture and goes *"off to make war with the rest of her children"* **v17** Do you see how clear this becomes.

In **Revelation 12**, Satan is thrown to earth with just *"a short time"* **v12** by who else **"Michael" v7**. Mentioned twice each time the women (the righteous seed) is taken away for **3.5 years** and the response for the first time *"Now the salvation and the power and the kingdom of our God ...have come ...and they overcame him ..."* **v10-11** then later the second time mentioned, *"rejoice O heavens and you who dwell in them"* **v12.** This time take notice of the victory statements as each declare victory **3.5 years** before the end. The kingdom is already come, and the heavens are spoken of as ever present. No where does it say where the wilderness or solitary place is, yet each is met with the hint that it is His kingdom come & Heaven come to earth. The first declaring Zion's arrival when the righteous Jews flee and are sealed the second declaring it slightly differently that those who remain now are joining Zion in the rapture.

In Jesus chronological timeline His appearing in **Matthew 24:30-31** occurs after the Day of the Lord in **Matthew 24:29** [when the moon is dark **cf. Revelation 8:12**]. Our departure occurs before the judgment portion of the Day of the Lord **v28-29** but after the Abomination **v15.** This means we are taken within a month of the Abomination setup by Government forces. Very quick and deceptive turn of events at an unexpected time period during the mantra "Peace & Safety", signs and wonders, a false Jesus coming, and many splinter religious groups claiming Jesus is with them!

Being that we are not taken off earth, but above we read these words. *"The serpent poured water like a river out of His mouth after the women, so that he might cause her to be swept away with the flood."* **Revelation12:15** My projection of this event is, we are seen above the earth as lights or stars so this possessed world leader persuades other nations to shoot nuclear weapons at us as if we are aliens invading earth. This could explain the term the descriptive portion of these passages best. Or possibly other nations intervene against His madness. The funny thing is we are aliens, not of this world, eventually invading earth with our King.

We see this truth again in the next chapter, in the vehement hatred consuming the Beast who *"blaspheme His name and His tabernacle (canopy above the earth) those who dwell in heaven."* **Revelation 13:6** So where is the tabernacle of God now, not on the earth surface but in the realm of earth above? Notice how the Beast anger is directed as though heaven's tabernacle is still in the *"room"* so to speak! Has not Jesus established His throne already above earth? These domino's have fallen from the time of the Abomination are a result of an unseen warfare in the heavens between Angels and Demons.

Now if we pay attention to His throne & tabernacle in **Revelation,** it is distinctly in Heaven far away in **chapter 4**, but by **chapter 7** we get a feel of angels above the earth sealing and His throne close to earth due to the sixth seal expressions of feeling His presence. In fact it is said, *"He who sits on the throne will spread His tabernacle over them."* **V15** revealing God's canopy is established at the beginning of the Trumpet period which the beast is preoccupied with in **chapter 13** as we saw. Don't miss this theme in **Revelation** of His tabernacle coming to earth like a canopy *"spread ... over them"*. If we are taken far away to Heaven, then what's the point of protection? For the Psalmist says, *"You hide them in the secret place of Your presence from the conspiracies of man"* **Psalms 31:20** and *"Let me dwell in Your (Chuppah) tent forever; let me take refuge in the shelter of Your wings"* **Psalms 61:4**

This brings us back to Peter's words, as to why in the heck would anyone be *"looking for and desiring the Day of the Lord"* **2 Peter 3:12** given the nature of it spoken as this scary period of destruction of the heavens and eventual burning of the earth; if we in fact remain on the earth? Unless we come to see this prophetic picture for what this period truly is. A triumph of our faithfulness to stay alert by our removal to our *"spacious place"* **Psalms 18:19**, *"secluded place"* **Revelation 12:7,14,** our honeymoon for where else do we fit this before the wedding feast?

UNDERSTAND OUR MARRIAGE TO CHRIST ISN'T CONSUMMATED YET! We are in the betrothal period where the groom has gone to prepare a place for us. **[Cf. John 14:3]** When He returns as the groom, there has to be a honeymoon phase before the feast mentioned in **Revelation 19**. Where else are we going to fit the honeymoon, the Jewish Chuppah or Huppah tent but exactly where multiple references imply a canopy shows up above the earth! How can Jesus even keep Heaven and earth separate? Isn't Jesus bringing Heaven with Him! For He taught us to pray *"Your Kingdom come Your will be done on earth as it is in Heaven"* **Matthew 6:10** In other words Jesus is connecting Heavenly Jerusalem to earth! This has always been God's intention!

Our Chuppah, our honeymoon, our tent before the wedding feast, is real! God will rescue the righteous. The prophets saw this, *"Come my people, enter into your rooms (honeymoon suite) and close your doors behind you until __indignation__ runs its course."* **Isaiah 26:20**, Which is a clear indication of the order as occurring before the end in the next verse *"For behold the Lord is about to come out from His place to punish ..."* **Isaiah 26:21** When is this? Starting at the beginning of the **1260 days** after the **30**, for Daniel uses the same language for the **1260 period** saying, *"He will prosper until* __indignation__ *is finished"* **Daniel 11:36. [Cf. Daniel 12:1,7]** Indignation occurs at the final 3.5 years and we are kept from it!

So let's review how we separate what is really going on in the final period we come out of. So deceptive is this short period which starts the Great Tribulation Period *"of those days"* **Matthew 24:21-22** in which we come out of **[cf. Revelation 7:14]** that **Daniel 11:32-35** needs to specifically tell us, *"not the appointed time"* **v35** of the end. Why? Because it will seem like the end. We see evidence of Christians around the world standing up! *"Those who know their God will display strength and take action."* **Daniel 11:32**

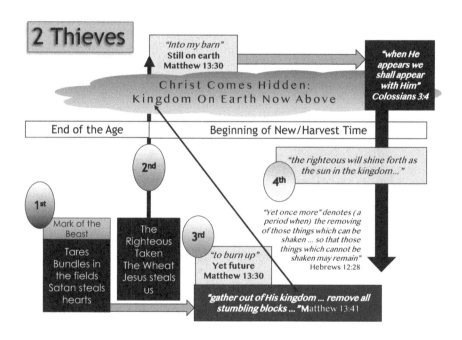

This is important to understand that only later does Daniel is told a time comes when *"everyone who is found written in the book will be rescued."* **12:1** Note that it says, *"everyone"* that includes you and I, the rapture. This *"great tribulation"* is then split in two tribulations according to Mark's account **[cf. Mark 13:24a]**. Why? Because what follows is the Day of the Lord judgment period or trumpet period of Revelation, in *"the sun will be darkened and the moon will not give its light."* **Mark 13:24b** So the first tribulation is for us to go through the other is forbidden, for it contains God's

223

judgments for the unfaithful & unbelieving. The reward of the faithful is not judgments.

When we enter this second tribulation, we see the Trumpet Period judgments are separating now the unready from the unbelieving. **[Cf. Revelation 8-13]** As this harvest shifts to its final process step in *"the hour of judgment"* or bowls which *"the wrath of God is finished"* **15:1,** Finally, we see Christ appear with His bride and the rest of the saints are harvested **[cf. Revelation 14:13]** with the commencement of judgment entirely reserved for the unbelieving **[cf. Revelation 14:14-19]**

THE TAKEN

*"See to it that you **do not refuse Him who is speaking**. For if those did not escape when they refused him ...much less ..."*
Hebrews 12:25-26

Hebrews 12 does a great job defining Zion **[v22-23]**, as Jesus coming with the *"church of the firstborn"* **v23** from heaven for our gathering above the earth in harmony with Paul's teaching bringing with Him *"those who have fallen asleep ... dead in Christ"* **1 Thessalonians 4:14-16** and again *"those who are Christ's"* **1 Corinthians 15:23.** Be careful to pay attention to what is SEEN at His coming. It is never Jesus Himself but His glory **[c.f. Matthew 24:27; Titus 2:13].** Think on this if Jesus appears physically no one need heed the warning, *"not refuse Him who is speaking"* **Hebrews 12:25** for the seeing would be enough.

Why did Jesus take special care to warn us of those who would say, *"Behold here is Christ' or 'there He is' do not believe him."* **Matthew 24:23** if He was first coming to be seen physically by the world. This must be considered strong proof that the **Matthew 24:30-31** event when He appears to the world and to gather us from the sky is not this same event being described here in the **Hebrews 12:18-28** which matches **Matthew 24:27** when we are gathered to the sky. Eventually yes, every eye will behold Him **[cf. Revelation 1:7]** but that context was never attached to the rapture of **Matthew 24:27-28** but of later in **Matthew 24:30-31.** Consider how brilliant God is in having a coming that is gradual. Concealing the truth of these days, because it simply goes against everyone's expectations of an all in one event.

Instead, this mysterious coming begins *"the days of the Son of*

Man" **Luke 17:26.** In this mysterious thievery which takes the faithful and catches the unready napping, the aftermath itself will not be what is expected as dead bodies fall to the ground all over the world. When people expect to see Jesus; God instead commands His sheep to hear His voice while watching for the glory! **[Cf. Titus 2:13, Matthew 24:27]** Thievery is about to take place, so settle in your heart which thief gets to take you! The fake Jesus on earth or the real one calling from heaven?

Consider the alternative if He gathers us at the very end of **the Day of the Lord Matthew 24:29-31** when every eye will behold Him. *WOULD THAT BE A SURPRISE AT ALL*? For starters nothing would be cut short! But NO! There would be no need to hear Him call. This book would not be necessary! God would be anti-climatic of a story teller, possibly cruel in the process. Yet the more and more we look at this, we see a beautiful picture instead. **Isaiah** is seeing the same event in **Hebrews 12**, when he paints a picture for us of the sudden appearance of glory across the sky in **Isaiah 59:19** declaring suddenly in the next verse *"A redeemer will come to Zion ...,"* **Isaiah 59:20** So let's look at the imagery.

> *"So they will fear the name of the Lord from the West and **His glory from the rising of the sun.** For **He will come** like a rushing stream which the wind of the Lord drives. A redeemer will come to Zion ..."* **Isaiah 59:19**

Notice the process starts with us and doesn't stop there but completes itself on the very earth with God's promise to the physical descendants of Israel in **verse 20.** Thus Joel declares God's deliverance occurring in two places. *"For **on Mount Zion** and **in Jerusalem** there will be those who escape"* **Joel 2:32** In that divine order first coming to Zion *"the church of the first born"* **Hebrews 12:23**, and then later showing how Jesus comes from Zion to the earth. *"The Lord roars **from Zion** and utters His voice from Jerusalem and the heavens and earth tremble. But the Lord is a refuge for His people [Zion] and a stronghold to the sons of Israel."* **Joel 3:16**

Which we should easily see the same picture in Jesus own words, as if He was leaning on **Isaiah** himself saying first, *"For just as lightning comes **from the east** and **flashes to the West** so will **the coming** of the Son of Man be."* **Matthew 24;27** Then later ... *"the Son of Man will appear"* **v30** when He comes *"from Zion"* **Joel 3:16** So we see this truth that God wants us to not live by entirely by sight but by His word, He comes shrouded in glory. For everything concerning this future revelation of a heavenly marriage with Christ was meant to be a great mystery! **[Cf. Ephesians 5:32]** The early church understanding the glorious nature of His coming being introduced by the Groom's best friend the Holy Spirit says, *"The Blessed Hope and <u>appearing of the Glory</u> of ..."* **Titus 2:13** making no mention of seeing Jesus physically first as Jesus didn't either. No where in scripture does it give us an indication He will be seen at first.

So as we return to the **Hebrews 12:18-28** event, we see it fits the **Matthew 24:27** event narrative at the beginning of the Day of the Lord and not the **Matthew 24:30-31** event at the end of the Day of the Lord. In fact, the picture we get here is of God shaking the tree so that the ripe fruit fall from it **[cf. 12:26-27]** or as we see in scripture elsewhere are taken. Harvest has begun and its a process as well is not a single event but occurs over 3.5 years. John the Baptist speaks of this day saying,

*"His winnowing fork is in hand and He will **clear His threshing flour** and He will **gather His wheat into His barn** but **He will burn up the chaff** with unquenchable fire."*

Matthew 3:12

Of course a basic understanding of this winnowing process is a fan is used to blow the chaff away from the wheat which then allows the wheat to be gathered leaving the chaff to be burned. Maybe we should think John the Baptist got the order wrong when Jesus seems to reverse the order with the tares gathered first. *"in the time of harvest gather up the tares and bind them in bundles but gather the wheat into my barn"* **Matthew 13:30**. Yet notice the tares are never removed from the fields at first, just bundled. The wheat are removed but not from the earth for Jesus will later say indicate when the tares are finally removed it is *"from among the righteous"* **v49** and from *"out of His kingdom"* **v41**?

Notice, His Kingdom is already on the earth and so are we still, just above it! **[Cf. V41]** As to the bundling, Paul describes *"a deluding influence"* **2 Thessalonians 2:11** which the word says, *"God will send upon them"* in order to make a clear separation *"for those who didn't love the truth."*. This might be the most logical explanation how God separates. Many say the mark of the beast found in **Revelation 13** to buy and sell as well is that identifiable marker for God.

This separation of the wheat and tares allows for a quick work for the one harvesting. Jesus describes this harvest uniquely saying, *"The angels will come forth and take out the wicked <u>from among the righteous</u> and will throw them into the furnace of fire."* **V49** In this occasion we can assume a further step was needed then the previous bundling of tares and removing wheat to the barn. The extinction of the tares now must occur in the fields and a sentencing to *"The place of weeping and gnashing of teeth."* **v50** Yet pay attention where the barn is located when it is said, *"... from among the righteous"* **v49.** We are still in the room so to speak!

Catch this revelation if you can, the barn isn't heaven away from earth because the tares are removed *"from among the righteous"*! We are above the earth surface but still in the earth's atmosphere. Where else can this barn be?! If it's some notion we stay on earth protected, then the barn would need to be in a separate location on the surface of the planet. Where would that be? We would be separated from *"the dead in Christ"* our other Bridal remnant & Groom above the earth, making no sense.

However, when we piece together all the different parables on the kingdom both given and then explained in **Matthew 13**, we see that the tares are first separated, then the wheat are removed first to the barn which must be within the earth's atmosphere *"just as"* the ark was above the earth! It is then that God removes the tares from the earth and reveals His Kingdom has already arrived to earth hidden. Thus now it can be said, *"The removing of those things which can be shaken as of created things, so that those things which cannot be shaken may remain"* **Hebrews 12:27** because we are never removed from the earth's atmosphere!

227

Otherwise **Hebrews 12:27** might gives us the idea that the tares are the ones removed at the rapture in the **Matthew 24:27-28** event, while we are protected on the earth surface! However this statement only reflects the end portion of the harvest process that we just saw explained in **Matthew 13**, when the tares are eliminated *"from among the righteous"* **v49** after we go to our barn leaves little room for another explanation other than we never leave earth for it is now His Kingdom!

Why is this debate so important to differentiate what happens? Because Jesus warns us not to be earth bound, thus the instruction, *"One in the field must not turn back"* **Luke 17:31** Our home isn't here; until Jesus is physically on the earth surface! The apostle John calling the rapture a test of faith says, *"so that when He appears we may have confidence and not shrink away from Him in shame at His coming."* **1 John 2:28** Be aware, many will believe Jesus has suddenly appeared on earth in the form of the Anti-Christ; but above the earth will be the real deal!

So tell me this doesn't matter! Jesus telling His own to *"lift up your heads"* **Luke 21:28** for your redemption is not down here. Verses later He declares our need for faith to have *"Strength to escape"* **v36** or in the King James Version it reads, *"to be found worthy"* **v36**. Found worthy to stay? No, worthy to leave.

For Jude informs us , *"To Him who is able to keep you from stumbling and to make you stand in the presence of His glory blameless with great joy ..."* **Jude 24** Many confuse Jesus warnings connected to the Abomination and a regional conflict which must happen first saying, *"flee"* with His warnings globally not to flee when he comes, but stand!

The author of Hebrews picks up this concern how we will react to His glory says, *"He who is coming will come and will not delay, if He shrinks back My soul has no pleasure in Him. But we are not of those who shrink back to destruction but of those who have faith to the preserving of the soul."* **10:38-39** Where would we shrink back to? Where will destruction occur but on the earth's surface? Not where Jesus is above the earth but on it! So Jesus asks *"will I find faith on the earth"* **Luke 18:8** Well will He? Where is your heart today, on things above or below?

We see the fan that winnows and separates is His glory seen before the commencement of Christ revealing in the sixth seal. His coming draws the righteous upward in anticipation until the event causes the unrighteous to retreat saying, *"hide us from the presence (glory) of Him who sits on the throne"* **Revelation 6:16**. At this point we can assume the voice has already called us up as we are found in **Revelation 7** with those *"who come out of"* which is a term for being taken not left!

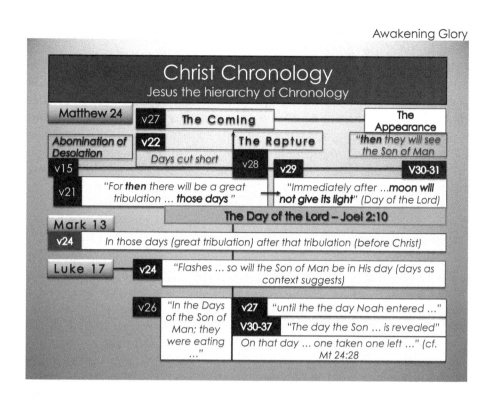

THE APPEARANCE

*"It will be the same **on the day that the Son of Man is revealed.** [gradual tense] On that day ... remember Lot's wife."*

Luke 17:30

Jesus just getting done describing the **"just as"** Noah parallel of His coming being period of **"days" v26** in which we follow Noah loading the Ark as the start of this period while there was peace & safety. Only four verses later and we discover another term for a different starting point called "**the day that the Son of Man is revealed." v30**? This reference is now a parallel of Noah entering the Ark the last time when God seals the door and the floods start. With this new use of **"day"** in **verse 30** we ask the question is this referring to an overlapping period as well of the flood or the event when God seals the door and the floods start as immediately after. **[Cf. This context Luke 17:30-37]**

Grappling with this question of how long & how Christ will be revealed my focused turned to two things in the passage. *First* it is

229

said to be *"the same on the day"* **v30** from the previous verse example of Lot. The main point being made is the righteous were taken before judgment came [not having to endure it but removed as seen in the context **v31-37**]. Again the word *"day"* is used, *"on the day Lot went out from Sodom it rained fire" v29.* Although the order is important with the solid truth of *"as soon as"* the righteous leave judgment starts without break, don't miss that the revealing part isn still unclear. So when we look at the corresponding verses in **Matthew 24** to this event in **Luke 17:31-37** starting with **v28,** as our marker for the rapture; we are really asking does this *"day of revealing"* include the next verse **Matthew 24:29** as well when it parallels the whole period of the flood in the future Day of the Lord.

I believe it does, for the clues are in the Lot example and the definition for the verb, *"revealing"* used. In the example of Lot, his *"day"* **Luke 17:30**, included the whole period it took Sodom to be destroyed. Granted it probably was quick, but the the other parallel of the flood and our future parallel of the Day of the Lord seem to have length to them. This brings us to the verb *"revealed"* **v30?** The verb *"revealed"* is *the present passive indicative*, which means it is ongoing or still happening or a process. The cross reference translators used for this same word in this very same tense is found in **Romans 1:17** when it declares *"righteousness of God is revealed from faith to faith".*

Okay, You can see how we understand our right relationship with our loving Heavenly Father through many places of trust being activated and not just from one event. Just as righteousness has a starting point so does the revelation to the world that Jesus must be above the earth, but only later is revealed physically. This itself is a very powerful revelation that Christ isn't revealed all at once! In fact the commencement of this *Day of His revealing* starts after He has already arrived! For again, the *Days of the Son of Man* in **Luke 17:26** starts before His revealing to us **v30**. For the world is making plans for the future in **v28** yet once the judgments start as implied in **v29** and seen in **v31-37** the world is thrust into a trap!

Stop the presses! Why hasn't ANY serious eschatological students cracked this. Consider, why would God test the world by being seen from the start? Even the book of **Revelation 10:7** refers to the trumpet period of testing as a mystery to be *"finished"*! Why? Well let's review. First glory appears, followed by dead bodies globally! Then we have a near end of the earth cataclysmic event that somehow doesn't end the earth but instead starts a prolonged 3.5 year period of strange occurrences. When you understand what actually is happening every word of **Revelation** begins to make sense! So to say that *the Day of the Lord* comes suddenly is only half the story. It also comes shrouded in a horrifying mystery.

The world wasn't aware Jesus had come, then thought for sure this is it but the Apocalyptic moment of the sixth seal occurs. What follows is the same as Mount Sinai. Darkness gloom terrifying moments as God comes but followed by seven days of clouds and glory seen through them. As we view Jesus words in **Matthew 24** it is clear; we will not see Him at first **v23-24** only the glory **v27** and we will be gone **v28** by synoptic Gospel passages and the way Jesus changes from a very personal dialogue to a very impersonal pronoun after saying, ***"They will see the Son of Man coming ..."*** **Matthew 24:30** when ***"every eye beholds Him"*** **Revelation 1:7** at the very end of His days. Leaving only one verse, **Matthew 24:29**, to explain the period of 3.5 years mentioned in **Revelation 8-11,12,13** for our honeymoon and Israel's deliverance!

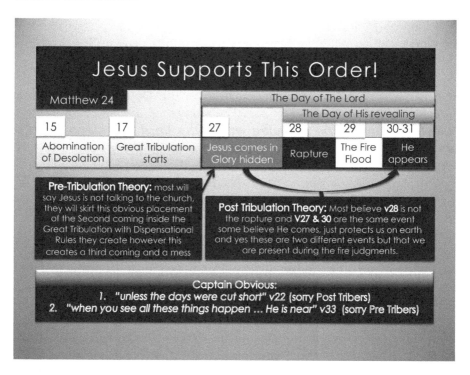

One could ask, how can this order be reversed? For focusing on **Matthew 24:31-32,** not only is the impersonal pronoun used **"they"**: but we are gathered from the sky *(not the earth)* only after the world has seen Him. Why would the world see Him first? Why are we being gathered from the SKY not earth? ***"from one end of the sky to the other"*** **v31** This is not the rapture. We are already in the sky with Him! How many examples can I give you to show you something is awfully wrong with our present day eschatology.

To understand this better we might want to examine how someone can appear at different times in different ways. In Paul's instructions to Timothy, he makes distinctions according to different appearances of Jesus all within the same letter. Notice, *"keep the commandment without stain or reproach <u>until the appearing</u> of our Lord Jesus"* **2 Timothy 6:14** which for us occurs at the rapture; for the context is us not the world. Yet before this Paul says, *"Now has been revealed by the appearing of our Savior Christ Jesus."* **1:10** which is looking backwards to His first coming as an appearance as well of Himself physically.

So the context is important! Towards the end of the letter, Paul states He will judge the world *"by His appearing and His kingdom"* **4:1** So now the context for appearing is the world. So what are we to think? If His kingdom is revealed when He appears to the world are we not His kingdom? **[Cf. Colossians 3:4]** If so has He not already arrived and taken us? Whatever the case, the distinctions are being demonstrated. First to us physically but not to the world, then later to the world with us displayed. This is called rightly dividing the word by contexts.

As to the timing of Christ appearance to the world, the word of God is clear. It occurs at the last hour of the Day of the Lord. For Paul locates it at the end of the **1260 days** of the beast authority, *"Lawless one will be revealed whom the Lord will slay with the breath of His mouth and bring to an end <u>by the appearance</u> of His coming."* **2 Thessalonians 2:8** Notice how Paul speaks as though His appearing is apart of the greater period of His coming or revealing. In this passage, Paul's contexts has shifted from explaining events that keep us from leaving to the mystery of the restrainer explaining our departure **[cf. v6-7]** to the perspective of the world in saying, *"they"* **v10** and *"them"* **v11** and *"they"* **v12**. Paul identifying this period of the Beast Authority/Trumpet Period/ Day of the Lord in **v8** bookended by two events; the revealing of the lawless one and his demise to Christ at His final appearing.

Again if Christ was to appear when he first comes, some inconsistencies arise in the scriptures. First we must relegate Christ coming to the end of the Beast authority **[cf. 2 Thessalonians 2:8]** and with that our departure. Remember **1 Corinthians 15:23** is clear the rapture is not separate from His coming. Yet before the Post tribulation crowd burst into cheers, there are several problems. The biggest in my mind at the start of this period of the Beast Authority **[cf. Daniel 11:36-45]** it is described as a period of *"indignation"* in the statement, *"he will prosper until the indignation is finished"* **v36**. By giving indignation a definite article *"the"*, it would appear as though it is assigned by God as *"the"* one. Well God tells us through Isaiah where we are, safe in our designated place.

*"You who lie in the dust, awake and shout for joy, for your dew is as the dew of the dawn, and **the earth will give birth to the departed spirits**.*
Come my people enter into your rooms and close your doors behind you; *hide a little while* **until indignation runs its course."**   **Isaiah 26:19-20**

Notice what has just happened and will happen next in **verse 21.** The dead in Christ have been gathered and with that it would be implied that those who remain also are taken. Indignation hasn't begun. What follows? ***"For behold the Lord is about to come out from His place to punish the inhabitants of the earth ..."*** **v21** So Christ has not been seen yet, He has not come out yet. We are taken, we hide while indignation occurs and at the end Christ comes out to be seen and judge.

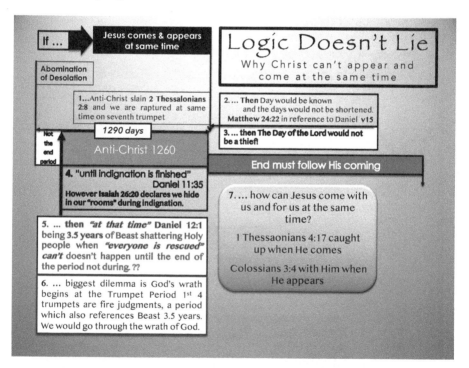

In every biblical context for the end of this age, especially the ones Jesus mentions **[Revelation, Matthew, Luke Mark]** we see evidence for *the Day of the Lord* **[cf. Matthew 24:29]** sandwiched between His arrival event **[cf. Matthew 24:27]** and His appearing to the world event **[cf. Matthew 24:30]**. This beginning of His coming being described as the sudden appearance of the glory or DOXA of God suggest since it was the hope of the church **[cf. Titus 2:13]** we are gathered in the next verses description **Matthew 24:28.**

233

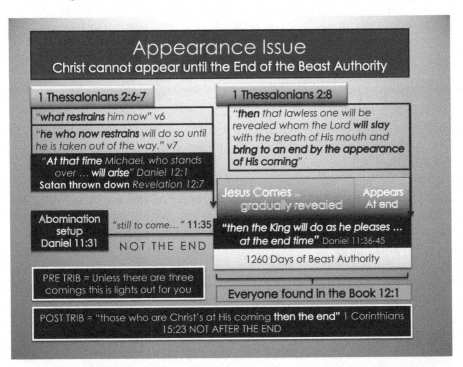

Appearance Issue
Christ cannot appear until the End of the Beast Authority

1 Thessalonians 2:6-7

"*what restrains* him now" v6

"*he who now restrains* will do so until he is taken out of the way." v7

"*At that time* Michael, who stands over ... *will arise*" Daniel 12:1
Satan thrown down Revelation 12:7

1 Thessalonians 2:8

"*then* that lawless one will be revealed whom the Lord **will slay** with the breath of His mouth and **bring to an end by the appearance of His coming**"

| Jesus Comes .. gradually revealed | Appears At end |

| Abomination setup Daniel 11:31 | "still to come..." **11:35** NOT THE END | "*then the King will do as he pleases ... at the end time*" Daniel 11:36-45 |

1260 Days of Beast Authority

PRE TRIB = Unless there are three comings this is lights out for you

Everyone found in the Book 12:1

POST TRIB = "those who are Christ's at His coming **then the end**" 1 Corinthians 15:23 NOT AFTER THE END

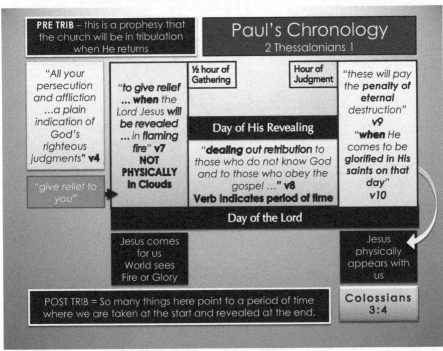

PRE TRIB – this is a prophesy that the church will be in tribulation when He returns

Paul's Chronology
2 Thessalonians 1

"All your persecution and affliction ...a plain indication of God's righteous judgments" **v4**

"give relief to you"

"*to give relief ... when* the Lord Jesus **will be revealed** ... in flaming fire" **v7**
NOT PHYSICALLY in Clouds

| ½ hour of Gathering | Hour of Judgment |

Day of His Revealing

"**dealing** out retribution to those who do not know God and to those who obey the gospel ..." **v8**
Verb indicates period of time

"these will pay the **penalty of eternal destruction**" **v9**
"**when** He comes to be **glorified in His saints on that day**" **v10**

Day of the Lord

Jesus comes for us World sees Fire or Glory

Jesus physically appears with us

POST TRIB = So many things here point to a period of time where we are taken at the start and revealed at the end.

Colossians 3:4

This is a dangerous proposition that nothing obvious signals us or leads us into a defined awareness of when we leave except what

Christ said not to miss; the Abomination of Desolation. God making the only sure sign an event easily missed by the carnally minded who look forward to the very thing that is an Abomination, the return of the temple and its sacrificial system. The Lord only giving them the sign they are looking for after we are gone in the lawless ones exaltations. For the Abomination will occur with trying to rebuild with the help of the Gentile Nations what God tore down.

Given this deceptive turn toward our departure, the glory of God appearing maybe your last hope to straighten up! Luke accounting for when Jesus was transfigured on the Mountaintop writes, **"appearing in glory"** and states **"Now Peter and His companions had been overcome with sleep; but when they were fully awake, they saw His glory" Luke 9:31-32** What did they see? The Glory! When? When they were fully awake! Church don't sleep through His coming! Awaken even now to the indwelling presence of God, the kingdom within! Understand, any hope that is earthly is your enemy to true readiness. Those who are not alert will miss this.

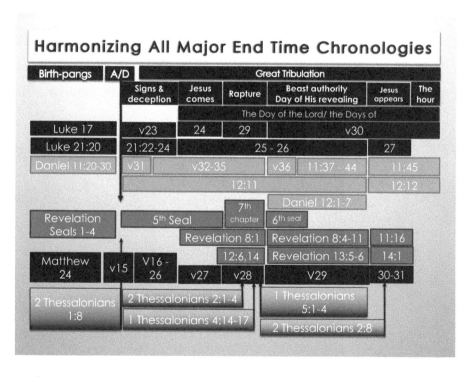

Consider the timing of Christ's appearance later to the world from Isaiah's words, **"so it will be when the Lord has completed all His work on Mount Zion and on Jerusalem (harvesting saints). He will say, "I will punish the fruit of the arrogant heart of the king of Assyria (the Anti-Christ Beast)..." Isaiah 10:12**. When does this dealing with the king occur but at the appearance of Jesus Christ to the world at the very end of the Day before Armageddon. **[2 Thessalonians 2:8]**. Notice this does NOT HAPPEN UNTIL *"all his work on Mount Zion"* **[above]** *"is completed"*. Is this not an indication of a gradual work of gathering His kingdom together, consummating His marriage and preparing His army. Before being seen by the world! In His words say, *"gathered the good fish into containers (PLURAL) but the bad they threw away!"* **Matthew 13:48** For Jesus will harvest the wheat and tend the vines of Israel as His word reads, and Jacob will be *"saved from it."* **Jeremiah 30:7**

As we transition into the final chapter, what are you expecting? After all my calculations you do not want to look forward to the wrong event! Will it be the appearance in glory or when every eye beholds?

9

Expecting:
Overspreading the Heavens

THE EXPECTATIONS

*"**Looking for and hastening** the coming of the day of God ... **since you look** for these things be diligent to be found by Him in peace ... **knowing beforehand** be on your guard."*
2 Peter 3:12-13

What are you looking forward to the most today? Think about it? The thought of many is: what I don't know can't hurt me. Many feel they have the luxury of denial or being unconcerned. Denying the amazing inheritance God has placed before us, choosing only to see our current situation and life seems normal to so many. The Apostles had nothing to do with living unconcerned or inattentive to what lied ahead. They never felt they had that luxury. Why, because Jesus never gave them that luxury? And the Word of God never gave their generation clarity. Yet today we have it and we are unconcerned. Consider many things in life are not important to us until we have enough understanding about it. For example technology, ask any gamer how they got into the addictive world of hours of playing? They will say it was because they finally tried it and learned how close to a reality it was.

237

The Apostles experienced their reality from Christ Himself, speak boldly to those who would *"go on sinning willfully after receiving the knowledge of truth"* **Hebrews 10:26** exclaiming that these people had to look forward to would be a *"terrifying expectation of judgment and the fury of a fire which will consume the adversaries."* **V27** They didn't withhold the truth that what occurs at the end depends on the focus of the life your living NOW! Why? Because we *"have need of endurance so that when we have done the will of God ..."* **v35** otherwise *"it is a terrifying thing to fall into the hands of the living God."* **v31** The contrast is vivid. There seems to be not much in-between these.

So we see this dynamic in our present world as so many are preoccupied and tested with what this world has to offer or not. As America riots we are tested where our hope and allegiance really lies. What if our great nation folds, divides or collapses, what kind of people are we to be? Any different? Paul aware of this phenomena of focus & conscience states, *"to the pure all things are pure; but to those who are defiled ...nothing is pure but their minds and their conscience are defiled."* **Titus 1:15**

Notice Peter balances the need to not go to that place of a defiled conscience that should fear the end. Instead he encourages the church to even *"hasten"* **2 Peter 3:12** that day, desire it as a choice to keep the embers burning for Jesus! Showing how important our focal point really is in forming whose we are, who we are, and where we will be! **[Cf. I John 3:2-3, Isaiah 26;3]** This chapter is about desiring that day, and why we should!

Looking at this command to *"hasten the day"*, the Pre Theory makes this desire not relevant at all since to them, the rapture stays clear of the Day of the Lord and we are sent away during it. For the Post position somehow we are *"sealed through the duration of that Day"* so why would we desire that either? Peter's comment seems way out of place with what we teach or believe today on the Bible. Why? Because we haven't been taught the proper placement of the rapture and the subsequent honeymoon of the chosen bride and the drama surrounding all this above the earth!

Yet here it is in the bible, our apostle of the church commands us to desire the very day! When left to today's experts its only darkness and judgment or complete separation from that Day. We are not taught how we overcome in that day is a marvelous beautiful thing. This only renders us confused about the veracity of scripture! How can we be an overcomer if we are not taught the truth! This is where it is not confusing to see why the Bethel crowd seek another answer that focuses on how the church overcomes and is empowered in the end. Since the reality of God's word is amazing for what's in store for those who await His physical return hidden above earth, this is your chapter!

Having settled too long on polarizing theories, in order to protect our precious truths; we have lost the amazing storyline that lies between these. So let's review, the Pre Tribulation Theorist have tried to honor the scriptural truth that **"God has not destined us for wrath" 2 Thessalonians 5:9** and Jesus firm words **"just as ... the days of Noah" Matthew 24:26-27** displaying our removal before destructive Apocalyptic events of the future. On the other hand the Post Tribulation Theorist seeing the weakness in the Pre Tribulation Theories argument for three comings and ignoring many other things have focused on only one event coming at the end. They will point to another conclusion that we are sealed by these words, **"take out the wicked from among the righteous" Matthew 13:49** or **"removing of these things ... so that those things that cannot be shaken may remain" Hebrews 12:27** not paying attention to how we never leave earth and do remain.

However I have guided you through this to the only answer that harmonizes with all passages, keeping to their context, with all parallelisms, types and shadows. The answer lies in the marriage of the actual truths they are protecting in this beautiful picture of the gradually revealed *Days of the Coming King*. Surrounding this beautiful sudden mysterious untimely arrival of Jesus Christ is His pursuit for His bride and their honeymoon, a truth buried within the pages of the Bible for us to search out.

THE VISIONS

"*For the vision is* **for the appointed time***; it* **hastens toward its goal** *and it will not fail. Though it tarries wait for it; For it will certainly come,* **it will not delay.**"

Habakkuk 2:2

Stretched across the writings of the prophets, you will see is this hope coupled with visions given from Heaven of what will occur when the Messiah would arrive. Many in our day read the prophets like it was a foreign language because we struggle to comprehend what they were looking at. We have no biblical foundation to place what they saw. Frankly most of us relegate anything they spoke to God's plan with the Jewish people not His bride the church. Today, when most of the voices of our day are ignoring their testimony as "old"; we have before us overwhelming harmony of a grand storyline & inheritance that should not be missed.

However I admit that if I didn't see what others aren't seeing, namely that Jesus is coming for a period hidden gradually revealed, I wouldn't have a grid to place what the old testament prophets saw. Peter above seemed to have this grid. Speaking in his first letter of how the prophets sought to know about this salvation **[cf. 1 Peter 1:10-12]** expands his own search into new discoveries acknowledging so in his second letter to the same churches **[cf. 2 Peter 1:19]**. In many places in this book especially in this last chapter we begin to piece together the prophets showing more than time codes, sequences of events and the like; but pictures drawn of this beautiful destiny for His own. Having hopefully established in your mind the analytics of God's end time plan in the last chapter, we can now place these beautiful visions in their respected order and appreciate God's painting.

Why is this so important to actually see and not just know the analytical stuff? Peter seems to think it motivates our obedience and generates greater levels of faith, saying, **"since you look for these things be diligent" 2 Peter 3:14** What things? Well, in the same verse he tells us, a new heaven and a new earth in which righteousness dwells, which is the fulfillment of God's words to the prophets! **[V13]** God keeps His promise, its not just theoretical but tangible now in the Spirit and soon in full view. For Peter says this will be **"according to His promise" v13** when others are saying, **"where is the promise of His coming" v3**. He read the vision of the prophets and took this as a promise, as a hope for His church. What God says He will do, Peter confirms He will do.

By the time we are taken we have shown how God splits the sky, which is heaven jumping dimensions, recreating the Universe in the process. We who are taken above the earth are the first to see this new creation, while the rest of the world is tested. This may seem like a fairytale ending only fit for Hollywood, too good to be true, but I'm here to tell you this is the picture God is painting through the prophets! Imagine God wants to display a new skyline to His bride!Remember Peter's words in this chapter are clear, the heavens are already dissolved before the earth is to be burned up and restarted, which only occurs during the trumpet period and the final hour of judgment **[Cf. 2 Peter 3:10]**.

God says, **"is anything too difficult for me" Jeremiah 32:27** Telling Sarah in her unbelief, **"is anything too difficult for the Lord? At the appointed time I will return to you at this time next year and Sarah will have a son." Genesis 18:14** God says to you and me, *'I will come at the right time, an appointed fixed time, and I will have children, and you will have fruit, you will have a reward.*

The promise will be fulfilled!' So we must ask ourselves where we are in this beautiful picture of God's grand finale. What will this look like *"a new heaven and a new earth"*?

However before we paint this glorious honeymoon suite God intends for us, let's make sure we have a handle on that day of our removal one more time. For it starts everything.

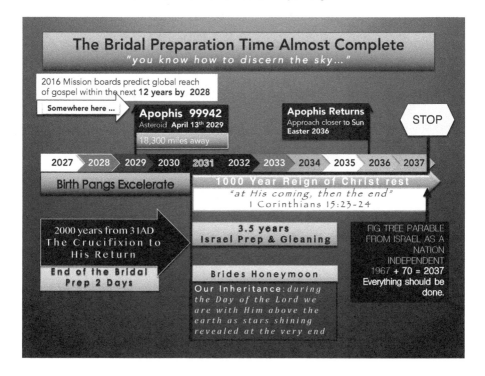

THE RAPTURE

> *"Like **the eagle** that stirs up its nest that **hovers over its young**, He spreads His wings and **caught them He carried them on His pinions... He made him ride on the high places of the earth."***
>
> **Deuteronomy 32:11-13**

The word rapture comes from the phrase *"we who are alive and remain will be caught up"* **1 Thessalonians 4:17.** This violent term for *"catching up"* is from the greek word *"harpazo"* in which we get our modern word for harpooning [I.e. spearing a whale]! Where are we taken? *"To meet the Lord in the air (lower atmosphere)"* **1 Thessalonians 4:17** Jesus in describing this event

241

that happens when He arrives **[cf. Matthew 24:27]** comes across very violent as well. Saying only, *"Where the corpse is, there the vulture will gather" v28* found also synoptically in **Luke 17:31-37.**

In both passages dead bodies are everywhere that "*aetos"* are; which is the word for *"eagles"* except translators see dead bodies and give it an alternative meaning. Excuse me, this is Jesus speaking the words given Him by the Holy Spirit directly from the Father. Maybe instead of believing translators, we should stand amazed at how well God concealed the truth of what happens here! For we read the passage above in our intro, that God is a mother eagle who *"caught"* her young and made for them to *"ride on the high places of the earth"* **Deuteronomy 32:11-13** Why stop there? For in **Revelation 12**, we read how God takes His own on *"two wings of the great eagle ... so she could fly ..." v14* referring to the rapture 3.5 years from the Seventh Trumpet *"end"*.

So why do we see corpses? Who is dying here? This is exactly what the disciples wanted to know from Jesus! Is it the people left behind or those taken? For Jesus just gave us two choices in **Luke 17:31-36.** The clue is definitely determined by how we translate the greek word *"aetos".* If the dead bodies are the left behind people than vultures, if the dead bodies are those raptured out of their flesh and blood with spiritual bodies than the answer is eagles.

In the context, Jesus has to tell us *"whoever loses his life will preserve it"* **Luke 17:33** Suggesting maybe the dead bodies are the winners of the day, the righteous. For who would be preserving themselves from the mighty presence of God but in the end losing their lives? Those left? Who would be risking losing their lives but the ones who face God and know they are forgiven! Here we are told to consider or *"remember Lot's wife"* **Luke 17:32** who desiring to go back from where she was being taken loses her life. The contrast is vivid here to the exhortation *"to look & desire that day"* **2 Peter 3:12** He comes versus the warning to not *"turn back"* **Luke 17:31**

Consider if you will Daniel's friends in the fire. The godless were not with them but Jesus was! They had resisted the mark of the Beast of their day by not bowing to the image of Nebuchadnezzar the king. The godless spoke, *"was it not three men we cast ...into the fire...Look I see four men."* **Daniel 3:24-25** So Shadrach Meshach and Abednego were removed from the rest of the world in the fire but within sight of the people, and Jesus of course shows up there with them as the fourth man! Think of their courage to enter that fire. This is significant parallel. Did you hear that? The world will see stars/lights in the sky and it won't be actual stars but the sons and daughters of God being manifested during the **3.5**

years. Who will be with us? That's right Jesus**.**

Finally, two scriptural references suggests to me what happens here is death at the rapture! For one it says, *"inasmuch as it is appointed for men to die and after this judgment"* which in context is followed by a rapture verse, *"so Christ ... will appear a second time"* **Hebrews 9:27-28** What is God saying? Can you be translated and that be considered a death? Most of us believe Enoch & Elijah never died, possibly returning to die as **Revelation 11's** two prophets. Not much changes in this debate of whether we leave our bodies behind or not. Popular Christian movie series had us vanishing. Non of this changes the need to be fearless in heeding the call of God to go up.

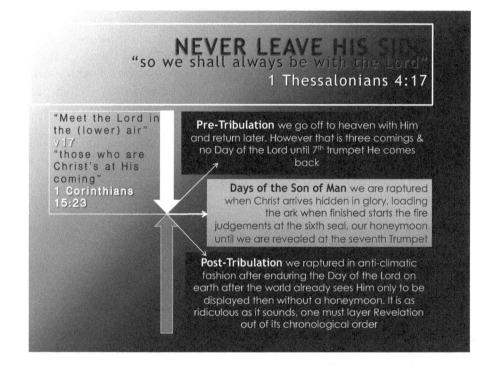

THE LAST TRUMPET

*"We will be **ALL changed** in a moment*
in the twinkling of an eye at the last trumpet
1 Corinthians 15:51-52

The second passage suggesting death at the rapture is from Paul's thesis on the resurrection process. We read in the clearest way, *"flesh and blood cannot inherit the kingdom of God"* **1 Corinthians 15:50** instead declaring for us *"immortality"* or that we will put on a new glorified body ay the very end or *"last trumpet"*. Paul working His message of resurrection in **1 Corinthians 15** chronological from the cross **v4** all the way to the Seventh trumpet or *"last trumpet"* **v52** reveals God's strategy for completing this transformation in the Resurrection process. *[See chart below]* For by **v23**, we taken to the proper placement of the rapture at His coming with still the end to come **[cf. V24]**.

At this point if you follow closely Paul's words, he will argue that *"there are also heavenly bodies and earthly bodies"* **v40** and the heavenly one cannot come to life unless the other dies. For *"it is sown a perishable body it is raised an imperishable body."* **V42** Of this raising up to life, God has already started this process, sowing inside us His Spirit regenerating ours! So that at the rapture we leave our bodies and await new ones as Spiritual beings having a spiritual body of light are seen for it is said, *"His glory will appear upon you. Nations will come to your light. ..."* **Isaiah 60:2**

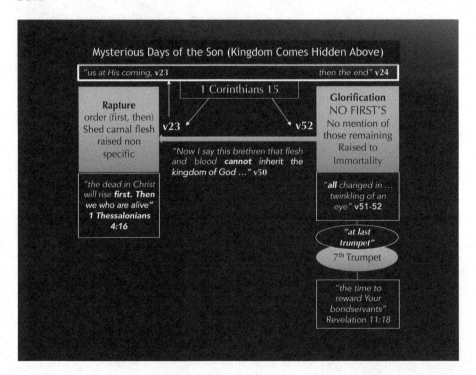

Given the nature of this process, would it be a surprise that God would await the final tally at the seventh trumpet to say, *"we will all be changed"* **v51**. For here it is said, *"the dead will be raised raised imperishable"* **v52** whereas Paul says elsewhere concerning the rapture, *"the dead will rise first"* **1 Thessalonians 4:16** Is this not the same event as some will point out? At this I say we have a contradiction forming! For how can *"all be changed in a moment in the twinkling of an eye"* **v52** if some are *"first"* **1 Thessalonians 4:16** and *"then"* **v17** others are raised after in order. No the dead are raised out of sleep and given spiritual bodies at the rapture then raised immortal, an upgrade. This is a process.

Many will argue that the last trumpet is the rapture because this does not refer to the Seventh trumpet of **Revelation.** Another words they believe this is the *"last call"* of this present age. Maybe they are right and I have this wrong, however the rapture has a specific order, whereas this event is all-inclusive raising at the exact same time. Again, God giving His word in a concealed way to make you and I take seriously every word.

THE LAST DAY

*"One who comes to Me I will certainly not cast out ... all that He has given Me **I lose nothing, but raise it up on the last day.**"*

John 6:37,40

Now we have one last mathematical problem, the rapture & the last day reference above? For the **Luke 17:30-37** event when we are taken is the same synoptic passage as the **Matthew 24:27-28** event. Only later does the **Matthew 24:30** event coinciding with the last trumpet of Revelation when it is said, *"The kingdom of the world has become the kingdom of our Lord and of His Christ and He will reign forever... have begun to reign"* and a verse later *"the time to reward Your bond servants the prophets and the saints and those who fear Your name small and great"* **Revelation 11:18**.

So what gives? For we just saw how Paul declared *"all"* would be changed at this time. Post Tribulation theorist believe this is the rapture at the very end, so they have no problem with Paul's words here. However, we showed how the rapture is not the very end, only the start of His coming and part of a resurrection process that has started for us when we were born again. So some things become evident and important here especially the words and placement in **chapter 15** at the very end of explaining this process of resurrection.

For starters, I believe Jesus uses the term *"last day"* **John 6:40** for the final prophetic day of a thousand years, which means Jesus can be raising for a period of time, gathering finalizing the resurrection during the days plural of His coming until like Paul says, *"all are changed in a flash!"* Otherwise we have the raising only at one 24 hour period at the very end of the age and we all should sign up to be Post Tribulation theorist. Otherwise, we are playing with words and creating new contexts as typical Pre Tribulation theorist need to do, and *"last"* is really not the *"last trumpet"* or the seventh trumpet of **Revelation** just of this age. Yet in that senario then there is no gleaning process to the harvest.

Yet many cannot conceive of a process. This is a constant theme if you didn't notice with my harmonizing scripture on the future, it's not a single event over and over. It is a process that culminates.

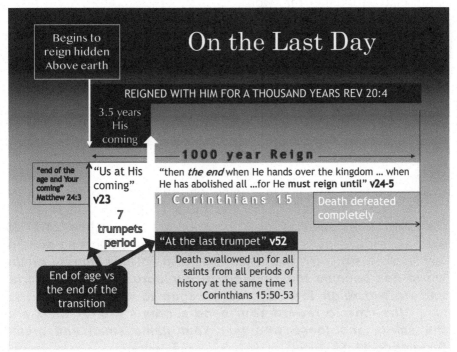

Although we see that not until the end of the **3.5 years** is it declared that, *"The kingdom of the world has become the kingdom of our Lord and of His Christ"* **Revelation 11:15** and it is observed rightly He has *"begun to reign"* **v17** in a physically seen way unlike what wasn't seen before.

This seems in connection with the final trumpet and Paul's words to the effect of describing not the end of this age but *"the end"*, or end of His Day. *"**Then the end**, when He hands over the kingdom to the God and Father when He has abolished all rule and all authority and power. He must reign until ..."* **1 Corinthians**

15:24-25 This leaves this transition period of 3.5 years as His coming days plural when all are gathered or harvested ending with all being changed together at the *"at the last trumpet".* My point is His coming goes from the end of this age to the end His day. *"At His coming then comes the end"* **v23-24** What happens at His coming? We are harvested for that period! *"After that those who are His at His coming"* **v23**.

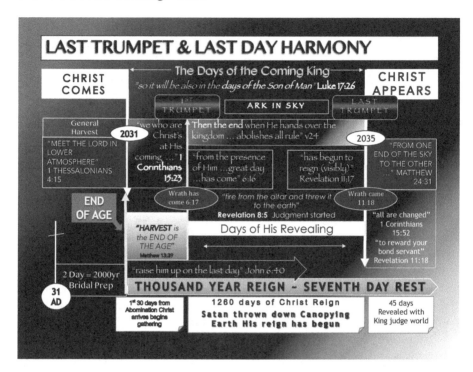

The harvest is the end of the age and the start of the new one. In other words Christ comes at the end of the age, announced by the Glory. Suddenly the ages change! The end of the age means the beginning of the last day or 1000 year reign of Christ. Christ has already arrived but in **Revelation 6** begins to be revealed but by **Revelation 11:17** finally it is seen and declared that His kingdom has overtaken the world's systems. The truth is He began to reign silently over the earth by expelling Satan. This revelation comes to us via **Revelation 12**.

Connecting *"at that time Michael, ...will arise"* **Daniel 12:1** with *"war in heaven, Michael waging war ...Satan was thrown to the earth."* **Revelation 12:7-9** and *"he (satan) has a short time when the dragon saw that he was thrown down to earth so he persecuted the women ...BUT"* **Revelation 12:12-14** This is a big BUT! For we read that God rescues His women for 3.5 years. So returning back a few verses after the first mention of satan being thrown to earth **v9**, we read *"NOW salvation ... and the kingdom of our God ...have come"* What is going on here is Jesus has followed Satan to earth but made residence above! He is already beginning to reign!

In a differing viewpoint of the Post Tribulation Theorist mind, the seventh trumpet would occur on the end of this age **2031**. His coming, the end of the age and the end are all the same. Christ doesn't begin to reign until the seventh trumpet. We can ask the questions that comes with it, what is really meant by *"the end of the age"*? Certainly the disciples asked it of Jesus **[cf. Matthew 24:3]** and His absence of rebuttal confirms Jesus coming is at the end of our present age not before the end of the age.

Yet so many things are left in disarray with this all in one coming at the very end that the Post argue. So the key in unlocking this is understanding His coming is *"days"* plural a final period of ministry, *"making firm the covenant for one week"* **Daniel 9:27** minus His first coming we have **Daniel's 12:7** three and half years to bring about righteousness in Jerusalem. Also we have two different terms, **"The end of the age"** and **"the end"**. These don't seem to be referring to the same thing. One deals with the ages and the big picture while the other more specifically defines the end of the transition or Seventh Trumpet, the end of *the Day of the Lord* or harvest. The harvest starts at the end of the age so this maybe the greatest rebuttal of all. For how can God harvest everything all in one event at the very end? This doesn't follow the pattern set for the Jewish people or feast.

Once we make the proper distinctions though, we can see harmony everywhere having a transition period for days called *"His coming"* *"the Day of the Lord,"* and *"Days of the Son of Man"*. Paul declaring suggesting days by the verb tense for abolish in *"then the end ... when all is abolished"* **1 Corinthians 15:24** means harvesting will continue 3.5 years until all is gathered and all is submitted to Christ.

Yet Jesus said, *"I reach My goal"* **Luke 13:32** on **the third day**, we must ask what is His goal? For this will finish **the 2000 years** and the age? For the Post Tribulation Theorist you would need to count **3.5 years** forward to **2028** for the Great Tribulation to start and the seventh trumpet being the end of the age versus *"the end"*. Yet notice Jesus goal is revealed after two days because it is connected to *the Bridal Preparation* in Moses example of two days, a return to *"revive"* Israel in Hosea's example.

Earlier I showed how He has already begun to reign silently from both accounts of **3.5 years** mentioned in **Revelation 12** with the corresponding victory statements at the beginning. Remember God says, He will *"laugh"* because He had *"installed My King upon Zion"* before even *"breaking them with a rod of iron"* Psalms **2:4,6,9** Our minds need to wrap around this, all of the drama of the **Book of Revelation** is carried out while the victory is already won **[cf. 6:16-19]** and we are safe in His wings! **[Cf. Chapter 7]** This fits the pieces together perfectly how the ages change at the beginning of His coming not the end.

THE PEOPLE

"For the Day of the Lord is coming; ... **As the dawn is spread across the mountains. So there is a great and mighty people**; *There has never been anything like it..."*

Joel 2:2

What a beautiful picture of the glory canopy that will cover the sky during *the Day of the Lord*. This contrast is seen again in **Isaiah 60:1-4** on the earth right after *"A Redeemer will come to Zion"* **59:20** two verses earlier. For the prophet declares at the start of *the Day of the Lord*, *"darkness will cover the earth and deep darkness the peoples"* but above in the sky to another people the prophet declares, *"the Lord will rise upon you and His glory will appear upon you. Nations will come to your light"* **v2** . Who are these people but those mentioned earlier in *"Zion ... the church of the first-born"* **Hebrews 12:23**.

The prophet Joel, so convinced with the magnitude of this vision, says, *"there will be nothing after it"* **Joel 2:2** too compare! For with this glorious canopy or *"dawn ... spread across"*, comes a revelation not of Jesus, or angels but His chosen people on display as lights in the sky. Daniel describing this phenomena in a similar way says at the beginning of this period of rescue **[cf. Daniel 12:1]** that *"those who have insight will <u>shine brightly like the brightness of the expanse of heaven</u>, and those who lead the many to righteousness <u>like the stars</u>"* **Daniel 12:3**.

Consider Jesus spoke of this day that starts with His coming being seen *"as the lightning ... and flashes"* **Matthew 24:27** across the entire globe of the planet but quickly becomes way more fierce. In **Luke 17:30-37** the same event is spoken of WHEN as one taken *(rapture)* and one left, with dead bodies left everywhere in the wake of this event. So when we return to Joel's description, many revelations begin to occur as we are able to align scripture references. For instance, Joel will describe this group as, *"a great and mighty people"* **Joel 2:2** and later as *"a mighty people arranged for battle"* **2:5**. Although they are described to be *"like war horses"* **2:4**, Joel doesn't call them *"angels"* or *"messengers of God"* but a people.

In fact in describing their appearance it's clear they have power over fire. Picture this, *"fire being consumed before them and behind them a flame burns"* **2:3** Almost like superhero's who cut through the glory of God's burning! In this description there is no question where the people are, for *"they leap on the tops of the mountains"* **2:5** They are still on the earth but above! The question then centers on when during *the Day of the Lord* is this? The Rapture saints at the start going up or the Army at the end coming down? Many questions circle this amazing vision.

Joel seems to answer though the effect of these many individuals have on blocking earth's view of the sky, *"Before them ... The heavens tremble, the sun and moon grow dark and the stars lose their brightness."* **2:10** For Jesus puts this very same description between the start and the end of the Day of the Lord. **[Cf. Matthew 24:29]** after the **verse 27** event before the end in **verse 30-31**. Notice the moon and sun are dark because of their presence is blocking their light, the magnitude of spirit beings in the sky is causing an eclipse. Next, we come to *"the Lord utters His voice before His army"* **2:11** and we ask: is this at the start when he is gathering or at the end dispatching them? Or is this an ongoing occurrence during? If you are inclined to see this the army above as one of the two witnesses during the 3.5 years causing issues for those who live on earth then this might just be a continuous occurrence during.

Maybe the insight we are looking for comes from another prophet seeing the very same event. For **Isaiah** uses the very same language as **Joel 2:11** declaring that, *"I have commanded My consecrated ones, I have even called My mighty warriors ... the Lord of hosts is mustering* [gathering, numbering, appointing] *the army for battle. They are coming from a far country,* <u>*from the farthest horizons*</u> *the Lord and His instruments of indignation"* **Isaiah 13:4** How else could the prophet describe such a thing; as Jesus reveals to John that we go to a *"wilderness"* **Revelation 12:14** or secluded place, and thus **Isaiah** says we come *"from the farthest horizons"* which suggest a global canopy spread across then when Jesus gathers us in **Matthew 24:31** its from the *"four winds"*! Either way we have a description of *the Day of the Lord* where His people are safely stored above the earth from one end to the other.

More insightful is the constant recognition of how organized this people are, *"they do not crowd each other, ... march everyone in his path, ...do not break rank."* **Joel 2:8** If these are angels this would make sense, especially in gathering the saints at the rapture. However what is occurring is judgment upon the earth by instruments who *"carries out His word"* **2:11** in this very same people. Where do we see this but in **Revelation**, both in the two witnesses who have power over fire during the Trumpet Period **[cf. Revelation 11:5]** and His heavenly army assembled at the very end **[cf. Revelation 19:14]**. Of this second option, His army are those *"clothed in <u>fine linen</u>, white and clean, were following Him on white horses."* **19:14** Excuse me but this is the Bride of Christ **v7** and possibly a more select group than the Great Multitude.

The Great Multitude are clothed in just, *"white robes"* because they have *"washed their robes and made them white in the blood of the Lamb"* **Revelation 7:13-14** However, another company seems to appear out of that Great Multitude later. Introduced to us as His army, they are given *"fine linen, bright and clean"* **19:8** to wear. What are we seeing here maybe a distinction between the masses washed in the blood and those who have accomplished *"righteous acts"* which are defined as those *"fine linen(s)"* **19:8** Most of this is speculative since nothing is definitive here, as in plainly said. For maybe God gives the whole Great Multitude an upgrade from **chapter 7 to 19**?

However, we must not live as though everything is on the level of salvation or not. We are encouraged by the scriptures to engage in a higher calling. Paul concerned, reminds the early church they are still being *"betrothed ...to one husband ... Christ"* **2 Corinthians 11:2**, therefore makes a plea for them to continue to engage in the love affair of a *"simple and pure devotion to Christ"* **v3**. Why? Because sitting on the fence or just inside the door of salvation is way to close to being on the outside and Paul says, *"your minds will (could) be led astray"* **v3** Since growth defines all organic beings, we cannot afford to be stagnant being that we are *"born again"*. We cannot afford the mindset to disengage in this pursuit of playing the role of the Bride awaiting her groom! Why neglect such a grand reward? Many circle wagons around these questions on whether all believers are His bride. Are there differing roles in His kingdom or heaven, distinctions if you will. Well the the book of **Revelation** is full of indications of them!

For in defining the dead in Christ, His kingdom that comes in the symbolic *"Mount Zion ... Heavenly Jerusalem"* **Hebrews 12:22**, for those who remain on the earth at His coming, the author will use different terms from *"the general assembly"* as though it is separate from what is mentioned next, *"and the church of the* *firstborn who are enrolled in heaven."* **v23** This should be obvious by the time we get to the description in **Revelation 20:4-5**, of who gets to reign with Christ is an obvious high calling with some very real restrictions! In fact this was embedded in early church doctrine and thought when Paul speaks a *"trustworthy statement"* then separates out *"if we endure we will also reign with Him"* **2 Timothy 2:12** possibly from those mentioned before and after as in, *"if we died with Him we will live with Him"* **v11** and *"If we are faithless, He remains faithful"* **v13** suggesting different outcomes.

In fact for our purposes of describing this amazing period when the glory covers the earth atmosphere and He takes His own, no where else can we fit the honeymoon which occurs before the wedding feast in the biblical Jewish culture but here! So there must be truth to differing functions in Heaven. Some are attendants and not the Bride and that's clear especially right before the feast. For why are the Great multitude announcing the bride if they all are the Bride? And why indicate there are those invited to come the feast if every saved person is invited or the Bride? Is this not declaring there are those who are not the Bride? **[Cf. Revelation 19:6-7]**

I leave this for you to be inspired. In two places **2 Corinthians 11:3** & **Ephesians 5:25** the verbs used are *"might"* not the greek mood for certainty *"will"*. In one case, Paul isn't positive scolding that they had the _"potential"_ and in the other speaking to a faithful church in Ephesus, that they had a _"high probability & desirable one"_ to God doing the action.

So there is this idea formed from scriptures that though Jesus brings with Him the general assembly, He chooses from these His government from what He defines as His body, His church and then specific group called His bride. Maybe this is where we see the **144,000** alongside the great multitude in the symbolic number **12** for government. They are sealed for they are allowed a front seat above the clouds to *the Day of the Lord*. Remember, the **144,000** are never expressly spoken of being on the surface of the earth. In fact we aren't told much until they are seen with Christ on Mount Zion later **[cf. Revelation 14:1-4]**. The only other alternative for the **144,000** is they are the remnant mortals sealed to survive on earth, descendant from the 12 tribes of Israel as His chosen remnant. Literal or symbolic, a select group or symbolically the whole, this age or the next, the options are too many to be dogmatic concerning the **144,000**. However nothing has intrigue our interest more concerning the end to the identity of these.

That said, both **Hebrews 12:22** & **Revelation 14:1** refer to this place as *"Mount Zion"* as distinct place separate from Jerusalem.

Notice Joel's use, *"On Mount Zion and in Jerusalem"* **Joel 2:32** later saying, *"The Lord roars from Zion"* **3:16** and Isaiah stating, *"The Redeemer will come to Zion"* **Isaiah 59:20.** So we are given this truth of Christ bringing with Him the city *"Zion"* which is distinctly different than the earthly location of Mt. Zion next to Jerusalem.

Since we never leave His side **[cf. 1 Thessalonians 4:17]** its hard to imagine the **144,000** by Jesus side in **Revelation 14** as anything but His bride, especially given the description, *"these are those who have not been defiled with women"* **14:4** For this symbolic gender specific instruction for a group was given only one other time in the bible, Moses to the people God wanted to be His bride after two days saying, *"do not go near a woman"* **Exodus 19:15** Moses is talking to men and woman so this is symbolic. Also in the **Revelation** *chapter 7*, they seem to be a separate group from the great multitude and in *chapter 14* from those left behind gathered at the very end later spoken in the context.   **[cf. Revelation 14:12-14].**

THE DIDACHE

*"The **sign of the outspreading** in heaven"* **chapter 16**
https://www.newadvent.org/fathers/0714.htm

Let us get sidetracked for a second here on purpose. Most scholars consider *The Didache*, a Christian treatise, to be a genuine first century statement of Creed passed down from the Apostles. The significance is it precedes the Nicene Creed and most likely was a reference in the making of the later one. What is intriguing is this early first century manuscript includes a section devoted to the Eschatological teaching of their day whereas the Nicene Creed avoids the topics as we do today. Many believe *the Didache* may have been the first concise statements of faith recorded by the patriarch of the New Covenant. For our purposes it works well right here at the end of the book as a supporting document into the harmony of scripture to early church faith. I encourage you to read Wikipedia explanation and resources on it.

Eusebuis (around 324AD, in History Ecclesiastica III, p25.), a renowned Christian bishop and church historian, mentions *the Didache* as the teaching of the actual Apostles and worthy of acceptance on a non-canonical level. The writings seem used by other notable disciples like Irenaeus, Clement of Alexandria,

Origen, with similarities to Ignatius & Polycarps writings to name a few. The reason I am bringing this into the picture is the clarity in which it summarizes what I have found to be true in the bible on the end times. All references are from its **final chapter 16.** Especially its reference to this phenomenon of God's canopy appearing. So let's dive in.

After some instructional warnings concerning the last days it reads as follows;

"Then shall appear the world-deceiver as the Son of God, and shall do signs and wonders, and the earth shall be delivered into his hands, and he shall do iniquitous things **[Matthew 24:15]** *which have never yet come to pass since the beginning."*

*Then shall the creation of men come **into the fire of trial,** **[Matthew 24:21]** and many shall be made to stumble and shall perish* **[Matthew 24:23-26]**; *but they that endure in their faith* **[Matthew 24:13,22]** *shall be saved from **under the curse** itself* **[Matthew 24:27-28]**"

Notice where we are saved from, from under the curse, not protected in the curse. The idea is we are taken above the cursed trap on the surface of the earth by stating where we are saved from. How does this happen? *The Didache* speaks very plainly from here.

*"**First the sign of an outspreading in heaven** [Our honeymoon canopy, the glory and tabernacle above earth arrives with Jesus]; **then the sign of the sound of the trumpet** [**Hebrews 12** voice calling us]; **and third the resurrection of the dead** [raising out of our bodies at the rapture]; yet **not all** [God is still gleaning to the very end of the 3.5 years] but as it is said; The Lord shall come and all His saints with Him. [At the very end God will have gather the rest so that all are changed together at the last trumpet when He is revealed] **Then shall the world see the Lord coming upon the clouds of heaven."***

When quoting this beautiful early church description, I have placed my interpretation of these words in brackets. So I will say it is clear according to this manuscript, we are taken before the very end from the surface where the curse is occurring and clearly during the "fire of trial". Many proofs have I given from the

254

scriptures first, and they all concur with this ancient manuscript basic premise. However notice the early church understood the revelation of the canopy of God that occurs. ***"The sign of the outspreading in heaven"***

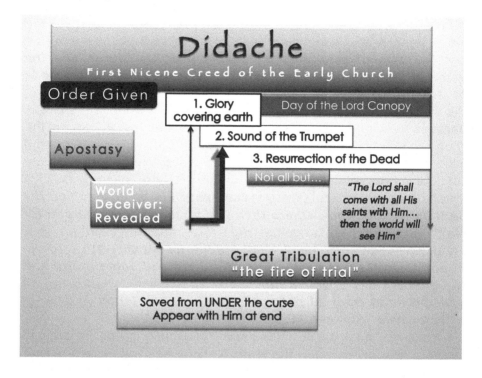

THE PSALMIST

"For in ***the day of trouble He will conceal me in His tabernacle*** *In the secret place of His tent He will hide me.* ***He will lift me up*** *on a rock"*

Psalms 27:5

Many don't think of David as a prophet who saw future events. Which is understandable since that skill set would seem to be overshadowed by a long list of titles and achievements for this shepherd boy from Bethlehem, who slew a giant with a sling shot and rose to be king. Yet in multiple places we find that God showed him this same picture of His arrival and the glories to follow in vivid detail. For instance the use of the words above "tabernacle" and "tent" (ABOVE) perfectly describe both the traditional honeymoon tent called, the Chuppah, and how God will make His residence above the earth as His tabernacle during the **3.5 year period** of *the Day of the Lord.*

Revelation offers us a glimpse into this reality of His coming tabernacle from heaven saying, *"get up and measure the temple .... And those who worship in it"* **Revelation 11:2** Now this measuring a temple is only found in **Ezekiel 40-43** concerning the future temple. And something very telling is said about this future temple, *"Son of Man, this is the place of My throne and the place of the sole of My feet, where I will dwell among the sons of Israel forever."* **43:7** When God speaks this prophetic word of His temple coming, He makes clear there will not be a mere wall between Him and the iniquity of the house of Israel. Notice the temple stretches from heaven to the surface of earth by the mention of it being His throne and also below where is feet touch. **[Cf. 43:7 above]** We see this again at the end of Isaiah's prophesying in his last chapter, *"The heaven is my throne and the earth is My footstool. Where then is a house you could build for Me?"* **66:1** which leads to the timing of Israel being birthed as a righteous nation again at the very end **[cf. Isaiah 66:7-9]** by Zion's, Heavenly Jerusalems might when *"the Lord will come in fire and His chariots like a whirlwind"* **v15** because Zion *"shall bring all your brethren from all nations"* **v20**. Thus *"all Israel [surviving] will be saved"* **Romans 11:26**

Focusing back on this idea truth of God bringing Heaven to earth in stages we see **Revelation**. God has vacated anything *"holy"* on the surface of the earth says, *"leave out the court which is outside the temple ... given to the nations and they will tread under foot the holy city 42 months."* **11:2** giving indication that all Jerusalem to God will be His future outer court when this is completed but for now God is vacating. What follows in **Revelation 11** is a firm count that this **3.5 years [cf. V3]** introduced as concurrent with *"two witnesses"* and *"two olive trees"* **[Cf. Revelation 11:3-4]** is representative of the Trumpet Period just mentioned in **8-11**. This drama leads to the concept of *"the beast ...will make war with them and overcome them and kill them and their dead bodies lie in the streets ..."*

The reality of what Jesus is revealing is deeply covered in symbolic speech to keep this a mystery. Yet, *"the great city which mystically is called Sodom and Egypt where the Lord was crucified"* **v8** is a clever way of concealing the location as earth itself. This is big picture stuff to me. For instance, our age according to Paul is one olive tree with both Jews and Gentiles grafted in **[cf. Romans 11:17]**. For there to be two olive trees that are synonym for the two witnesses, then might we be instead of two individual prophets in Jerusalem, seeing two groups from two ages witnessing across the globe. This is big picture stuff.

Revelation is showing you how God is bringing together everything, heaven connected to earth at the end. This age above the earth in His tabernacle connected to the remnant mortals of the next age given power to frustrate Satan's system. This changes everything we see here. For 3.5 days would be masking what it is truly representing, the 3.5 years spoken verses earlier, when our dead bodies from the rapture are left and celebrated over as a triumph of the Anti-Christ system, redefining what *"overcoming the saints"* represents! The world is being convinced by their man & system that the rapture was a removal of the problem.

We see that God has made His tabernacle with those he has already gathered above the earth, during this period of the Beast authority, for **3.5 years**. David saw this! Check out where God is. *"Bow Your heavens, O Lord, and come down; <u>touch the mountains</u> that they may smoke. Flash forth lightning and scatter them; send Your arrows and confuse them. Stretch forth Your hand from on high; rescue me and deliver me out of great (many) waters (peoples) ..."* **Psalms 144:5-7** Isn't this perfect, God has come down to the lower atmosphere just as it says, Jesus will meet us in the 'aer' in greek or lower air.

From the earliest Psalms comes this revelation of a mystery so deep. How God would secretly *"installed My King Upon Zion, My holy mountain"* **Psalms 2:6** while all the nations get to experience His *"anger ... fury"* **v5** and God is said to be laughing! **[V4]** What happens next is an amazing conversation between God the Father and Christ His Son that includes us as His body the bride in *"I will surely give the nations as Your inheritance and the very ends of the earth as Your possession."* **Psalms 2:7-8**

The references continue from this powerful songwriter prophet. *"In the shadow of Your wings I will take refuge until destruction passes by"* **Psalms 57:1** When are the righteous taken to heaven but before judgment occurs or is finished. And who is He taking according to this chosen spokesperson for God? *"Gather My godly ones to Me, those who have made covenant with Me by sacrifice."* **Psalms 50:5** Don't be distracted by the lingo, *"sacrifice"* which means by the blood of Jesus. God isn't taking any run of the mill professing *"Christian"* but those who have exchanged their lives for His live through His blood thus making covenant.

This message so far is aligning with everything we have been saying, for the very next verse after gathering us he transcribes this, *"The heavens (sky) declares His righteousness, for God*

Himself is judge." **50:6** What happens after the rapture is *"the day of His revealing"* **Luke 17:30**, when a great mystery is unveiled above the earth. For from the sky will come judgement and certain eyes opened that those taken weren't as the beast proclaimed. The evil ones being judged but the righteous are as shining lights. The world will see His righteousness displayed. Those left behind, will declare, *"Oh crap we missed it!"*.

By the time we read **Psalms, 18 & 97,** David is almost giving us a complete account of the second coming of Jesus Christ. In the first it is as if God came for him at a time in his struggles with Saul, much like He will on *the Day of the Lord* for it seems like a personal account.

In the vision he says, *"then the earth shook and quaked; ...He bowed the heavens also and came down with thick darkness under His feet ... He sped upon the wings of the wind. He made darkness His hiding place, His canopy around Him"* **Psalms 18:7-11** Next we read that His voice is being uttered as in prophetic account of **Hebrews 12:28**. Simultaneous lightning flashes which take us all the way up to, *"He sent from on high, He took me; He drew me out of many waters."* **V16** Oh my gosh here we have **Matthew 24:27** followed by **v28** being our removal. As if lightning flashes are angels taking the righteous region by region.

Notice if this was just a testimonial from David of an event we know not of, he would not say, *"out of many waters"* **Psalms 18:16**. For how could that be David is one not many so how can he personally come out of many? No, David is prophesying of a future event where many David's are gathered. Where will these righteous people after God's heart go but to ... *"He brought me forth also into a broad place; He rescued me, because He delighted in me."* **Psalms 18:19!** Which is very similar to what it will feel to have the ability to fly around the globe canopy! God delighted in him, because he had obtained God's heart! **[Cf. 1 Samuel 16:7]** So we must ask ourself does God find delight in me? In spite of my sin or struggles with addictions, behavior based on protection devices much like David struggled, do I have a heart after Him? If so then, God wants to bring you to a spacious place! Put an end to your sin nature and be your triumph. This is good news!

Revelation 12 calls this a *"secluded place"* or *"wilderness"* **12:14** and David calls it a *"broad" "spacious" "large place"* **Psalms 18:19**; I believe we are talking about the same place! Why is it spacious? Because it covers the globe as a canopy! *"His lightning lit up the world. The earth saw and trembled... the mountains melted like wax at the presence of the Lord of the whole earth ... all the peoples have seen His glory."* **Psalms**

97:5-6

Notice, His canopy of glory covers the entire globe! Who do they see? Not Jesus but His glory! *"For You are the Lord Most High over <u>all the earth</u>. Who preserve the souls of His godly ones; ..."* **Psalms 97:10** How are we preserved but in the glory, *"Light is sown for the righteous"* **v11** In other words we are saved from this earth as stars in the heavens because we can stand in the fire of His glory! **"among whom you appear as lights in the world" Philippians 2:15**

So David delineates where salvation will come from for the physical nation of Israel who are held captive in the **final 3.5 years**. *"The salvation of Israel would come out of Zion, when the Lord restores His captive people."* **Psalms 14:7** David associates Israel's survivors and nation born in a day again like Isaiah does *"com(ing) out of Zion"*! In another **Psalm**, David again refers to this tent or canopy, *"Their voice is not heard, their line [rapture= harpooning us] **has gone out through all the earth and their utterances to the ends of the world. In them He has <u>placed a tent for the sun</u>"* **Psalms 19:4-5**. God after creating this place and likens the whole thing as a *"bridegroom coming out of His chamber."* **v5** Jesus has just spent His consummation with us and now is rejuvenated saying, *"rejoices as a strong man to run its course. It's rising is from one end of the heavens and its circuit to the other end of them and there is nothing hidden from its heat."* **Psalms 19:5-6**

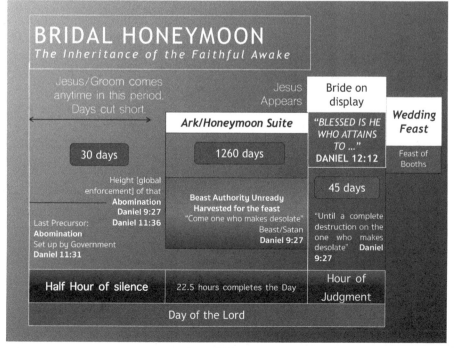

THE CANOPY

*"For I, declares the Lord, 'will be **a wall of fire around her** and I will be **the glory in her midst"***

Zechariah 2:5

The prophet Zechariah saw precisely when this canopy of glory would enter the earth's atmosphere prophesying that during a time Israel would return to her land and be fooled into false security, **"without walls" v4**, God would show up in glory to protect her **[passage above v5]**. The prophet then speaks another telling thing saying, **"after glory" v8** *[towards the end of the Day of the Lord]* He would go out to plunder nations. Why? **"For he who touches you, touches the apple of His eye." V8** Are you getting this? What are we looking forward to? For not only are we to experience a deliverance into an amazing supernatural atmospheric Holy Ghost extravaganza with our fellow believers but we get see God's jealous love poured out during the trumpet period until we finally ride to victorious battle with Him by His side!

Understand this is a love affair of the bridegroom for His bride, a Father for His children and a God for His heritage Israel. Each group in its order, first the church, then Israel, then the nations. The prophet Ezekiel as well was hit on this vision of this coming canopy while prophesying to Egypt saying, **"when I extinguish you, I will <u>cover the heavens</u> and darken their stars; I will cover the sun with a cloud ... all the shining lights in the heavens I will darken over you ..." Ezekiel 32:7-8** Some think this is the very end or during Armageddon but it is not. For the events that follow this canopy of darkness being established is the invasion of Egypt by **"the king of Babylon" v11** or the same king described doing the same thing in **Daniel 11:42-43** at the start of His crazy phase or towards the beginning of the 3.5 years.

More events follow this one in the next verses. **[cf. Daniel 11:43-45]** My objective here is to demonstrate that the canopy does not occur at a very short period at the very end as some might try to suppose. It stays over the earth for a lengthly period as did the waters that covered the face of the earth during the flood **[cf. 313 days in Genesis 7]**. When this covering begins Isaiah is clear what happens. The glory comes **[59:19]** followed by a Redeemer with Zion **[59:20]** followed by darkness and the phenomena of the rapture found in the following words that follow **v20**.

*"For behold **darkness <u>will cover</u> the earth** and deep darkness the peoples; but the Lord will rise upon you. ... <u>**Who are these who fly like a cloud**</u> and like the doves to their lattices."*

Isaiah 60:3,8

THE REDEEMER

*"Who is this that comes from Edom, ... This one who is **majestic** in His apparel, **Marching in the greatness** of His strength? It is I who speak in righteousness mighty to save."*

Isaiah 63:1

As previously established, Jesus shall suddenly arrive with Zion, the dead in Christ. **[Cf. Isaiah 59:19, Joel 2:32]** Only at some point later to roar from Zion. **[Cf. Joel 3:16]** Here in this chapter we have seen the reality of His canopy arriving over the earth. Later Christ appearing from it in the clouds **[cf. Revelation 1:7; 14:15, 19]** with

261

His army for battle. So this section we look at what happens when the redeemer comes to Israel.

Starting with the very end, **Isaiah 63:1** above is a beautiful indication that after being seen by this world, He will enter into judgment personally. For it says, ***"Why is Your apparel red"***. When this occurs it seems he has come from the vicinity of the Southeast where ancient Edom was located. This is home now to Saudi Arabia or the wilderness territory the children of Israel crossed. Habakkuk one of the minor prophets says, ***"God comes from Teman [Edomite country], and the Holy One from Mount Paran. <u>His splendor covers the heavens</u> and the earth is full of His praise. His radiance is like the sunlight; He has rays from His hand, and there is the hiding of His power."*** **Habakkuk 3:3-4** Yes, it actually says there, He was hiding Himself for a period of time before unveiling Himself before the world in. ***"There is the hiding of His power"*** **v4**

Next though the prophet sees this, ***"before Him goes pestilence and plaque comes after Him. He stood surveyed the earth; He looked and startled the nations."*** **3:6** Hello, Jesus here. Do you get this? The nations are startled because He hasn't been seen yet, otherwise there would be no surprise. Remember we saw the same effect ***"the mighty people"*** **Joel 2:2** had on the earth in **v3**. This is another angle on the **Matthew 24:30-31** event, the first sighting of an extraterrestrial being, Superman in the flesh! Can you blame the world for being shocked? All of a sudden the canopy opens as Jesus defines it as, ***"Then the sign of the Son of man will appear in the sky"*** **Matthew 24:30** and who is with Him but His army.

For Jesus is not alone. For Habakkuk describes God riding ***"on Your horses [plural] On Your chariots of salvation?"*** **Habakkuk 3:8** Jesus is only one person so He cannot ride on plural horses and chariots can He? Stating the obvious for you, the answer is this is the same picture of the mighty people in Joel. When we are called His body then we are one with Jesus, we must always be present with Him. This is how God sees the King Jesus riding with His bride, one person!

The vision continues. ***"Sun and moon stood in their places; they went away at the light of Your arrows at the radiance of Your gleaming spear. In indignation You marched through the earth; ...trampled the nations. You went forth for the salvation of Your people, for the salvation of Your anointed."*** **Habakkuk 3:11-13** Again we see two groups, His people Israel and His anointed, His bride. This occurs during the *final bowls of Revelation* as part of the judgment of Babylon *[the world system]*

262

when many nations will be drawn into battle at Armageddon. When does that happen but *"in those days"* **Joel 3:1** referring back to the period called *the Day of the Lord*. Prophesying over this period He is clear, *"When I restore the fortunes of Judah and Jerusalem I will gather all nations and bring them down to the valley of Jehoshaphat." 3:1-2* and *"For I know their works and their thoughts; the time is coming to gather all nations and tongues. And they shall come and see My glory." Isaiah 66:18*

As this final battle is about to occur, Joel hears these words, *"bring down O Lord Your mighty ones."* **Joel 3:11** Did you hear that, He calls you His mighty one! Again we see our calling to never leave His side. Our destiny if we choose to accept it, is be His lover & fellow warrior in His army in order to reign with Him!

So let's get this straight. After taking His faithful bride to her honeymoon suite, Jesus will come out of His tent with his bridal army to restore the true remnant of Israel's fortunes to the point of drawing all nations for judgment until finally He comes physically to Israel. When? When Israel is said to be *"scattered among the nations"* yet again because of the Anti-Christ/Beast, and two when *"they have divided up My land" 3:2*. This has not occurred yet. Yet God promises it during the 3.5 years in order to *"shatter the power of the holy people"* **Daniel 12:7** in order to *"remove ungodliness from Jacob"* **Romans 11:26** How does Israel return to her land at the end but by returning from all the nations they were dispersed to at the time of the end. **[Isaiah 60:4,9 66:20]**

THE OVERCOMER

*"... **What sort of people ought you to be** in holy conduct and godliness ...**be diligent** to be found by Him in peace spotless and blameless ... knowing this beforehand **be on your guard** so that you are not carried away by the error of unprincipled men and **fall from your own steadfastness.**"*

2 Peter 3:11,14-15,17

In following Peter throughout His second letter, we find that he is now bringing his arguments for a timely end of this age and our future hope in His return in for a landing on the airstrip of our due diligence. Repeating over and over, the importance of being steadfast, observant, diligent and on our guard to this cause due to *"unprincipled men"*. Peter speaking of God's *"patience"* **2 Peter**

3:15 directly connected to our salvation. Why? Because this is an active partnership, that needs time to take root, and when taken root spreads becomes secure in the knowledge of Him and infects others.

One thing is for certain God will press out every soul from the earth that is His own. For He says, *"all that He has given Me I lose nothing but raise it up on the last day"* **John 6:39** *"no one can come to Me unless the Father who sent Me draws him ..."* **v44** *"no one can come to me unless it has been granted him from the Father"* **v65**

As for the dangers that exist, Peter concludes that many *"unprincipled men"* **v17** are among us wolves selling shortcuts. These are those who bend the meanings of passages instead of harmonizing them with others. The Apostle gives us the idea our planes would crash under these mindsets of both entitlement or a legalistic approach! Whether it's the approach that His return doesn't matter because he can come anytime or that we better do things because He is only coming for a victorious church; it's all unbiblical unprincipled conclusions.

Yet in all this Peter, for his part, doesn't give these obstacles as the motivation for our drive, but instead states a fact, *"Since you look for these things"* **v14** We are fueled by a proper understanding of what we are looking at from His word! I have demonstrated to you how the pulpits has stolen our vision of how amazing all this is ahead of us! For we aren't being fueled by opposition to error, but our *"blessed hope in the appearing"* **Titus 2:13** which has already appeared to us inside us by the Holy Spirit!

The Holy Spirit has given us enough, a taste of Heaven, *"a pledge of our inheritance, with a view to the redemption of God's own possession ..."* **Ephesians 1:14** God is saying through Paul, we have been given a *"view"* in which *"the eye of our hearts are enlightened"* **Ephesians 1:18a** Seeing what exactly? *"The riches of the glory of His inheritance in the saints, ..."* **v18b** Understanding that all this comes down to a love affair birthed by the Spirit in which we become partakers and citizens of heaven! Paul says, *"The Spirit Himself testifies with our spirit that we are children of God and if children heirs also ..."* **Romans 8;16-17**

Inheritance of what exactly? For much of the Christian perspective seems like this earth is there concern! Yet the Word says, *"Our <u>citizenship is in heaven</u> from which also <u>we eagerly wait</u> for a Savior the Lord Jesus Christ; who will transform the body of our humble state into conformity with the body of His glory ..."* **Philippians 3:20-21** Did you hear that? Paul even tells us

NOW God has *"seated us with Him in heavenly places"* **Ephesians 2:6** Even NOW are hearts are being fueled by this love and acceptance of what will be! Even NOW we are enrolled in Zion!

Jesus revealing the nature of those who are triumphant over this world calls them the *"overcomer"* **Revelation 2-3** who come out of the seven churches types who seem to be present at the end of this age. Possibly giving a distinction between those *"whoever calls on the name"* versus *"those whom the Lord calls"* **Joel 2:32**. Yet given the perfect harmony of John's teaching who says, *"For whatever is born of God overcomes the world; and this is the victory that overcomes the world — our faith [puts confidence in]. Who is the one who overcomes the world, but he who believes [thinks to be true, persuaded, trust in that fact] that Jesus is the son of God?"* **1 John 5:4-5** One would have to take a pause and think maybe those who call on Him are the called of God and we shouldn't be devalue salvation as anything but overcoming.

Maybe there is no distinctions! Maybe Christ kingdom is all that heaven is? Not some will reign with Him while others play the flute. So it is here many preach a separation must exist between those who *"overcome"* and are apart of His kingdom and the rest who just dwell in Heaven. They do this by cleverly dissecting Christ Kingdom coming to the earth from Heaven far away. Yet we have shown God is breaking down that divide in His coming itself, there will be no separation! Heavenly and earthly Jerusalem will be connected. Heaven will come to earth. Yet these preachers will point to Jesus own famous words, *"Unless one is born again he cannot see the kingdom of God... enter the kingdom of God."* **John 3:3,5** The absence of heaven is mentioned. Yet when Jesus runs through the beatitudes **[cf. Matthew 5]**, he seems to use *"the kingdom of heaven"* **v3,10** interchangeably with those who *"inherit the earth"* **v5** as the *"sons of God"* **v9**

Be careful here to join your heart with a desire for the lowest common denominator. God's not here to lower standards but raise them. Many thinking God lowered the standard from the law to grace are mistaken. For God never had any other standard than the *"cleansing their hearts by faith."* **Acts 15:9** God has always wanted a people whose hearts were invested not trying to figure out how to manipulate the system (the Bible). Yet returning to Jesus message on being born again, he uses *"see"* **v3** and then *"enter"* **v5**; one for the present reality tasting the kingdom NOW within us *"see"*, and the other for the future reality of being apart of His kingdom coming *"enter"*. This undeniable connection exist between already experiencing His kingdom authority within us, to desiring its ultimate fulfillment that draws us deeper into it. Thus Peter understanding the dynamics of organic life, starts **[cf.1 Peter 1:8]** & finishes with the growth reality that is a certainty tied to birth, or being BORN AGAIN *"but grow in grace and knowledge of our Lord"* **2 Peter 3:18**

What is clear is from **John 5:4** is that those born again are the overcomer period end of story! These have the right kind of faith as Peter is targeting. **[Cf. 2 Peter 1:1]** So returning to John's introduction to His vision, he addresses the *"seven churches"* **Revelation 1:4** as those *"released from our sins by His blood"* **v5** stating that, *"he has made us to be a kingdom"* **v6.** Although this is John's hope for all, Jesus will not be so kind knowing tares are amongst the wheat. His words blast the churches with warnings and the reality of what lies amongst them. In this harvesting struggle to bring out of this world the wheat from amongst the tares we have the drama that will be played out in **Revelation.**

Everybody wants their Aunt Susie to be with them in Heaven. I understand. We struggle to understand passages that leave us with the impression the standard for heaven is irrational. For example, *"<u>they overcame him</u> because of the blood of the Lamb and because of the word of their testimony and they did not love their life <u>even when faced with death</u>."* **Revelation 12:10-11** Being a bullied child growing up in fear, I always wrestled with this possible reality of death. Being sent before a firing squad for my confession of my faith would dance in my head as a new born believer. It didn't help that later this theme is repeated in **Revelation,** *"I saw the souls of those who had been beheaded because of their testimony of Jesus and the word of God... and they came to life and reigned with Christ for a thousand years."* **Revelation 20:4** with the idea that only those martyred reigned with Him. God seemed so selective and impossible, until I learned to observe, ask questions and view the context of these scriptures.

For these the hard statements in **Revelation** tend to be very symbolic in nature. For example, *"beheaded"* **20:4** and *"did not love their life even unto death"* **12:11** are both concepts of the new birth from the start. Paul saying, *"I die daily"* **1 Corinthians 15:31** and *"I am crucified with Christ no longer I who live but Christ ..."* **Colossians 2:20** When we look close at *"they overcame him ..."* **Revelation 12:11** it includes and starts with ONLY *"the blood of the Lamb"* yet we must assume since it is a seed that reproduces itself, it already has the DNA of *"even unto death"* the conclusion of that process. God's not requiring anything beyond where we actually are in our growth. Remember the covenant of Abraham made by God with Himself only needing

Abraham laying on the altar at rest symbolically! God creating the motion and change not us, yet inevitably there is a partnership and consistency for evidence of growth. A plant never struggles in the ground to grow, any less than a baby can command itself to grow. *"But God causes the growth"* **1 Corinthians 3:7**

So though some want to make room for others not submitted to God's way, the scriptures are clear, if they do not submit they do not grow and get rejected! For **John 5** dedicated to what is true faith that overcomes, argues that three witness not just one or two. **[cf. John 5:6-8]** Having these three; the clean conscience from the blood of Jesus, the witness in indwelling Spirit partnering with ours, and the witness of Christ death working death to our selfishness as represented in submerged water baptism. Many try to make sense of what they do not understand by creating doctrines for others like *"all the good people just get in with a confession"*. Until you read haunting passages spoken by Jesus, *"Lord, Lord"* **Matthew 7:21-22**, **25:11** and *"Lord permit me first to go ... "* **8:21** showing our confession alone is not enough, a life of lip service won't cut it!

John finishing his letter makes some firm declarations like, *"no-one born of God sins"* **1 John 5:18** Which means goes on sinning habitually without a check and struggle from another contrary nature from God, or the need to be sanctified. In the end, John defining the root of sin as *"All unrighteousness is sin"* **v17** and thus brings us to the conclusion of what God looks at; the heart, the roots through which our actions reveal the fruit. The issue of identity, son-ship and destiny are all tied to the salvation issue. Being defined not by our actions but by our proper approach to God, we should fear & honor Him even more! For God's never fooled. We must ask how am I approaching my Father as a Father should be approached as a GOD should be who can destroy me? Am I honoring Him the right way? Is it righteous? For in saying, *"Christ who became to us wisdom from God and righteousness ..."* **1 Corinthians 1:30** reveals God chosen pathway and only way to come and to honor Him, through His sons sacrifice but it never stops there it must grow!

It is these people who become an overcomer, from *"from faith to faith; as it is written, 'The righteous man shall live by faith'"* **Romans 1:17**. I can't see this seed growing but I feel it, I see change! So I apply more faith, I continue to water it. With this confidence, we aggressively partner with the Holy Spirit to aggressively attack the entrance to His kingdom. No apathy, no room for anything but a full assault on heaven!

MY LAST WORD

*each man's work will become evident; **for the day** [of the Lord] **will show** it because it is **to be revealed with fire** [when the King Groom comes] and fire itself will **test the quality of each man's work**. **If any man's work which he has built remains he will receive a reward** [departure to be with Him above] **If any man's work is burned up, he will suffer loss; but he himself will be saved yet so as through fire** [purified in the tribulation period]."*

1 Corinthians 3:13-15

How can I conclude something so intricate & amazing as His Word on our future. Where this book ends, your journey of discovery must begin. Destiny is a choice made out of awareness of His ability & design for you given in time. We can never divorce ourselves from the day He choose for us to live in. The question isn't where do we go from here, but how will we allow the vision of what lies ahead to make a deciding resolve in our faith in the role we are to play in His story. Is it His story or yours?

I never promised to answer all your questions, or even that everything I wrote would make perfect sense or be what you should believe. Just that I would make every effort to give you something to move forward your discovery and in the pursuit of Him hopefully we would all awaken!

Awakening Glory Ministries

Established as a John the Baptist generational message & encounter ministry to prepare His bride for her day. Through worship, a word of readiness and watchful anticipating prayer, Join the revolution for His kingdom coming through empowering the Kingdom NOW! www.awakeningglory.com **partner with us through prayer, financial support and the creation of Encounter weekends**